WHITE MUSICAL MYTHOLOGIES

**Sensing Media: Aesthetics,
Philosophy, and
Cultures of Media**
EDITED BY WENDY HUI KYONG CHUN
AND SHANE DENSON

WHITE MUSICAL MYTHOLOGIES

Sonic Presence in Modernism

EDMUND MENDELSSOHN

STANFORD UNIVERSITY PRESS
Stanford, California

Stanford University Press
Stanford, California

Printed in the United States of America on acid-free, archival-quality paper

Library of Congress Cataloging-in-Publication Data
Names: Mendelssohn, Edmund, author.
Title: White musical mythologies : sonic presence in modernism / Edmund Mendelssohn.
Other titles: Sensing media (Series)
Description: Stanford, California : Stanford University Press, 2023. | Series: Sensing media: aesthetics, philosophy, and cultures of media | Includes bibliographical references and index.
Identifiers: LCCN 2022052438 (print) | LCCN 2022052439 (ebook) | ISBN 9781503636347 (cloth) | ISBN 9781503636637 (paperback) | ISBN 9781503636644 (ebook)
Subjects: LCSH: Modernism (Music)—History—20th century. | Avant-garde (Music)—France—History—20th century. | Modernism (Aesthetics)—France—History—20th century. | Music—Western countries—Foreign influences. | Music—Philosophy and aesthetics. | Philosophy, French—20th century. | Postcolonialism and music.
Classification: LCC ML3877 .M46 2023 (print) | LCC ML3877 (ebook) | DDC 781.1/7—dc23/eng/20221108
LC record available at https://lccn.loc.gov/2022052438
LC ebook record available at https://lccn.loc.gov/2022052439

Cover design: Daniel Benneworth-Gray
Cover photograph: Alfred Stieglitz, *Georgia O'Keeffe*, 1920, platinum print, 19.5 × 24.5 cm, George Eastman House International Museum of Photography and Film
Typeset by Elliott Beard in Minion Pro 11/14

To Xiansheng and Furen

CONTENTS

ACKNOWLEDGMENTS

In ancient culture, and therefore well before Christianity, telling the truth about oneself was an activity involving several people, an activity with other people, and even more precisely an activity with one other person, a practice for two. . . . [I]t is a question of taking care of the soul and of fixing a regimen of life, which includes, of course, the regimen of passions, but also the dietary regimen, and the mode of life in all its aspects.[1]
—*MICHEL FOUCAULT, from* The Courage of Truth

This book is the result of a decade of generous support from others. Those who know me today would not recognize who I was in 2011. My deepest gratitude is owed to Fuoco B. Fann and his wife Wenxiang Zeng, who transformed me from an obese alcoholic with neither hope nor direction into a healthy, happy individual who slowly learned— with frequent error and constant need of help—to read, write, and listen. Formerly a fine arts and art theory professor in China, Mr. Fann came to the United States in the late 1980s with his wife and eventually founded the Philosophy and Art Collaboratory in Northern California, at which I began studying in 2011. Mr. Fann is a rarity of our time: he possesses an incredible ability to penetrate through texts by many of the most insightful (yet opaque) thinkers of western modernity— Derrida, Foucault, Baudrillard, Lyotard, Bourdieu, Deleuze, Barthes, Arendt, Kristeva, Lévinas, and others. He wields these various philosophers' ideas to rearticulate questions of reason, the subject, language, and knowledge in continental philosophy from Kant to Heidegger and toward French poststructuralism, always with an encompassing view of contemporary life.

I owe my life and this book to Mr. Fann and Mrs. Zeng's constant support. To me, they embody a time-honored figure—that of the pedagogue, the caretaker of the self, the spiritual and intellectual guide, and the medicinal discipliner of the mode of life in all its aspects: this mysterious "other person" that Foucault found in ancient Greek texts. Mr. Fann trained me to read and write, spending countless hours coaching, critiquing, and lending me his insights. At first, I did not even know how to use footnotes and had not read a page of philosophy: over the course of a decade, this mentorship made possible my completion of a PhD at UC Berkeley in 2021. The most crucial concepts and terms in the present book are owed to Mr. Fann. Readers of his own book, *This Self We Deserve: A Quest After Modernity* (2020), may find many of these terms explicated in the clearest way there, including: ontology (as the mainstream of western philosophy); the modern phonetic language (as the medium through which this philosophy has been articulated); ethno-, logo-, phallocentrism (as the ethical problematic of this philosophy); and, of course, presence (a metaphysical ideal presupposed by this philosophy as by the language through which it is articulated).

James Clifford once remarked to me that *This Self We Deserve* conveys a serene radicalism, peering into the indeterminacy of our time and handling otherwise obscure topics with lucidity. Addressing themes such as the instability of contemporary knowledge, the ontological question of the modern phonetic language, the self-consumptive inner narratives of the modern speaking subject, and the inversion of Descartes's *cogito, ergo sum* into "We think therefore We are" in our post-aesthetic age of simulation, Mr. Fann suggests that knowledge, in his own words, may be "unlearned and relearned," refocused toward "know-how, knowing how to live, and the care of the self," and made part of a "practice of shifting a life situation from a discordant condition to a harmonious one, so that understanding is practically mediated by actual experience." He writes:

> We have come this far only to realize that "we are stuck." With our great intellectual power—in Derrida's words, "the great

metaphysical, scientific, technical, and economic adventure of the West"—we are stuck. Of course, we continue to produce more theories. In the human sciences, which have become "dangerous intermediaries in the space of knowledge," through a process that Foucault calls *anthropologization*, we believe that modern "man has emancipated himself from himself." That is to say, we hope and we think we can "talk" or "write" ourselves out of the trouble since "Western culture has constituted, under the name of man, a being who, by one and the same interplay of reasons, must be a positive domain of *knowledge*."[2]

The present book is meant as a modest contribution to the guiding hope opened up by *This Self We Deserve* and other works yet to come: that *real philosophy* (profound thoughts, not only ontology)—as the Greeks wished once upon a long time ago, and as Foucault also wished during his last few years—may become a vehicle for unlearning and relearning, for mediating understanding with actual experience. Perhaps to see through this modern dream (or delusion) to apprehend something of the present life, which is, as Mr. Fann has said, however limited, always boundless.

• • •

I am also indebted to Mary Ann Smart's mentorship at UC Berkeley. As my advisor, she went beyond the call of duty, reading multiple drafts of crucial documents right up to the deadline, diving deep into my unformed prose to suggest new ways of phrasing and formulating what I was trying to say, and offering invaluable guidance on the structure, content, and flow of each chapter included here. I am not alone among Berkeley alumni for thinking of Mary Ann as an academic mother. I wish to thank Nicholas Mathew for his generous support of my writing and his willingness to share with me (and others) his own ambitious ideas about the humanities, weaving virtuosic connections between texts, modeling the kind of erudition and interdisciplinarity toward which I aspire. My gratitude is owed to James Q. Davies, whose guidance with my prose and intensive coaching to read, synthesize, and interpret texts in seminars during my early years at Berkeley, as well as his warmly trenchant wit, made a deep impression. I also wish to thank Bonnie Wade, Ken Ueno, Ramona Naddaff, Lester Hu, Delia Casadei, Emily Zazulia, and Sean Curran for their support and brilliance, as well as many friends who read my writing and/or with whom I shared ideas, gripes, and laughs through the years, including Christina Azahar, Susan C. Bay, Nadia Chana, Arathi Govind, Melanie Gudesblatt, Peter Humphrey, Edward Jacobson, Alessandra Jones, Daniel Legrand, Amalya Lehmann, Gabrielle Lochard, Kirsten Paige, Nour El Rayes, Kim Sauberlich, Melissa Scott, Desmond Sheehan, Saraswathi Shukla, Danielle Simon, John Walsh, Parkorn Wangpaiboonkit, and many others.

Paul Rabinow (1944–2021) constantly pushed me to be as rigorous and imaginative as possible. He never tired, usually with a distinctive glimmer in his eye, to bring me back to basics and encourage my curiosity. His memory lives on. Richard Taruskin (1945–2022) was the first musicologist I ever read, and I will never forget his patience during the fall of 2014, his last and my first semester at Berkeley. It is an honor to have braved his proseminar in musicology (200B), where he encouraged my growth by challenging me to speak louder when too shy, to speak slower when nervous, and to speak less when too confident. He was a generous and candid reader of this manuscript in its original form. While I will miss receiving his witty no-punches-pulled penciled comments in the margins of future drafts, I also will never forget his basic lesson about writing: to work harder so your reader doesn't have to.

Having begun research on the idea of presence and having studied some of the authors cited in Hans Ulrich (Sepp) Gumbrecht's *Production of Presence: What Meaning Cannot Convey*, I am very glad that I worked up the courage to email Sepp, who immediately offered support. He patiently read my writing, offered invaluable suggestions, and productively challenged the Derridean views on presence, ontology, and metaphysics that shape my study. This book in its present form would not have been possible without Sepp's work and his help. I wish also to thank Erica Wetter for her helpful editorial advice.

I thank James Clifford, whose essay "On Ethnographic Surrealism" catalyzed the present study by offering an inroad to approach Derrida and company by way of the artists and ethnographers of an earlier generation, the precursors to mid-century French theory. I am also grateful for his correspondence as well as his introduction to Santa Cruz by way of the Giant Dipper and his photography. I thank Anna Maria Busse Berger for generously encouraging me to attend a seminar at UC Davis—my first grad seminar—in 2013. Her patience with me—her sincere criticism, willingness to push me, and her kindness and humor—left a deep impression. Carol Hess, too, encouraged me during my pre-grad-school stage, and also more recently, providing helpful questions about and insights into my chapter on Boulez and Candomblé. Thanks are owed also to Beth Levy and Alex Stalarow.

I thank Benjamin Piekut, who gave a seminar on experimental music at Berkeley during the fall of 2014, which spurred my interest in John Cage and twentieth-century music in general. I thank Suzanne Guerlac for her insightful work on Bergson and for her willingness to go deep into my prose, to pause over every step of my argument, and to encourage adequate framing and clarity (particularly in my first chapter).

I am grateful to John Lagerwey for his generous correspondence and his insights, in his writings, into western and Chinese dualisms, differences in written systems, and Derrida's deconstruction of western metaphysics from a sinological perspective. I wish also to thank Ning Zhang for her brief correspondence and for her published work in which she has captured Derrida's most concise and (uncharacteristically) simple explanations of what his philosophy was all about.

I thank Caroline Potter and Peter O'Hagan, whom I briefly met in London and whose correspondence about Satie and Boulez (respectively) encouraged me to write about these composers. I am also indebted to and continue to take inspiration from Michael Gallope's work, as well as that of Karol Berger, Brian Kane, and Carolyn Abbate.

Finally, I wish to express my gratitude to the musicians and philosophers described and cited here, who have left us with the gift of their music and their ideas—as contentious, perplexing, yet profound as these ideas are.

WHITE MUSICAL MYTHOLOGIES

Prelude

A SILENCE FILLED WITH SPEECH

> But bid life seize the present?
> It lives less in the present
> Than in the future always,
> And less in both together
> Than in the past. The present
> Is too much for the senses,
> Too crowding, too confusing—
> Too present to imagine.
>
> —ROBERT FROST, from "Carpe Diem"

• • • An oft-recounted event. The audience entering the Maverick Concert Hall in Woodstock, New York, on 29 August 1952 came to hear a program of new music by members of the budding New York School. To start the penultimate piece on the program, pianist David Tudor walked onstage, sat before a piano, and quietly held a stopwatch. He turned the pages of a blank score (that was marked only with a title, vertical lines, and time indications), opening and closing the piano lid to frame the three precisely timed movements of John Cage's "silent prayer." "What they thought was silence," said Cage of the audience, who, as he chided, "didn't know how to listen, was full of accidental sounds."[1] As the story goes, wind stirred outside during the first movement; rain began to patter the roof during the second; and once it was too clear that Tudor would not play a note, audience members began to whisper and walk out during the third.

In the decades following the premiere of *4'33"*, a flood of ink has filled Cage's silence. *4'33"* demands that one make sense of it, perhaps by

1

reading the composer's well-known reflections about his experience the previous year in an anechoic chamber at Harvard University: hearing his blood flowing with the tinny ringing of his nervous system, Cage proclaimed there is no such thing as silence.[2] One can also read, in his book called *Silence*, Cage's affirmation that any listener is free to unite the hodgepodge of sound around them into their own perceptual composition.[3] Anything can be music when so heard. The reader may soon discover that Cage envisioned an "all-sound music of the future," redefining the role of the composer as an "organizer of sound," one who, with the aid of emerging technologies of sound reproduction and an ever-growing body of recordings, "will be faced with the entire field of sound."[4] In Cage, this entire field of sound, or "all-sound," becomes totalizing: a philosophical sound, present now and present always. "Until I die there will be sounds," Cage averred in 1957: "And they will continue following my death. One need not fear about the future of music."[5]

4′33″ was not only a precisely timed frame or blank canvas for "all-sound" but was also a precisely timed frame for all sorts of inaudible chatter: the inner speech of Cage's listeners. We do not know what really happened in the Maverick Concert Hall (any more than we can know what happened in any unrecorded performance), but we do know that a murmuring stream ran through it: speech—Cage's speech, and the words of Cage's critics, followers, and listeners. We can read this stream through the decades leading up to 4′33″, in Cage's own writings, and we can listen to the murmurs since 1952.

The legacy of Cageian sound depends on this endless murmuring flow of speech, narratives and questions about what music is, what the musical work is, and about the status of the author and of western musical aesthetics.[6] 4′33″ may be read to anticipate various discursive threads in the arts and philosophy, including the "Death of the Author" that signaled the "birth of the reader," since, as Roland Barthes affirmed in 1967, "a text's unity lies not in its origin but in its destination."[7] Whole books have been devoted to 4′33″.[8] It has been read as a symbol of the blurring of art with life, or of aesthetics with banality, that art and music critics have traced backwards at least to Cage's predecessor Erik Satie, and forward through Marcel Duchamp toward conceptual art.[9] It has been read as a liberation of sound on par with Cage's French senior (who spent most of his life in New York), Edgard Varèse, and as a quest for the "all-sound music of the future" à la Pierre Schaeffer's *musique concrète*.[10] Douglas Kahn has described the rise of "all-sound" as a theoretical category in twentieth-century modernism, a conceptual shift made possible by new technologies and by musicians who—like Cage—faced the entire field of sound: "sound accumulated across a discursive diapason of *one sound* and *all sound*, from isolation to totalization."[11] Reading Cage's above-quoted aphorism about the eternal presence of sound beyond the composer's own life: "[i]t is here that Cagean *all sound* melded forever into *always sound*."[12] While some affirm that Cage flattened music into sound, thus flattening the composer's ego, Richard Taruskin (citing Lydia Goehr) claims contrariwise that Cage elevated sound into the aesthetic realm of the nineteenth-century European concert hall, ultimately affirming the composer's own writerly authority.[13] Still others locate this authority in the inner space of the listener. Philip M. Gentry reads *4'33"* as a "window into the tense negotiations between one's private sense of self and one's relationship with the world."[14] This refrain echoes others who take Cage's silence to have been a reaction against the intense and bombastic expressions of, say, avant-gardist Pierre Boulez, Cage's French correspondent, or even a queer resistance to the abstract expressionist ego.[15]

4'33" has been read to anticipate now-current questions of identity politics, of self-formation and sexuality. It has also been read as a denial of any overt questioning, a "Beat Zen" resistance to meaning.[16] It has been read, in short, as both an affirmation and denial of authority and of romantic aesthetics, as a refusal and profusion of meaning, and as an effacement and disclosure of selfhood.

4'33" has been read, and therefore has been written.

• • •

A DICHOTOMY OF PRESENCE

Despite appearances, John Cage is not the subject of this book. To re-tell a re-telling—with all the possible ironies inherent in "reading" a piece like *4'33"*—is to perform the kind of problem that the following pages will examine. The reader need not hurry to the back of the book to read the flurry of notes that has already commenced; this flurry performs the problem in question. To speak of "reading" a piece of music (especially a strange one like *4′33″*) is already, borrowing a phrase from Paul de Man, to allegorize reading, which is to make the act of interpretation a central feature of a work at the same time that a single definitive reading is precluded—the work thus deconstructs itself.[17] Every Cage scholar knows that to write about *4′33″* is already to write about other writings, to wade through a sea of ink. I begin by observing that this condition, "writing about writing," does not just pertain to *4′33″* but also characterizes much of twentieth-century music.

It is as if, by the time Cage and Tudor premiered *4′33″*, Euro-American art music had already prefigured the expansion and radicalization of the notion of "writing" that Jacques Derrida describes, with an air of mystery and of catastrophe, during the opening chapter of *Grammatology* (1967). "The concept of writing, no longer indicating a particular, derivative, auxiliary form of language in general," Derrida writes, "no longer designating the exterior surface, the insubstantial double of a major signifier, *the signifier of the signifier*—is beginning to go beyond the extension of language. In all senses of the word, writing thus *comprehends* language."[18] Derrida portrays this *"overwhelming"* or "comprehension" of writing as a "profound reversal," almost an invasion: writing effaces its limits, "reducing all the strongholds, all the out-of-bounds shelters that watched over the field of language."[19] Following Derrida's words, one gets the sense that an epochal change had occurred: the term "writing" would no longer simply connote the material double of something that is present—the signified, which is *here* in a moment, present to the mind and pronounced in an act of speech. Whatever is here, whatever is signified, becomes in Derrida's view just another signifier among others.

The imperative of Derrida's view on writing has been well examined.[20] Derrida's "profound reversal" means a subversion of western phonocentrism, the belief according to which speech is the ideal medium for thought, expressing the soul through the breath; writing, on this view, would have to be the merely material double of speech, a breathless supplement lost if there is not a voice to speak it. To quote sinologist John Lagerwey's succinct *précis*:

in *Voice and Phenomena* and *Of Grammatology*, Derrida denounces the Western metaphysical prejudice against writing—a
prejudice that he traces from Plato through Rousseau to Lévi-
Strauss—and he also critiques the constituent opposition between the "dead letter" and the "living voice." In admirable pages
on Plato, he shows the equivalences in the Platonic system between the notions of father, sun, voice, and life, in opposition
to mother, moon, writing, and death. . . . The Latin West will
think in terms at once ethical and metaphysical regarding the
lexical couples of body/soul, matter/spirit, woman/man, politics/
religion (or State/Church), always giving a negative value to the
first term of each couple.[21]

When he writes of the "overwhelming" or "comprehension" of writing, Derrida flattens the field, undermining the privilege granted in
western thought to the voice and mind above writing and the body,
hence of man above woman or of "the West" above the other. Each of
these metaphysical oppositions springs from "the metaphysics of phonetic writing (for example, of the alphabet)," which, in Derrida's words
from the opening page of *Grammatology*, had been "nothing but the
most original and powerful ethnocentrism, in the process of imposing itself upon the world."[22] Once *écriture* expands to encompass "not
only the physical gestures of literal pictographic or ideographic inscription, but also the totality of what makes [inscription] possible; and also,
beyond the signifying face, the signified face itself," then the privilege
granted to speech as the living vehicle for thought can no longer remain
unquestioned.[23]

   While Derrida does not make the historical configuration about
which he writes too clear, during the opening of *Grammatology* he implies that prior to the modern epoch writing had only been derivative,
auxiliary, and a supplement to spoken language, but then it became revealed (as if on its own) that supplementarity in fact defines the possibility for any kind of signification to occur at all.

   And thus we say "writing" for all that gives rise to an inscription
   in general, whether it is literal or not and even if what it distrib-

utes in space is alien to the order of the voice: cinematography, choreography, of course, but also pictorial, musical, sculptural "writing". . . . All this to describe not only the system of notation secondarily connected with these activities but the essence and the content of these activities themselves. One might also speak of athletic writing, and with even greater certainty of military or political writing in view of the techniques that govern those domains today.[24]

I have wondered about the "we" ("*on*") implied in this passage. On one hand, Derrida performs his own thesis, giving an air of historical inevitability to this "profound reversal"—as if suddenly, *aujourd'hui* during the 1960s, writing "invaded" language, exposing the play of difference and deferral at the heart of any and every act through which meaning may be conveyed. But, on the other hand, if we take Derrida's "we" to refer to a milieu or to a moment during the mid-twentieth century, a set of historical questions emerges. What was going on in Derrida's world? What choreographic, pictorial, sculptural, musical, or political writing was he reading? If a larger milieu (and not just one philosopher) hailed the radicalization of *écriture*, then what role(s) might other thinkers, and particularly artists, have played in signaling this "profound reversal"?

The philosopher was likely unaware of what Cage had done, yet his words well describe the premises and consequences of works like 4'33". Cage expanded the notion of writing—as composition—to encompass any and every sound, including whatever sounds happen to be *here* during the blank temporal frame of a "silent" piece. Cage can be said to have deconstructed the hierarchized binary oppositions between music and sound, the written and the oral, notation and audition, exposing the movement of all sound that is the condition of possibility for any such distinctions. The composer can also be said to have deconstructed the privilege that western musical traditions had granted to the author and to the urtext: he reduced music to the bare play of sounds, present for a moment, echoing in memory yet never to return. Any sound present *is* the composition. But, as we shall see, even as the composer went far to expand the notion of composition, to unseat composerly intention and to turn the performance venue into an empty frame—devoid of signification, of meaning and *logos*—he also retained something of the western metaphysical tradition that Derrida set out to deconstruct. Cage deconstructed the notion of composition but reserved—in fact, he intensified—a belief in the power of voice, of spontaneous utterance—*here*, this very second—as the model for creation. He was a thinker of presence.

The expansion of "writing" in twentieth-century music is the first theme that will organize this book. To interpret Cage's music, and even to experience this music, is already—whether one means to or not—to dive into a bath of ink. Cage made explicit a tension that characterizes perhaps all Euro-American art music, a tension that may be termed a *dichotomy of musical presence*. Performed music is alive for its moment and then vanishes; ephemerality is its nature. Every special experience—the goosebumps, the shock, the reverie—comes after the moment in which sound is created. Like the "now" moment, music in performance constantly slips away—or, as Henri Bergson had it, "nothing *is* less [present] than the present moment."[25] One can only account for the present (from French *le présent*, or Latin *praesentem*, "immediate" or "in sight") in retrospect. Since many traces of absent pasts linger in every experience of the performed present, music embodies a distinct temporal structure. It is here and then gone, and every movement of a finger on a key or of breath through a horn is afforded by, and is only thinkable in relation to, whatever one retains from the past.

The experience of music "in the present" may be termed the *performed presence of music*: music's transient life in a specific space for a time. This sense of presence aligns with the usual connotation of the term in and beyond music scholarship. Presence usually refers to that which is beyond meaning, or, to paraphrase Hans Ulrich Gumbrecht, that which is beyond meaning-based modes of interpreting the things of the world.[26] Presence has to do with sensation, immediacy, and with discarding modes of interpretation that would privilege textuality, discourse, *écriture*. This is the sense of presence that Carolyn Abbate invoked when, in "Music—Drastic or Gnostic?," she called for a new ethics of musical interpretation that would direct the scholar's gaze toward the transient, or "drastic," effects of music in performance as opposed to the meanings that may be summoned through "hermeneutics"—that is, through the exegetical reading of musical works as texts.[27]

Yet the performed presence of music is already gone. As soon as one recalls a musical moment, music is but a lingering trace: an echo, a memory that is shaped in part by how one wields words. A basic—though perhaps counter-intuitive—premise of this book will be that the lingering trace of music, whatever one grasps or refers to when one writes, *is another form of presence*; in fact, it is the only presence we can really *know*. This claim is counter-intuitive because to speak of presence is usually to infer that one can wade backward through the lingering traces of absent music to recapture something of the one-time-only event. Presence, in performance studies in the mode of Peggy Phelan or Erika Fischer-Lichte, means bodily immediacy or co-presence, that which is "unmarked," un-repeatable in a performance.[28] However, since the now in which music occurs is always outside itself, hollowed out by its relation to the near future while already shot through with traces of many absent pasts, our very experience of this present is already marked, already interpreted, already loaded with latent meanings. It is already shaped by lingering memories, by conscious or unconscious biases, the filter of what we know and of what we have practiced. *Presence cannot be said to exist*, never purely, never simply. There "is" no presence other than the leftover trace, the echo or double that one may mold through words to become something else.

In contrast with the performed presence of music, this other form of presence, which is somewhat like a linguistic double, is what might be termed the *written presence of music*. This is to paraphrase Derrida again, who claimed that Being or presence, a central notion of Euro-American (i.e., "Western") philosophy, had only ever been a "written being" (*l'être écrit*).[29] This claim was part of Derrida's deconstruction of foundational metaphysical beliefs that had structured western philosophical thought. He derived the term "deconstruction" from Martin Luther, who used the Latin *destructio* to connote a method of questioning and de-constituting the theological heritage of the Church, and from Martin Heidegger, whose *Destruktion* carried Luther's quest further, referring to an unravelling of the founding concepts of *ontology*: the discourse, science, or knowledge (*logos*) of being (*on*).[30] The distinction between the performed presence of music and the "written being" of music may be understood, along these (dense) Derridean lines, as a modulation of the Heideggerian distinction between lowercase "being" (in German *Seiend*, or French *l'étant*, often translated as "entity" or "existent") and uppercase "Being" (*Sein* or *l'Être*). "What do we mean by saying 'this is a being'? What does it mean to be?" During a seminar given in China late in his life, Derrida answered: "*Être/Sein* is nothing. You can never find anything anywhere that we can call *Sein*, and yet *Sein* is presupposed each time we say 'this is a being.'"[31] Being/*Sein* is not an entity: it is something of a mirage created by a language built on the distinction between ideal and sensible, signified and signifier.

The most significant part of Derrida's deconstruction for this study will be his conviction that western thought in general rests on a faulty ground because every form of idealism, and even the metaphysics of the phonetic writing used in the west, presupposes that the "now" moment, the present, is somehow stable and self-sufficient. Derrida's manner of approaching the philosophical question of the "now" or of presence was consistent throughout his career from his early studies of Edmund Husserl. Peter Salmon succinctly sums up Derrida's early critique of Husserl's concept of the "living present" (*der lebendige Gegenwart*):

> Deconstruction is . . . born with Derrida's analysis of Husserl's "now"—that originary moment, that imaginary vantage point, where one can carry out a phenomenological description of the world as though time does not exist. . . . Husserl relies on this "now" to generate his philosophy and to set its limits, but the concept "now" is itself assumed, unquestioned. For Derrida this is an example, par excellence, of the "metaphysics of presence"—the unexamined assumption and therefore privileging of the notion that consciousness is fully present, that the world is fully present, and that we can analyse it with concepts which are fully present and that, in some sense, exist as things. Metaphysics privileges presence over absence.[32]

If the "now" is the basis of any idea—any referent—then "now" is no longer a spatio-temporal specificity but rather a general form: Being. This is what is meant by presence in the sense of *praesentia*, an abstract form of *there-ness* that is the condition for any ideality to be plausible. Derrida's oft-mentioned "deconstruction of the metaphysics of presence" can be restated (in a less modish way) as a questioning of the presumed stability or endurance of presence. "What I tried to do," Derrida stated during the China seminar, "was to deconstruct the main prescription of ontology as a science of something that can be considered present. That is to say, I tried to deconstruct the privilege granted to the present."[33]

Music is an embodiment of this philosophical dilemma of the "now," since by its nature, performed music strikes the senses right away, yet can seem to recall or manifest something that endures, or that has been present all along. Michael Gallope has termed this dichotomy a "paradox of the ineffable," citing Arthur Schopenhauer's affirmation that "music is as *immediate* an objectification and copy [*Abbild*] of the whole *will* as the world itself is, indeed as the Ideas are, the multiplied phenomena of which constitutes the world of individual things."[34] It is Schopenhauer's use of the term *Abbild* that most intrigues Gallope. The paradox of ineffability connotes the strange situation that music is immediate to perception yet "copies," and hence mediates, something else; in his own words, "music appears as a sensuous immediacy at the same time that it is mediated by forms and techniques."[35] An immediate mediation? Perhaps this duality is best understood, as Gumbrecht has suggested, "if one replaces Schopenhauer's reference that music is an 'immediate copy of the will itself' with the formulation that it is 'the embodiment of the will,' less an *Abbild* than an alternative modality of its [the will's] reality."[36] But whether one takes music as a copy or an embodiment of the will, the basic "paradox," or dichotomy, still characterizes what music *is*: a "now" moment that is always outside itself. Music is a movement of *différance* as Salmon understands the term. "Différance . . . is the moment before this founding act of violence, where we are held before the decision," that is, the decision about what to name something, the effort to oust indeterminacy in favor of the fixity of meaning: "[différance] is the moment of aporia, before there is a road taken and a road not taken."[37]

To put it more boldly: *music is presence.* The very dichotomy of musical presence is the very dichotomy of western philosophy as ontology:

the "now" moment is already gone, yet it leaves its trace. I will suggest throughout this book that the always vanishing nature of musical sound, instead of revealing or supporting a fixed, stable, and indeed "ontological" understanding of things, *avowedly destabilizes ontology.* The "now" is but a trace, and a trace of the erasure of the trace, yet western philosophy has always striven to deny the trace structure.[38] As Fuoco B. Fann has it, "Western philosophy from Plato to Heidegger is," according to Derrida, "ontology that attempts to delimit 'being present' or 'now' in the Logos; in other words, there has to be a way we can settle 'being present' or 'now' in writing!"

> We are sitting here now getting older. Every second slips out of our fingers and there is nothing we can do about it. That's the very nature of life. But since Plato, Western philosophy has taught us that we have to hold on to it because we can make it *ontologically* permanent. We must *philosophize* it so that is becomes permanent. This particular inquiry develops into written philosophy, namely Ontology.[39]

The will to settle the now in words—to make it "*ontologically* permanent" or present—also characterizes musicology, or music as an *-ology*, a *logos*: a discourse, science, or knowledge. *How do you write about music?* That is, how do you write about something that vanishes, that seems to resist language even as it moves like language and invites language? This book begins from the conviction that the dichotomy of musical presence, the "paradox of the ineffable," is best understood as a shifting *historical ratio.* Musicians and other thinkers in different historical configurations have given more priority to "sensuous immediacy" or to "forms and techniques," depending on their aims and means. An overall trajectory can, however, be discerned.

Whereas in nineteenth-century contexts the performed presence of music in concert halls and private venues came conceptually before music's discursive elaboration—inspiring composers and their critics to write about what music can mean and what music can do to the self or to the soul—by the twentieth century it became possible for this relationship to be reversed. In short, *whereas music once came before writing, during the twentieth century, writing began to efface music.* When

E. T. A. Hoffmann wrote of Beethoven that the composer took listeners "out of the everyday into the realm of the infinite," for instance, or when Schopenhauer wrote that music allows a listener, through the paradoxically immediate medium of sound, to experience a torrent of emotions—joy, anger, striving, and melancholy—in their pure form (i.e., without attaching these feelings to a specific worldly referent), one can presume that when these philosophers wrote about music, it was the performed presence that inspired their awe.[40] The profound experiences of music in the concert hall—and the intimate experience of studying this music in private with four-hand piano transcriptions, or, in Schopenhauer's case, by playing Gioachino Rossini's melodies on a flute—aided these thinkers on a spiritual journey.[41] They then articulated ideas about music's metaphysical import that would become emblematic (and, indeed, something of a historiographical caricature) of (German symphonic) romanticism.[42]

The era of Hoffmann and Schopenhauer inaugurated the modern form of the "written being" of music, its double that arises, specter-like, in the virtual space of language. After the turn of the twentieth century, however, as French modernists brought listeners down deliberately from Hoffmann's "infinite realm" to the everyday, and as avant-gardists laughed in the face of meaning, things changed. Which leads us back to where we started, not specifically to 4′33″, but to a dichotomy that characterizes perhaps all music, a dichotomy that Cage seems to have exploited for all it was conceptually worth in 1952.

• • •

Unlike a painter's paint or a sculptor's stone, the sonic material of music is elusive. Its ephemerality is part of what makes it meaningful for philosophers as for musicians and their listeners. It can seem so close, so present. We chase its trace down many curves of a pen impressed in paper, through grooves dug in a record, through data encoded in files, through movements trained in a musician's muscles, and through the distant memories impressed in one's self. And then, looking back, we see a pile of words in place of the absent sounds, a specter that threatens musical presence. By chasing music's presence, we inevitably create more traces, more writings. Perhaps, after all, "the present" can only ever be a figment or mirage, something we can only recognize after the fact, in the movement of writing, once the game of references, deferrals, and differences has begun. When we return to the present, we have already fallen. The *real* present, the fleeting here and now, is, to paraphrase Robert Frost, perhaps too crowding, too confusing—too present to imagine.

THE CLAIM

Three main premises structure this book. The first has already been stated: music embodies the philosophical question about the "now," or about the present; the "now" always vanishes yet presence is the basis by which anything can be known. The language we use, the designations we make, refer to something that is *there*, hence a stable presence, a general and abstract sense of *there-ness*, resides in the metaphysics of our language. Second: this question of the "now," of the present, is at the heart of ontology—*any* ontology. A discourse on Being presupposes that Being has a stable existence. There is always "now." But since there *is* no present, and the present is only knowable as a trace of a now-absent past, it is fair to say that *presence is an ontological idea.*[43]

This brings me to the third, and most important, theme of this narrative: that *presence is a distinctly western idea*, since ontology is a western thing. It is, in Emmanuel Lévinas's words, a "philosophy of power" because to think ontologically is already to bring the other, that which is unknown and yet to be settled in words, into the domain of Being. Whatever is distinct and incomprehensible must be illuminated by the light of Being. "The relation with Being [*l'être*] that is enacted as ontology consists in neutralizing the existent [*l'étant*] in order to comprehend or grasp it."[44]

It is worth pausing over the term "ontology," and I will do so later. For now, it suffices to say that the idea of ontology that informs this book is drawn primarily from thinkers who have contended that the philosophical discourse on the nature of being has always amounted, in the west, to a kind of power game: Lévinas and Derrida, and—as I will describe below—Sylvia Wynter and Tendayi Sithole.[45] Lévinas writes of (uppercase) Being as a light (a metaphor that Derrida, as we shall see, also employs): "[t]he neutralization of the other who becomes a theme or object—appearing, that is, taking its place in the light—is precisely his reduction to the same." To "know ontologically" is to turn that which is yet to be named and yet to be written into a general object of knowledge, an illumination that "[removes] from being [i.e., the entity] its resistance" and its alterity, "because light opens a horizon and empties space—delivers being out of nothingness."[46] Derrida would later voice a similar idea when, during a conversation with his Chinese translator Ning Zhang, he defined the *logos* as a "gathering":

> If one tries to think, strictly speaking, what is philosophy (what you call the philosophical consistency), from that point of view, I have tried quickly enough, at once in the footsteps of Heidegger, but also turning away from Heidegger, to see there an acknowledgement of, or submission to the authority of what one calls in Greek the *logos*, meaning at once reason, discourse, calculation, speech—*logos* means all that—and also "gathering"; *legein*, that which gathers. Thus, the idea of a system.[47]

White Musical Mythologies: Sonic Presence in Modernism reassesses twentieth-century modernism by examining musicians who "gathered" various non-European and pre-modern forms of expression under the banner of sound. I describe some of the means by which a series of modernists—including Satie, Varèse, Boulez, and Cage—strove to intensify the performed presence of music, seeking to strip music bare of its normative syntax, to rid us of the historical baggage of (German/romantic or Italian/operatic) tradition(s), and therefore to construct various forms and figures of the primitive. The musicians studied here sought to convey—through sonic violence, shock, revelation, or even boredom—an abiding sense that something is wrong with us, and that the estrangements of modern society—of rationalism, capitalism, consumer culture, what have you—might be shorn in a profound moment of presence. This is the story of an irony, however, since while these modernists sought to amplify the performed presence of their music, they wound up foregrounding music's "written being," forging an ontological understanding of sound that persists in the pages of sound studies today. The presence that they sought is, after all, dichotomous.

Composers of art music had long sought fresh styles and new sounds by reconstructing a non-European other, whether through Mozart's imitations of Turkish music, the exoticized characters of Bizet's *Carmen*, or the rhythmic counterpoint that drew Debussy to Javanese gamelan. I suggest that these endeavors to imagine and to appropriate extra-European sounds became specifically "ontological" by the mid-twentieth century. This occurred as composers approached sound by way of primitivist musical tropes and techniques, referencing non-European peoples, quoting, mimicking, and re-imagining the sounds of the other (while not always citing their sources). The central idea that will join my descriptions of the composers studied here—whose works and thoughts will often appear quite distinct, demanding patient study on their own terms—will be that *primitivism was the means through which twentieth-century Euro-American creators of avant-garde and experimental music forged an ontological understanding of sound.* In other words, through various encounters (or encounter narratives) with otherness, a central philosophical idea of sound emerged, a kind of trans-historical figure of sound like the "all-sound" that we have already "read" in Cage. *Sound became ontological.*

Otherwise stated, *White Musical Mythologies* describes the emergence of the modernist credo that sound *has* an ontology, or a metaphysical reality that a composer or a scholar might reveal, and that may become the basis of art practice or of scholarly authority; once again, ontology is a power move. This book may therefore be read as a prehistory of our contemporary thought of sound, noting that sound studies is, by and large, just as Euro-western-centric as the form of modernism studied here.[48] Sound is only thinkable today because of the modernists who have made it for us, and through the pages to follow, a collection of diverse—sometimes incompatible—beliefs about sound will emerge, many of which may be familiar.

Sound is the real itself, present here, now, and always; sound is a vibrant, immersive materiality out of which any particular music or human utterance emerges, and into which our voices die away; sound is therefore beyond perception and even beyond the human, an eternal energy in itself; at the same time, sound is also a vital resource for musicians; it is productive of musical form and technique, inspiring methods of organization, inscription, analysis, reproduction, visualization, simulation—in short, the media of *écriture*; sound may be liberated, dematerialized or idealized; it may also be banalized, returned to its inert, meaningless vibratory nature and made to fill the room like light and heat, as comfort in every form. But most crucially: sound emanates from the ethnographic other; it vibrates in the unseen realms opened by ancient spiritual practices and by hypnotic repetition and psychological experimentation; it echoes in the cacophony of the modern city as in ritual dance or chant; sound is something feminine, Black, beyond. Yet, even as the musicians studied here sought (in a deconstructive mode) to destabilize western traditions and the metaphysics of romantic music, they wound up ontolog*izing* sound, re-affirming in a new and inextricable way the metaphysical beliefs about musical sounds that they sought to bracket. To quote Zakiyyah Iman Jackson,

> appeals to move "beyond the human" may actually reintroduce the Eurocentric transcendentalism this movement purports to disrupt, particularly with regard to the historical and ongoing distributive ordering of race—which [tacitly] authorizes and conditions appeals to the "beyond," maybe even overdetermining the "beyond's" appeal.[49]

By casting sound as the beyond and casting the other as sound, these musicians wound up re-inscribing Eurocentric transcendentalism.

The "white mythology" named in this book's title is, I will demonstrate, the myth of "pure sound," the sound that Varèse sought to liberate, that Boulez sought to neutralize, and that Cage—following Satie's half-winking quip that sound is an inert, meaningless comfort, a vibrating *Furniture Music*—cast as all-sound and always-sound. I describe the emergence of sound as these composers constructed a "West" against a "non-West," the Same against the Other, taking cues, arrogating ideas, and appropriating forms of expression from this other. This primitive other was sometimes to be found within Europe or the United States, for instance, in medieval Catholicism or nineteenth-century transcendentalism, in the realm of the unconscious (newly discovered by the late nineteenth century), in the unorganized sounds of the modern cityscape, or in the incantatory clash of verbal sounds—the letters and syllables stripped of representational function in Dadaism and the murmuring streams of consciousness characteristic of surrealist poetry. But primarily, the other was reconstructed as avowedly outside the center, that is, as a voice, a dance, a ritual, or a vision emanating from the Global South.

The chapters to follow will trace these exoticist tendencies across modernist musical practice: the fascination exerted on Satie and *fin-de-siècle* mystics in his circle by medieval Catholicism (northern Europe's pre-modern other, ever since the early romantics) and by the unconscious states revealed through hypnosis and other more occult practices (Chapter One); the inspiration Varèse took from the sounds of the New York cityscape and Dadaist sound poetry, on one hand, and from ethnographic surrealism on the other (Chapter Two); Boulez's musical approximations of the shouts, noises, and rhythmic effects of Antonin Artaud's screaming voice as the actor mimicked the sounds of Rarámuri ritual, as well as the composer's appropriation of the poetics of Bahian Camdomblé in *Le Marteau sans maître* (Chapter Three); and the fascination exerted on Cage (and Derrida) by Wiener's *Cybernetics* while Cage flattened composition into "all-sound," appropriating words and ideas willy-nilly from Eastern thought (Chapter Four).

By examining musicians who strove to produce sonic presence, specifically by re-thinking the concept of musical writing (*écriture*), my inquiry opens into philosophies of sound and writing in twentieth-century France. I place these musicians in dialogue with contemporaneous French philosophers and theorists, pairing Satie with Bergson, measuring Varèse by Georges Bataille, listening with Boulez to Artaud, and, finally, examining Derrida's notion of the "overwhelming" or "comprehension" of *écriture* alongside Cage's effort to expand the notion of composition. The process of learning moves in both directions: *White Musical Mythologies* positions each of these modernist musicians in an anticipatory position leading to Derrida, suggesting that musicians already prefigured the "deconstruction" of western metaphysics before Derrida wrote his books. Deconstruction was always already musical.

And yet . . . Even as these modernists sought to destabilize the norms and mores of their musical pasts, they also intensified something of the Euro-western tradition, something very old and very white: *ontology*, the belief that the reality of things, whatever is foreign, unwritten, and unknown, may be given form, brought into the light, made part of a method or technique, and written into being. Musical modernism well embodies a tension that Geoffrey Bennington stated succinctly, summing up the consequences of Derrida's body of thought: "deconstruction maintains that we are always in a *tension* between the metaphysical and its undoing."[50] These musicians, like other thinkers in their surrounds, worked stubbornly within this tension between, on one hand, the fixity of meaning and the monumentality of tradition, and on the other, the deconstruction of "the West." Modernism was perhaps always in a tension between Hoffmann's realm of infinite yearning and the formless indeterminacy of *différance*. *White Musical Mythologies* uses philosophy to illuminate music and uses music to open a new perspective onto the 1960s French intellectual milieu commonly grouped under the banner of "French theory." We cannot fully understand French theory in its novelty and complexity, I suggest, without music and sound.

"WHAT HAPPENED TO MUSIC?": THE SCAFFOLD

Before wading further through the philosophical waters, some context may help. Around 2010, as a bright-eyed and naive jazz student who had left sunny California for the east coast during his late teens, I found a spirit in the prestigious New York jazz scene quite unlike what I thought I heard in the great jazz albums produced by Impulse or Blue Note records during the 1950s and 60s. Not only was the jazz scene dominated by institutions that pumped out hundreds of talented (or not) student performers every year into a jobless market, but the academicization and specialization of "contemporary improvised music" made it seem that one needed to be dry and cerebral to be hip.[51]

At a certain point along the jazz school road, I stopped loving what I was doing. In hindsight, I see that while my experience was in many ways idiosyncratic, my (limited) time in the jazz world (such as it was in Manhattan of the early 2010s) reflects an overall disenchantment that had already occurred in classical genres. What I did not (yet) know was that the story of the over-intellectualization of twentieth-century

Euro-American art music was already familiar to musicologists. "Advanced" music in the United States became, more and more, an intellectual pursuit by specialists in ivory tower enclaves after the inauguration of the first PhD programs in music composition. In Taruskin's words, the post–World War II age was an "age of technocrats."[52] It is well known (by now) that the academic field of music composition became ever more specialized during a Cold War era in which the American academy placed high value on personal autonomy—an autonomy that composers like Milton Babbitt sought through aesthetics.[53] In Europe, though the composers associated with Pierre Schaeffer's *musique concrète* studio at the Radiodiffusion Française or with the Studio für elektronische Musik in Cologne did not have the academic pedigrees like Babbitt in the United States or like Wolfgang Steineke at Darmstadt, the competition for ever-more technological innovation and for ever-more theoretical sophistication, following music's increasing specialization, fueled these early electro-acousticians' researches in sound.[54] Cage and Tudor, meanwhile, read Norbert Wiener along with Marshall McLuhan, and their use of new technologies—contact microphones, homemade oscillators, and, eventually, computers—inspired generations of composers in academic settings to make the medium central to music's message.

Studying this prehistory gave me some solace that the difference I sensed between the old records and the "technically advanced" jazz of the twenty-first century—prolix and impressive yet often, to my mind, vapid—was not altogether unjustified. The lengthy road leading to this book therefore began with a simple question (which then required a great deal of help to articulate and to pursue). *What happened to music?* And less simply: how and why did twentieth-century musical modernism, based in an ethos of being heroically of the present (as Michel Foucault said of Baudelaire's modern attitude), and composed of musicians who constantly sought to amplify the momentary effects of sound in *le présent*, tossing off the discursive norms of the past, evolving through tense relationships with many pasts, often through a restive and self-reflexive spirit that we can call avant-garde—why did this heroic modern tradition wind up giving so much weight to discourse after all?[55]

My experience in New York was the first catalyst for this study. Jazz, which had been live and present once upon a time—in my admittedly impressionistic imagination, anyway, but the stories I heard from the old-timers seemed to support my intuitions—had already been recast as an object of heady discourse and an ignored historical relic thanks to the late-twentieth-century culture industry and academic institutionalization. This is not to say, of course, that the music stopped happening—there are probably more jazz players now than there ever were during Miles and Coltrane's day—but rather: many of the students and professionals I encountered seemed to echo, wittingly or not, the infamous question attributed to Babbitt—"Who Cares If You Listen?" The obscurity of the contemporary art music scene seemed compounded by the baffling situation of contemporary visual art. On one hand, there was pop, bright and colorful with cartoon clarity and shiny hyperreal patina; and on the other, there were objects and events that, to my naive eyes at the time, seemed bizarre or sterile or just opportunistic: readymades and concept art, endurance art and body mutilation, political slogans and sales pitches.

The final catalyst for this book came by way of a fortuitous event: a decade of study with Fuoco B. Fann, who has trenchantly joined the thoughts of several late-twentieth-century French intellectuals to inquire into the instabilities and indeterminacies of our present—including the situation of contemporary "post-aesthetics" in the art world, which, in his view, cannot be separated from the situation of modern knowledge, the self, or language. In *This Self We Deserve: A Quest After Modernity* (2020), Fann embarks on an incredible project, drawing together Derrida's critique of the west's logo/phonocentric metaphysics; Foucault's narrative of the archaeological mutation that produced the figure of Modern Man (*l'homme*) through the "dangerous intermediaries" of the modern human sciences; Jean-François Lyotard's characterization of "postmodern" knowledge as "discontinuous, catastrophic, nonrectifiable, and paradoxical," "producing not the known, but the unknown"; Lévinas's contention that western philosophy has most often been a form of "ontological imperialism"; Gilles Deleuze's declaration that "we have become simulacra," forsaking "moral existence in order to enter into aesthetic existence," which, in his view, is a positive alternative to the metaphysical dualisms that have long burdened western aesthetics (i.e., original/copy, true/false, God/man); and Jean Baudrillard's contention, contra Deleuze, that simulacra and simulation signal an ever-deeper alienation (in a Marxian sense): the vast landscape of consumer goods and the "dizzying whirl of reality" on screen convey a fictive sense of communal warmth when in fact we moderns are more alienated than ever.[56] Reduced to the system of signs and objects that constitute contemporary "post-consumption," we are plagued by the danger of becoming simulacral reduplications of ourselves.[57]

In short, the instability of our present knowledge runs deep. Through the course of Fann's exegesis, one gets the sense that western metaphysics *is premised on something that does not exist*, the fictive "now" that has been written into being in Derrida's sense and that Fann incisively links to the fictive self-assurance of the modern subject, one who is gifted with a kind of ontologically endowed speech to *say what is*. This "modern speaking subject, being self-conscious of one's freedom," nevertheless stands on empty ground. In one of many striking reversals described in *This Self We Deserve*, Fann suggests that Descartes's famed *cogito, ergo sum* should be recast today as "We think, therefore We are": this modern subject, who "uniquely simulates a self-projected autonomy as the individual," winds up thinking, speaking, and consuming the same mass-mediatized images, the same inner narratives, and the same salable goods and ideas as everyone else.[58]

To make clear the kernel that *White Musical Mythologies* takes out of Fann's *Quest After Modernity*: this flourishing moment in French thought—from Derrida and Foucault's 1960s through Baudrillard and Lyotard's 70s—appears as the most prescient, most potent, and most revealing descriptors of our contemporary time, marked as it is by an egotistic, ethnocentric, screamingly desperate spirit of Modern Man that is waning and washing away yet whose specter still walks among us. *White Musical Mythologies* tells part of the prehistory of this contemporary problematic, examining musicians who seem both to have embodied this figure of Modern Man and also to have destabilized his metaphysical ground, struggling in the tension between the metaphysical and its undoing.

It was only after taking a long detour through these French thinkers—poetically opaque and contentious yet insightful—that I came full circle to understand the baffling cultural situation that I had faced as a young wannabe modernist in a world "after" modernism. It is Fann who states most succinctly the view of artistic modernism that informs this book:

> A *specter is haunting the West*—the heroic spirit of modernism— even if we keep acting as if it no longer matters. It was depicted as a timelessly screaming, violent, narcissistic, and unending self-contradictory project that is waning away. Now the specter of the waning of affect is haunting us in the world of postmodernism.[59]

I, too, understand modernism as a self-contradictory project that aimed to recuperate a form of non-alienated experience, but that also necessitated and even presupposed the development of ever-more sophisticated discursive apparatuses—music criticism, academic and technological jargon, specialized elite knowledge—that led to a different kind of alienation.

While it is certain that Baudelaire's modern attitude has faded into the past, it is nevertheless difficult to know what to call this world "after" modernism. Perry Anderson noted that the advent of the color television, the supreme technology of simulation, announced a new cultural logic during the early 1970s—one that Fredric Jameson famously described as a superstructural expression of a late capitalist economy driven by the multinational corporation.[60] Yet "postmodernity" as a period marker seems no longer in vogue, perhaps because the term lacks specificity. As Lyotard conjectured even before the term became an academic shibboleth, postmodernity perhaps "is not modernism at its end but in the nascent state," a "state [which] is constant."[61] Otherwise said, any given stage of modernism can give way to a "post"-modern moment, which becomes the basis for a new modernism, and so on. There are always "counter"-modernisms within modernism.[62] Some now prefer the term "contemporary" to refer to the period—anywhere from 1945 to the present—during which modernism became historical.[63]

The main thread of the world "after" modernism addressed in *White Musical Mythologies* will be the increasing centrality of the concept of writing for how "presence" was understood and produced, since modernists in Paris and New York began to think of music as primarily a written form, something produced by and in writing. By claiming that presence does not actually exist except in the form of a linguistic double or lingering trace—the written presence of music—I do not, however, mean to repeat the "linguistic existentialism" that Gumbrecht identified as a common post-linguistic refrain: "the sustained complaint and melancholia (in its endless variations) about the alleged incapacity of language to refer to the things of the world."[64] This is the danger of wholeheartedly taking on a Derridean view of presence (as I do): one risks joining the ranks of a horde of "soft terrorists," to quote a phrase from Gumbrecht.

> Despite all its revolutionary claims, and its confidence that it has the intellectual potential to bring "the age of the sign" to "closure," deconstruction has . . . to a large extent relied on soft terror to shore up the existing order in the humanities.[65]

I am too young to have experienced the "soft terror" directly, but I gather that the issue had more to do with certain Derrideans. Derrida seems to have been subtler (and better dressed). In *Grammatology*, he writes that the "epoch of metaphysics" or "the age of the sign," which was "essentially theological," "will never *end*. Its historical *closure* is, however, outlined."[66] An end is not the same as a historical closure: Derrida insisted that deconstruction was not a destruction of philosophy.[67] One Derridean, Bennington, goes so far as to insist that deconstruction in fact amounts to a "demonstration": it *"repeats metaphysics differently,"* first unravelling "the hierarchization of the speech/writing opposition," and then demonstrating such binaristic oppositionality to be fictive. To repeat metaphysics differently would be to uncover its inherent difference with itself, for Derrida the *différance* that makes possible the whole play of presence and absence from the start.[68]

Readers of Gumbrecht may find that *White Musical Mythologies* contributes to a growing body of literature that subverts the "soft terror." Adriana Cavarero's *For More Than One Voice*, for instance, theorized an ethics of listening meant to de-center the "one voice" of western philosophy, and hence to destabilize European thinkers' obsessions with meaning and *logos* by training philosophy's attention toward an individual's distinct voice, present in the flesh.[69] In a similar fashion, I draw from Lévinas to suggest that the avant-garde ideal of pure sound always involved silencing other voices, and part of the present endeavor is to find (some of) those voices. Readers may therefore find that this book, despite obvious differences in subject matter and method, aligns with recent monographs by Fumi Okiji and Dominic Pettman, both of whom theorize voice and sound differently yet with a similar imperative: to use sound to think beyond entrenched ethnocentric, anthropocentric, and logocentric biases.[70] *White Musical Mythologies* is meant to contribute to this body of literature in two main ways: by reexamining the artistic history of sound and by revisiting the intellectual prehistory of Derridean deconstruction with music and sound in view. After all, it was poststructuralism's deconstruction of the author and of "the West" that ultimately made way for our various present-day post-west posthumanisms to develop.

My project of re-approaching mid- to late-twentieth-century French theorists by way of artists and thinkers of a prior generation builds off the work of a few crucial predecessors. In "On Ethnographic Surrealism" (1981), James Clifford suggested that French ethnographers and surrealists active during Paris's interwar years prefigured a view of cultural order that "can be called, without undue anachronism, semiotic" à la Roland Barthes.[71] What a surrealist poem or painting has in common with a colonial exhibition is an underlying conviction that culture is a collection of objects, signs, and myths that may be juxtaposed in the purportedly neutral analytical space of an ethnographic museum as on Lautréamont's operating room table. The surrealist penchant for re-combining unlike, incompatible signs in a poem or a painting provides, in Clifford's words, an important continuity in the ongoing relation of cultural analysis and surrealism in France, "[linking] the twenties context of surrealism proper to a later generation of radical critics."[72] In this vein, Lydia H. Liu has suggested more recently that Derrida's thought experiments with "typographical inscriptions and spaces . . . (arche-writing, spacing, trace, différance, and so on)" were the philosopher's response to "the pressures of biocybernetics" and to the threat of James Joyce's "'hypermnesic machine' designed to anticipate all one

can possibly say in a language and exhaust every conceivable combination of verbal elements."[73] Joyce is known to have influenced Derrida's
prose style, but Liu pushes a step further, recasting the Derridean project as a kind of philosophical-poetical inheritor of Joycean abstraction
through the filter of information theory. "Derrida's work is a modernist
event in the larger narrative of contemporary technoscience." Finally,
in musicology, Mary Ann Smart has broken the path leading from
early-century ethnographic surrealism toward mid-century theory,
suggesting that Michel Leiris's writings about opera and his studies of
the language of the Dogon people of West Africa anticipated Derrida's
inquiries into the status of voice and the deconstruction of western
phono/logocentrism. "Leiris's beliefs that voice and melody were keys
to understanding the past, and that both music and language were most
powerful when they were destabilizing each other, prefigure ideas that
would be explored in more disciplined terms by Barthes, Derrida, and
others."[74]

Examining the artistic prehistory of late-twentieth-century French
thought offers a way to approach Derrida that is distinct from the early
importations of deconstruction into music studies during the 1980s
and 90s. Most of the music scholar's ink back then seems to have been
spent explicating Derrida's terms—which was not unhelpful but was
certainly long-winded—or by scouring historical composer's scores in
search of *suppléments* and traces: the pivotal chord towards the end
of Chopin's Prelude in A minor that makes the whole piece pop with
presence; the marginal grammatical elements that make a Mahler symphony resound with metaphysical depth; or the "deconstructive play
with unity and plurality" in works by Beethoven or Schumann that, in
Lawrence Kramer's words, "model a general cultural practice: a practice that resists as well as pursues, challenges as well as embraces, the
nineteenth-century ideology of organic unity and subjective whole-
ness."[75] In short, the underlying question seems to have been: how do
we *apply* deconstruction to music? Or, how do we use deconstruction
to re-hear the music we know?

White Musical Mythologies neither takes issue with this question
nor pursues it further. The main thing that seems to be missing from
most previous musicological importations of Derrida is an acknowl-

edgment of—and a method of grappling with—what was really at stake
in his deconstruction of western logo- and phonocentrism, the ethnocentrism of western metaphysics, and the idea of ontology. Approaching Derridean thought through the back door (so to speak)—trying to
re-examine, terror free, so-called French theory through the screen
of music and sound—seems to offer a way to address this ellipse and
(perhaps) to re-open a body of thought that some scholars may tend to
regard as a thing of the past.

However, no matter how one approaches Derrida, and no matter
how cleverly a music-historical approach may seem to obviate the Derridean "soft terror," at some point latter-day Derrideans (like me) must
address a common characterization: French poststructuralists were obsessed with language, after all, and music is not (quite) a language (most
of the time). To quote Abbate, "[a]dopting a deconstructive apparatus
and scoffing at presence like a man can truly seem perverse when real
music is at issue," since, "[w]hen [music] is present, it can ban logos
or move our bodies without our conscious will."[76] A language-focused
philosophical view would therefore be inadequate—a thing of the past.

On this point, it helps me to recall that Derrida fundamentally
had a problem with the occlusion of things under the heavy weight of
language—that is, under the modern phonetic language. Language carries a power to produce presence, to have an enduring sway over what
music may be taken to mean or to be. This power is not simply the
power to forge meaning: as Steven Rings pointed out, language has a
"deictic" power to shape how one even hears music in the first place.[77]
Derrida seems to have been aware of the danger that follows when the
language we use becomes split off from the things we designate, seeming even to override the world we experience. Of course, this is to be
a bit loose with the philosopher's own words, but looseness does not
imply imprecision. When he stated that "Western metaphysics, as the
limitation of the sense of being within the field of presence, is produced
as the domination of a linguistic form," I would wager that we can take
this "domination of a linguistic form" to refer *precisely to the kind of
linguistic domination that musical or artistic experience might resist.*

Derrida was somewhat (though not completely) unique in his insistence that this "domination of a linguistic form," or the occlusion of

things under the heavy weight of words, came by virtue of the nature of phonetic language itself. As Fann has demonstrated, Foucault, too, shared Derrida's basic view that phonetic writing—which Derrida called "the medium of the great metaphysical, scientific, technical, and economic adventure of the West"—was always bound up with ethnocentrism and with the very idea of ontology.[78] Whence came Derrida's elusive idea of the "overwhelming" or "comprehension" of writing: phonetic language *already* overwhelms and comprehends. In his own elusive poetic (French) way, Derrida throws the "overwhelming" of writing back in the face of western logo-, phono-, phallocentrism. In other words, by reconceiving *écriture* as something comprehensive (i.e., as the movement of deferral, difference, and delay always already at the heart of any system of meaning, signification, expression, gesture, etc.), Derrida sought a way out of the phonetic-alphabetic "domination of a linguistic form." On a basic level, then, ineffable music and effable language are beholden to the same play of traces, to a fundamental indeterminacy: to *écriture* as *différance*. And thinking *différance* allowed Derrida to destabilize the philosophy that wants always to solidify things, to settle the "now" in words: ontology.

It is time now to clarify this term. The title of this book derives, of course, from Derrida's "White Mythology: Metaphor in the Text of Philosophy" (1971), in which the philosopher sets himself the imposing task of analyzing the role of metaphor in all western philosophy from the Greeks to Hegel and Heidegger.[79] The next section, which will be the final framing gesture of this Prelude, will examine some of the poetically elusive figures in "White Mythology" to describe a link Derrida establishes between the supreme metaphor of the sun (the heliotrope) and the Hegelian *Erinnerung* (the *relève* or *Aufhebung*). I will assemble Derrida's ideas with other thinkers of alterity including Wynter and Sithole, for it is Blackness that is the obverse, occluded figure under the light of the west's philosophical sun. My aim is to suggest that everything Derrida says about metaphor in "White Mythology" pertains to a single, unified sense of ontology as the *logos* of Being. It is this single, unified sense of ontology that I will use throughout the present narrative, since my aim is not to recuperate the term—as in recent scholarship that attempts to reconceive ontology beyond Euro-western centeredness. I do not believe that ontology can be successfully decolo-nized; it is colonial, always already. Ontology is the movement of ideal-ization, the turning of the sun, the gathering of otherness into the *logos* of the same.

"WHITE MYTHOLOGY": ONTOLOGY AS MODE OF INCORPORATION

"White Mythology," like virtually every text by Derrida, employs imag-inative plays with words that tend either to charm, baffle, or infuri-ate his readers. As Salmon notes, many followers of Derrida "end up talking to themselves in a sub-Derridean word salad—full of puns, neologisms, scare quotes, parentheses, footnotes and clubbable jokes, none of which Derrida was averse to himself (he was just better at it)."[80] Any commentator on "White Mythology" risks falling into the trap of obscuring Derrida's already opaque prose by extending his metaphors and adding more sub-Derridean poetry. The main thing that distin-guishes Derrida from (some) Derrideans, in my view, is that Derrida's wordplays always tend to imply something clear and distinct—even and especially when he seeks to destabilize the (ethnocentric) privilege that philosophy grants to clarity and distinctness.

"White Mythology" begins:

> From philosophy, rhetoric. That is, here, to make from a volume, approximately, more or less, a flower, to extract a flower, to mount it, or rather to have it mount itself, bring itself to light— and turning away, as if from itself, come round again, such a flower engraves—learning to cultivate, by means of a lapidary's reckoning, patience. (209)

In this opening flourish, Derrida either makes explicit or hints at almost every metaphorical figure that will appear throughout his essay, and that he will use to clarify what metaphor is and does in the text of philosophy.[81] Philosophy *extracts* a flower—it reduces a volume or plurality to one figure; like metaphor itself, this flower offers *more or less* than whatever it is meant to represent—the extracted figure, the supplement, substitutes for a presence while offering an excess of presence; this flower grows in the light of the sun, which is up in the sky in the transcendent realm of ideality—as in the light of Being; this flower is also cultivated from the ground of the earth—the foundation;[82] like a sunflower, it turns, following the sun across the sky; this sun moves from east to west like Hegel's Spirit, and the turning of the flower is analogous to the turning of soil in the cultivation of the earth; cultivation recalls tilling, which recalls inscription: the farmer's tool inscribes the soil as a lathe turns stones; hence Derrida invokes lithography, cutting, engraving, or polishing; and, finally, he seems to ask the reader for her patience, thus bringing the reader's own temporality into play. Turning means tracing: spacing and temporalizing. The metaphorical flower (or the flowering of metaphor) is, in this context, an allegory for writing.

Each of these figures is taken up throughout "White Mythology," but rather than attempt to untangle each of them, I would suggest that there is one more metaphor presented during the opening pages that gets more directly to the point of the essay: money, which Derrida approaches via wordplay on the French term *usure*. "Metaphor seems to involve the usage of philosophical language in its entirety," he writes, and soon clarifies that "use" or *usure* has a double meaning: it connotes "erasure by rubbing, exhaustion, crumbling away"—to use something up or to wear it out—"but also the supplementary product of a capital, the exchange which far from losing the original investment would . . . increase its return in the form of revenue, additional interest, linguistic surplus value" (210). Use means using up and usury, an effacement of *use value* and the promise of a fictive surplus value—more meaning, significance, or interest than a sign (a coin, a word) might seem to offer.

The metaphor of *usure* allows Derrida to toggle between two related forms of value, linguistic and monetary, which he approaches by a rather odd detour through Anatole France's novel, *The Garden of Epicurus*. Derrida focuses on a moment in the text toward the end of the novel during which one of France's characters, Polyphilos, remarks in a dialogue with another character, Aristos, that "Metaphysicians" are like knife-grinders "who instead of knives and scissors, should put metals and coins to the grindstone to efface the exergue, the value and the head" (210). Derrida brings in Polyphilos and Aristos's exchange out of context and with minimal preparation, but the content of their dialogue clearly involves the role and value of metaphysical language. Polyphilos commences an eccentric ramble about an old adage he found in a text by Jules Lachelier: "The spirit possesses God in proportion as it participates in the absolute." Polyphilos claims that each of the figures in this phrase—"spirit," "God," and "absolute"—are "a collection of little symbols" and are rather like coins with effaced surfaces. These words are mythic symbols "much worn and defaced" (212), whose original meanings were, once upon a time, much more colorful, dynamic, and mysterious. In Polyphilos's reconstruction, "spirit" connotes man's breath—a breath "seated on the shining one in the bushel of the part it takes in what is altogether loosed," or a breath of "divine fire, the home and source of life"; man receives ("by the demons, I imagine") the power to project his warm breath, his "little invisible soul, across the free expanse (the blue of the sky, most likely)" (213). Though it is unclear how he arrives at such a vision, Polyphilos concludes, in the manner of one restoring a palimpsest, that he has "found symbols and a myth in a sentence that was essentially symbolic and mythical, inasmuch as it was metaphysical." Conspicuously, this reconstructed fable is like "a Vedic hymn, and smacks of ancient Oriental mythology." Polyphilos's point (and Derrida's) begins to become clear: "any expression of an abstract idea can only be an analogy"; "By an odd fate, the very metaphysicians who think to escape the world of appearances are constrained to live perpetually in allegory." These metaphysicians are but a "sorry lot of poets" who "dim the colors of the ancient fables, and are themselves but gatherers of fables. *They produce white mythology.*"

Derrida's oft-quoted words follow:

> Metaphysics—the white mythology which reassembles and reflects the culture of the West: the white man takes his own mythology, Indo-European mythology, his own *logos*, that is, the *mythos* of his idiom, for the universal form of that he must still wish to call Reason. (213)

The "white" in white mythology carries a double connotation, not just white in the sense of Euro-western whiteness, the white race, *l'homme blanc,* but also "blanc" in the sense of "blank," effaced and colorless like Lachelier's mythic symbols. The two *blancs* are closely related, since whiteness obliterates, blanks out: the white man whitewashes.

Over the course of "White Mythology," one gets the sense that metaphor *is* a whitewashing, an effacement of the exergue and a circular movement of using up and supplementation. Metaphor is a "double effacement":

> The primitive meaning, the original, and always sensory and material, figure . . . is not exactly a metaphor. . . . It becomes a metaphor when philosophical discourse puts it into circulation. Simultaneously the first meaning and the first displacement are then forgotten. The metaphor is no longer noticed, and it is taken for the proper meaning. A double effacement. Philosophy would be this process of metaphorization which gets carried away in and of itself. Constitutionally, philosophical culture will always have been an obliterating one. (211)

The kernel of "White Mythology" is right here: "philosophical culture will always have been an obliterating one." Derrida states that the "movement of metaphorization" is "nothing other than the movement of idealization" (226), the Hegelian *Aufhebung*, which translates as "removal" or "cancellation" but is usually rendered as sublimation—that is, raising up to a higher status. Derrida translates *Aufhebung* in French as *relève*, which carries a double connotation of raising up and replacing, and along with a second Hegelian term, *Erinnerung*, "the memory that produces signs," *Aufhebung* and *relève* come to mean interiorization, "an interiorizing anamnesis (*Erinnerung*), a recollection of meaning" (269).

In perhaps the most important gesture in "White Mythology," Derrida connects this idea of the *relève* with the heliotrope, which becomes an explicit object of his analysis during his explication of metaphor in Plato and Aristotle. In Plato's *Republic*, "the sun appears," "producing the essence—Being and appearing—of what is. . . . Keeping itself beyond all that which is, it figures the Good of which the sensory sun is the son: the source of life and visibility, of seed and light" (242). The sensory sun is a metaphor of the intelligible sun, which shines the light of Being across the land, making everything that exists intelligible along "the

great immobile chain of Aristotelian ontology." Philosophy wants clear
and distinct ideas, and "its logic, its epistemology, and more precisely
its poetics and its rhetoric" aim to bring these ideas—which must be
unambiguous, impossible to be misread—into the light (236). (*Idea* is, as
Derrida points out, from the Greek *eido*, "to see" [254]). Bringing things
into the light of the intelligible sun requires passing through the detour
of externality—a detour that, in *Grammatology*, Derrida figured as the
supplément, and that in "White Mythology" defines what metaphor is
and does. It is "an expropriation, a being-outside-one's-own-residence,
but still in a dwelling," "a detour within (or in sight of) reappropriation,
Parousia, the self-presence of the idea in its own light. The metaphorical
trajectory of the Platonic *eido* to the Hegelian idea" (253).

"White Mythology" is rigorous and subtle, seemingly soft, but suggests a thesis that hits hard. Later in life, Derrida was sometimes more
blunt about things. In an interview during the early 1990s with Swedish
writers Daniel Birnbaum and Anders Olsson, he made explicit one of
the central contentions in his writings about Hegel, and particularly
what he termed in "White Mythology" the "the philosophical desire to
summarize-interiorize-dialecticize-master-*relever*" (269):

> In *Glas*, my work on Hegel, I had already become interested in
> the figures of incorporation that are to be found in speculative
> thought—the very notion of comprehending as a kind of in-
> corporation. The concept of "Erinnerung," which means both
> memory and interiorization, plays a key role in Hegel's philos-
> ophy. Spirit incorporates history by assimilating, by remember-
> ing its own past. This assimilation acts as a kind of sublimated
> eating—spirit eats everything that is external and foreign, and
> thereby transforms it into something internal, something that is
> its own. Everything shall be incorporated into the great digestive
> system—nothing is inedible in Hegel's infinite metabolism.[83]

"Eating" is another way of saying "gathering," the *logos* as expropriation.[84] Western philosophy *eats* the other. "The movement of metaphorization" is "nothing other than a movement of idealization" (226)
because, by naming something with a borrowed term, metaphor brings
one, unambiguous meaning out from a plurality of possible meanings,

reducing polysemia and casting light upon the Truth. In his own poetic way, Derrida assembles the philosophical quest to deduce an original meaning from polysemia with the movement of Spirit (*Geist*), which, in Hegel's *Phenomenology*, progresses through History like the sun, moving out from itself only to return to itself, rising in the East and setting finally in Germany.

> This *return to itself*—this interiorization—of the sun has marked not only Platonic, Aristotelian, Cartesian, and other kinds of discourse, not only the science of logic as the circle of circles, but also, and by the same token, the man of metaphysics. The sensory sun, which rises in the East, becomes interiorized, in the evening of its journey, in the eye and the heart of the Westerner. (268)

Though Derrida does not make this explicit in "White Mythology" (perhaps because the implication is obvious enough yet would necessitate an entirely different kind of analysis if he were to state it), the white light of Being must produce a shadow. If the white man ascends into the light, the Black man descends into the dark. Derrida never (to my knowledge, anyway) discussed one of perhaps the most nakedly ethnocentric characterizations of the sensory exterior that needs to be interiorized: Hegel's caricature of Africa as "the land of childhood," "beyond the day of self-conscious history, . . . enveloped in the dark mantle of Night," "exhibiting the most reckless inhumanity and disgusting barbarism." In his *Philosophy of History*, Hegel shines the light of Reason toward the South:

> Tyranny is regarded as no wrong, and cannibalism is looked upon as quite customary and proper. Among us [westerners] instinct deters from it, if we can speak of instinct at all as appertaining to man. But with the Negro this is not the case, and the devouring of human flesh is altogether consonant with the general principles of the African race; to the sensual Negro, human flesh is but an object of sense—mere flesh.[85]

Fann, quoting Hegel, remarks: "[i]n the most ruthlessly derogatory tone and ethnocentric view, Hegel now kicks Africa out of History"; "[h]is reconciled synthesis of conflicts"—his dialectical progression—

"preserves only the best elements of an 'ontological imperialism.' In other words, his idea of freedom is granted only to the Western world."[86]

It seems strange to me, especially given our present-day sensitivity to such matters, that while every PhD student in the humanities must gain some familiarity with Hegel, *simply quoting* Hegel's words from *The Philosophy of History*—who does this?—is enough to uncover the epic, teleological, and dialectical progression of the Spirit that becomes itself through a heroic propulsion across time and space as something of an *ontological cartoon*. Hegel's *Philosophy of History* lays out the empirical "evidence" for the abstract claims he makes in his *Phenomenology*: the movement of the Spirit encountering its other, clashing with it, finally internalizing or sublating alterity, has a real-world correlate. This dialectical movement structures the whole of Hegel's *Philosophy of History*, in which the Greeks sublimate the Persians, the Romans sublimate the Greeks, the Germans eventually sublimate the Romans, and so on: in each case, Hegel wrote, "the superior principle overcame the inferior," a universal principle that he termed an "*a priori* proof."[87] Fann quips: "[i]t sounds like '*gangster proof*,' but is indeed an ontological proof that has dominated the world since the nineteenth century."[88]

My purpose in recapitulating Derrida's "White Mythology" and casting the essay as an anticipation of his later ideas about Hegel's infinite metabolism is to suggest that this greedy egotism, this white will to dominate-dialecticize-master-*relever*, *is the foundation of ontology*. The contours of the term become especially clear—cast (quite literally) in black and white—in *The Black Register*, in which Tendayi Sithole states, in an elegant turn of phrase, that "the modern colonial world cannot be divorced from the processes that brought the human into being."[89] Bringing the human into being connotes the rise of a modern view according to which "the black subject represents a body not in the ontological sense, but the body of the non-human, a distinct category of the living, whose death cannot be seen as transgression but [rather as an] act which can be justified."[90] Here, Sithole draws (tacitly at first and then quite explicitly) from Wynter, who theorized the "over-representation of Man" as a condition of Euro-western modernity.

Wynter frames this historical emergence of Modern Man under Foucault's aegis, drawing from *The Order of Things* to suggest that along with the "archaeological mutation" or epistemic rupture that occurred during the late eighteenth century, producing Modern Man as both an object of discourse and a knowing subject, an old cosmic scheme according to which "all human groups had millennially 'grounded' their descriptive statement/prescriptive statements of what it is to be human" disappeared. This larger cosmic scheme found its basis in a set of distinctions, "mortal/immortal, natural/supernatural, human/the ancestors, the gods/God," whereas the birth of Modern Man brought about an "overall devalorization of the human species," of the old mode of the human being, and a valorization of "our present hegemonic Western-bourgeois biocentric descriptive statement of . . . Man, over represented as if it were . . . that of the human" itself, or the one, correct measure of the human.[91] In other words, the old dualisms were wiped out and replaced by one simple binary: that between the human and the sub-human. This, for Wynter, set the condition for the modern invention of race.[92]

Sithole's essential view (reminiscent of Lévinas) is that ontology has captured (i.e., metabolized or obliterated) blackness, and it is only through a process of reversal and by recourse to that which is outside (crucially: not "beyond") the ontological that some form of justice may be rendered. He defines the black register as "blackness rewriting its own name," a manner of "thinking, knowing, and doing" that moves "against any form of injustice" and "the force of critique that comes from thinkers who are dehumanized": "the liberal triptych of liberty, equality, and justice is, in an antiblack world, a register that renders blackness absent and mute."[93] This black register is an "ontological scandal," which implies that blackness—theorized as something extra-ontological—scandalizes the whole category of ontology. Though Wynter also does not cite Lévinas directly, she sounds the refrain that ontology imposes "'the unbearable wrongness of being,' of désêtre . . . upon all black peoples and, to a somewhat lesser degree, on all non-white peoples."[94] Zakiyyah Jackson, meanwhile, directs Wynter's critique toward "Eurocentric humanism," which, in her own words, "needs blackness as a prop in order to erect whiteness: to define its own limits and to designate humanity as an achievement as well as to give form to the category of 'the animal.'"[95] Something of Derrida's spirit can be read in Wynter and Jackson's trenchant reflections on the white mythology of Man-versus-animal, Being-versus-*désêtre*, since reversing these binarisms is a step on the way toward a "revalorization of the human being itself, *outside* the necessarily devalorizing terms of the biocentric descriptive statement of *Man*."[96]

Having traveled through these citations—the early Derrida's subtly poetic words about the heliotrope; the later Derrida's much-less-subtle words about Hegel's metabolism; Hegel's own blunt degradations of Africa; and Wynter, Sithole, and Jackson's respective takes on Blackness—I hope that the reader will understand at this point why I cannot convince myself that ontology could ever be anything like a neutral historical term or stand-in for "being," why the scholarly argument in favor of polysemy (*Derrida or Lévinas offer only one historical understanding of the term "ontology," after all, there are many others . . .*) has not convinced me. It would appear easier to ignore Derrida and company (to relativize or to sequester deconstruction as a thing of the past, to over-write it or to seek some disciplinary higher ground) than it is—borrowing a key phrase from Fann—to "unlearn and relearn" their ideas.[97]

In lieu of recasting the term "ontology," I instead endeavor to show that there are always cracks, always traces that cannot be completely blanked out under any ontological notion of . . . well, anything . . . but for the purposes of this study: sound. Throughout "White Mythology," Derrida hints at a strange excess, an "Oriental difference" (269), or a "differential syntax," "a properly *unnamable* articulation," something "irreducible to the semantic *relève* or to dialectical interiorization" (270). He refers obliquely to something other that cannot be eaten by ontology, and on the final page, states that metaphor—like the "I"— "always carries its death within itself."[98] "And this death, surely, is also the death *of* philosophy" (271). He closes by distinguishing the heliotrope of Plato and Hegel from that of Bataille, for whom, to quote Derrida's last words,

> there is always, absent from every garden, a dried flower in a book; and by virtue of the repetition in which it endlessly puts itself into *abyme*, no language can reduce into itself the structure

of an anthology. This supplement of a code which traverses its own field, endlessly displaces its closure, breaks its line, opens its circle, and no ontology will have been able to reduce it. (271)

I will return to the idea of ontology throughout the narrative to follow, addressing other, more recent takes on the term—particularly in sound studies and the "anthropology of ontologies" (see the end of Chapters One and Three especially). For now, it may suffice to state that the problem I see is not with the ethical thrust of recent endeavors to recuperate or reconfigure the term, but rather with the basic conviction that "ontology" can ever be other than a white science, that old Greek *logos* of Being.

ON METHOD: FIELDWORK IN MUSICAL PHILOSOPHY

Many composers may have featured in the present study. The selection of these four—Satie, Varèse, Boulez, and Cage—came partly through happenstance and partly through my gradual realization, through a long course of study, that these composers form a coherent historical lineage around the themes of sound, presence, and writing. The links between them are concrete: Satie corresponded (very briefly, anyway) with Varèse and crossed paths with him at the Schola Cantorum (and elsewhere) in Paris during the first decade of the twentieth century (plus, Louise Varèse visited the old cynical Satie before his passing while Edgard was at work in New York); Varèse corresponded (briefly, again) with Cage and certainly influenced both him and Boulez; Cage and Boulez corresponded for several years around 1950 (and then basically ignored each other for the rest of their lives after Boulez disdained Cage's use of chance operations); and, as if to make a full circle, Cage studied Satie's old manuscripts and writings during his travels to Paris, claiming Satie as one of his heroes. In addition to these concrete historical connections, each of these four musicians took cues from non-European (or archaic western) cultures (as already suggested), whether in Satie's dabblings with mysticism and exoticism in bohemian Montmartre of the 1890s or Varèse's experience of ethnographic exhibitions and surrealist poetry in 1930s Paris, or in Boulez's incorporation of a

South American sound world, or in Cage's (haphazard) misappropriations of Eastern thought when we wrote about sound, silence, and chance. And finally, they each developed new ideas about *écriture*, whether in Satie's (half-winking) *phonométrographie*; in Varèse's (more serious but no less metaphorical) notion of a "telegraphic" or "seismographic" writing that he wanted to use to compose for new electronic instruments; in Boulez's concept of *écriture*, which he theorized during lectures given at the Collège de France; or in Cage's notion of the expansion of "composition" to include "all-sound," which amounted, for him, to the discovery of "composition itself."

The most compelling links among these musicians began to surface for me (and perhaps this will be the case for the reader), however, when I sensed a deep connection between their works and contemporaneous philosophy. This (more or less) coherent historical "lineage" between musicians, which could have been constructed otherwise, began to mirror a French intellectual lineage. *White Musical Mythologies* is a kind of double narrative. One historiographical line I describe leads from Satie to Cage, from late romantic music through the French avant-garde toward New York experimentalism—the three origin points of basically all present-day Euro-American art music. The other historiographical line leads from Bergson and the beginnings of phenomenology, through Bataille's base materialism, toward Barthes's *Mythologies* and Derrida's grammatology. These musicians' endeavors to rethink the nature of sound through techniques of *écriture* offer a new lens into contemporaneous theories of presence and writing from Bergsonian *durée* to the Derridean *trace*.

I trust it is apparent by now that the present study is meant to be both historical and philosophical. This is a challenging pair, since one seems to always want to "sublate"—or dominate, or simply refuse—the other. Rather than subsume music into a pre-given Theory (which would be my own brand of "ontological imperialism"), I endeavor to examine historical actors on their own terms while also presenting concepts that seem appropriate to each composer individually, and to the greater historical span that *White Musical Mythologies* will narrate.

One might call this endeavor a *fieldwork in musical philosophy*—with full acknowledgment that I am not doing "fieldwork" in any literal sense.[99] Instead, the term "fieldwork" is meant to capture a commitment to the specificity of actors in their contexts, following them on their own terms, and also a conviction that we can relive their works in creative ways that go beyond laborious decoding. Therefore, while I describe specific works, I wish to keep technical jargon to a minimum. While re-telling parts of these composers' biographies will be a crucial part of the narrative to unfold, biography, strictly speaking, is beside the point (since multiple biographies already exist for each of these composers). Though I will occasionally use music theory terms when describing specific moments in these composers' works, the reader need not pay too much heed to the minutiae of the score or the language of analysis. The excerpts provided from musical scores are meant as visual samples of a sort. No knowledge of musical notation on the part of the reader is assumed, nor is such knowledge necessary. Rather, the excerpts are intended to bolster the prose description by letting the reader see (quite literally) certain features in the music—for example, to see how Satie repeated certain melodic phrases with subtle variations, or to see how in his late style the composer crafted works by juxtaposing short musical fragments; to see how Varèse constructed his music by assembling discrete blocks of sound (or sound masses); or to see the "cryptographic sublime" at work in Boulez's *Le Marteau sans maître*. The reader is invited—but by no means expected—to listen to recordings of the compositions described (each of which may be easily found on any number of online platforms). By the end, one will have experienced a sample platter, sometimes sweet and sometimes sour, of modernism in music.

A fieldwork in musical philosophy offers a way to re-engage with what music can do to the self without falling into what I see as the main pitfall of the "drastic" musicology called for by Abbate in "Music—Drastic or Gnostic?" Prior forms of hermeneutics—or simply the laborious decoding of hidden musical meanings—were dismissed, yet a new form of analysis was lacking. We were left with first-person narrative descriptions of "what I felt and thought about during x performance."[100] Instead, I will endeavor to take each piece described here in its historical specificity as a *vehicle of possible experience*. Less emphasis will be placed on completing the hermeneutic circle, returning the work to its context (or vice versa), and more on describing how the composers *might* have engaged—and how we today can engage—with music as a means to imagine a self and world otherwise. This is meant to shift the focus away from the more limited terrain of what I, the specific narrator, experience inside myself to the possible modes of experience that music can afford for us, as listeners and scholars.[101]

A fieldwork in musical philosophy, therefore, takes a cue from the ethical orientation of "Music—Drastic or Gnostic?," which, though it failed to provide a lasting method, nevertheless touched on something that musicians always know yet scholars sometimes forget. Music is meaningful not because it is a work, an object of laborious decoding, or a revealer of ontology—this is what music becomes when we write. Rather, music is a compelling object of study because it can always become a medium. Music lets us dive in. Yet scholarly habit seems to divert us away from the obvious.

One

THE ONTOLOGY OF THE INEFFABLE

Satie and Bergson

• • • The pianist's left hand shifts in a serene back-and-forth, as if a vaudeville stride pattern in slow motion, a dance turned into an exploration of chordal color. The *Trois Gymnopédies* (1888), perhaps Erik Satie's (1866–1925) best-known early compositions for piano, each feature an oscillating rhythmic pattern, the left hand moving to and fro between a bass note and chord to accompany the right hand's sparse melodies. This repetitive movement is partly an affordance of the *Gymnopédies*'s generic ties to dance forms: the Greek title aside, the *Gymnopédies* (from *gymn*—naked; *pais*—child; one of Satie's many nods to antiquity[1]) are like any number of *valses lents* that Satie must have accompanied as a pianist at the Chat Noir or the Auberge du Clou, two Montmartre cafés. After escaping the Paris Conservatoire by opting for military service, and after escaping the military by exposing himself to the cold and taking to his bed with bronchitis, the itinerant young Satie found solace amid a crowd of fellow night owls and misfits in these bohemian dens. One can imagine the composer churning out repetitive loops on a piano to accompany any number of then-popular chansons before a hodgepodge of bourgeois Parisian onlookers and their alluring *demi-mondaines*, symbolist poets and introverted painters, violent anarchists and smoke-shrouded mystics. Strangely, in works like the

Gymnopédies there are echoes of an ascetic ideal, the stripped-bare simplicity that would characterize the composer's whole *oeuvre*, but which took form in Satie's early years through his dabblings with Catholic mysticism. I would suggest that these blocks of literal repetition for Satie were, at this time, both a generic habit learned in the café and a grasp at the kind of mystical effects that one might experience through hypnotic induction, a bid towards a purer state of being.

In the *Première Gymnopédie*, the oscillating left hand creates an ostinato, a repeated rhythmic phrase. It alternates at first between two chords in a bright (major) mode and then proceeds through a series of (modal) chords—ambiguous and colorful—to accompany Satie's melody, which is characteristically simple: the first phrase arching downward, unfolding slowly (in stepwise motion), the next repeating and then extending the first phrase by a note or two, and the next moving upward, almost a mirror image of the first phrase. As is well known, this movement divides into two nearly identical halves, and toward the end of each half, as Satie approaches the final cadence, the melody leaps upward to a high pitch (a G natural) and then steps down (Figure 1).

FIGURE 1. Toward the end of the first half of the *Première Gymnopédie*. The arrows indicate the leap upward to a high G and the downward half step (semitone) to an F sharp, the pitch that will affirm the D major tonality.

Satie's downward-stepping melody anticipates the return to the key of D major, the bright tonality in which this *Gymnopédie* began. Then pause, and then repeat. The stride pattern restarts; the arching melody recommences. This melodic gesture, a subtle step downward, gains significance with its repetition in the second half. When the melodic leap comes around a second time, however, a sudden dissonance rings out as the high G steps downward, not to the familiar F sharp this time, but slightly lower, to an F natural (Figure 2).

The gesture recalls a sigh. But whereas sigh figures in nineteenth-century piano repertoires typically step downward to resolve a dissonance, here—as if with a smirk—Satie lands on a dissonance. The F natural clashes with the other notes below it, and especially with the lowest pitch, the bass note (E, with which the F natural forms a minor ninth, perhaps the most unstable interval in western music theory). This sigh lends the *Première Gymnopédie* an arc, as if the turn to minor was always meant to be the destination of all this colorful wafting. The repetitive rhythms move from major to minor; through bright naivete

FIGURE 2. Toward the end of the *Première Gymnopédie*. This gesture (circled) is almost identical to the prior one, with the crucial difference that the high G moves downward (as indicated by arrows) to an F natural rather than an F sharp. This difference of one semitone, though slight, signals a change of mode, leading to a final cadence in D minor.

to melancholy, ceasing with a final cadence that rings somberly only after we have been lulled, through all this repetition, into a trance.

Around the time of Satie's convalescence after his discharge from the army and in a different domain, Henri Bergson prepared to publish *Time and Free Will: An Essay on the Immediate Data of Consciousness* (1889), which includes this query:

> When the regular oscillations of the pendulum make us sleepy, is it the last sound heard, the last movement perceived, which produces this effect? No, undoubtedly not, for why then should not the first have done the same?[2]

The movement of a hypnotist's pendulum is an apt analogy not only for Satie's oscillating left hand, but also for Bergson's *durée*. The philosopher affirms that a pendulum's repetitive motions may lull our consciousness through an inexplicable effect of accumulation. It is neither the final sound nor the final swing of the pendulum, captured like a still life, that sends our consciousness away. Rather, it is the accumulation (in Bergson's term, the contraction) of the past into the present, of multiple pendulum swings and copious sounds, that produces an effect that is more than the sum of its parts. An effect like Satie's sigh: the step downward to an F natural conveys more than a momentary dissonance since so many preceding oscillations affirm, again and again, the association of F sharp with D major, reintroducing the major mode, circling always back to it.

It is not often noted that Bergson elaborated his ideas about duration by invoking the experience of art, and specifically of rhythm and meter. In *Time and Free Will*, he avows that "the object of art is to put to sleep the active or rather resistant parts of our personality, and thus to bring us into a state of perfect responsiveness [*docilité*], in which we realize the idea that is suggested to us and sympathize with the feeling that is expressed." He continues:

> In the processes of art we shall find, in a weakened form, a refined and in some sense spiritualized version of the processes commonly used to induce the state of hypnosis. Thus, in music, the rhythm and measure suspend the normal flow of our sensa-

tions and ideas by causing our attention to swing to and fro between fixed points, and they take hold of us with such force that
even the faintest imitation of a groan will suffice to fill us with
the utmost sadness.[3]

Bergson endeavors to put his readers in touch with an experience that
he trusts we will already know. By moving one's attention to and fro,
it is as if music's rhythms, arcing back and forth like Satie's left hand,
can arrest the flow of time. The philosopher evokes the work of a hypnotist: think of a rhythm, he suggests; follow its oscillations; recall a
melody moving with your own breath, mimicking your voice. Once we
are sensitized, the slightest imitation of a voice that moans [d'une voix
qui gémit] fills us with the utmost sadness: music can make us sigh.

The experience that Bergson describes may be termed a musical *illusion*. From the Latin *illusionem*, the word refers to a deceptive appearance, a guise or an apparition, and also a play (*illudere*). The visual arts,
for instance, work by illusion: by the appearance of a three-dimensional
figure on a flat canvas; by the sense of depth or of motion, or even
the evocation of narrative, which may seem to spring out of a static
image. Bergson's description of the heightened sympathy that graceful
movement or rhythm and meter may bring about suggests that music,
too, works by illusion. Though not often used in relation to music, in
Magician of Sound: Ravel and the Aesthetics of Illusion, Jessie Fillerup
demonstrates that illusions may occur in musical works when a composer simulates the sound of a trumpet through just the right combination of winds or recalls a harp glissando through cascading arpeggios
across an orchestra. A trick of perception ensues when one instrument
(or group of instruments) imitates another. Beyond tricks of timbre,
musical illusions also include the eureka moments in which we, led
through a gradual ascent toward a climax or propelled by rhythmic
repetition, experience transformation along with the characters portrayed in a ballet or an opera.[4] Illusion therefore involves real sensory
stimuli, not mere fantasy, as when music suggests motion or stasis or
when music seems to imitate a voice that sighs.

In the pages to follow, the idea of illusion will expand beyond the
typical connotation of the term. One may already intuit that Bergson

found music to be a compelling vehicle for reflection because music is a time art: the experience of music occurs with music's passing. Through its very disappearance, it beckons the philosopher toward lasting ideas. This vanishing nature of music is part of its illusion, an illusion that has compelled philosophers at least since Pythagoras heard universal harmonic laws echoing in the tones of his monochord; since Schopenhauer and nineteenth-century aestheticians heard in music an embodiment of the soul or the will; and since twentieth-century philosophers in a phenomenological vein, Bergson included, found that music opens the door for meaning while also always escaping or deferring its meaning, a temporal play akin to what Derrida later termed *différance*.[5] Musical sounds vanish yet timeless knowledge may seem to remain.

For Bergson this knowledge of absolute conditions was, like musical temporality, elusive and fleeting. Music was not only an apt metaphor for the imaginative *durée* in which our inner life takes place: the philosopher believed that music is best thought as a modality of *durée* itself.[6] Musical experiences, for him, did not function as "examples" meant to prove a philosophical point—music was not just a metaphor, nor was it a literary trope. Rather, Bergson (like Satie) wanted to *make his readers move*, to recall the movements of a melody or to oscillate with music's rhythm and measure. It is through artistic illusion that we might come to understand the true nature of temporality, the true nature of life. The Bergson of 1889 seems therefore to have shared an orientation toward aesthetic illusion adopted by Oscar Wilde, who called art the "telling of beautiful untrue things"; or by Friedrich Nietzsche, who claimed that art's status as a beautiful semblance (*Schein*) allows art to reveal Truth; or, finally, by Jean Baudrillard, who would later call the whole world "a twofold illusion," a play between objectivity and subjectivity, neither of which exists except through their mutual ghost-like oscillation—like a rhythm to and fro.[7] Fuoco B. Fann, explicating Baudrillard's notion of aesthetic illusion, writes:

> [Baudrillard] affirms that "all the great cultures" have accepted the world as illusion and "striven to manage the illusion by illusion—to treat evil with evil, so to speak." Only the Western world seeks "to reduce the illusion with truth." However, this

Western "ultimate truth" "is the most fantastical of illusions." This Western ultimate truth, as the "final solution, is the equivalent of extermination."[8]

I will focus on this interplay between "illusion" and "reality," taking illusion in music to connote the charming and deceptive appearance of something more real emerging from behind the screen of musical experience, as when the musical imitation of a sigh, brought about through the gentle pulling and pushing of repetitive rhythms, sensitizes us to the real movements of temporal life. By the end, I will argue that to disavow illusion in favor of the real (a disavowal that is characteristic of any effort to ontologize music and sound) is to reduce and to miss— even to exterminate—what makes musical sounds so compelling in the first place, for philosophers, musicians, and for us.

• • •

I have begun from what may seem at first to be a random concordance in the flow of human thought. Bergson never met Satie and surely had not heard the then-obscure *Trois Gymnopédies* when he wrote of music's oscillating rhythms and the mysterious imitation of a groan (and who knows what music Bergson *was* thinking about). The composer and philosopher are seldom examined together, yet during their own day, music critic Alexis Roland-Manuel noticed a similarity. In 1916, Roland-Manuel suggested that Satie's use of repetition, especially in humoristic works of his later period (some of which I will describe later), was the composer's means to satirize the mechanisms of banal bourgeois life. In an essay that examines the Satie–Bergson connection via Roland-Manuel, Ann-Marie Hanlon demonstrates that Satie's cynical wit accords with the philosopher, who, in an oft-quoted phrase from *Laughter: An Essay on the Meaning of the Comic* (1900), stated that laughter is a kind of corrective when one witnesses "the mechanical encrusted upon the living": laughter ameliorates the feeling of estrangement caused when social mechanisms impose a kind of artificial temporality on human life.[9] One of Satie's parodic "Memoires of an Amnesiac," which appeared in the *Revue musicale* in February 1913, is perhaps best appreciated in light of Bergson's resistance to mechanism:

An Artist must regulate his life.

This is the precise timetable of my daily acts:

I rise: at 07.18; inspired: from 10.23 to 11.47. I lunch at 12.11 and
leave the table at 12.14.

Constitutional ride around my estate: from 13.19 to 14.53.
Further inspiration: from 15.12 to 16.07.

Various activities (fencing, reflection, immobility, visits,
contemplation, dexterity, swimming, etc.): 16.21 to 18.47.

Dinner is served at 19.16 and ends at 19.20. Followed by
symphonic readings, aloud: from 20.09 to 21.59.

I retire with regularity at 22.37. Once a week, I wake up with a
start at 03.19 (on Tuesdays).

I eat only white victuals: eggs, sugar, grated bones; the fat of
dead animals; veal, salt, coconut, chicken cooked in white
water; fruit mold, rice, turnips; camphorised sausage,
pasta, cheese (cream), cotton salad and certain kinds of fish
(without the skin). . . .[10]

Of course Satie had neither an estate nor a horse on which to take
constitutional rides. By this time, very much in poverty, the composer
had moved away from the bohemian heart of Montmartre to an unheated apartment in Arcueil-Cachan to the south of Paris, where he
never received visitors; upon his death, his apartment was found to have
been in an utter state of filth.[11] His musical compositions from this later
stage of his life were just as fragmentary and gnomic as his memoires,
and in this short writing, the composer mocks the very clock-like regularity of external societal time from which Bergson sought, in his own
way, to free himself. Matei Calinescu puts the modern consciousness
of time in a nutshell, stating that European modernity gave birth to an
irresolvable dilemma between, on one hand, "the objectified, socially
measurable time of capitalist civilization (time as a more or less pre-
cious commodity, bought and sold on the market)," and, on the other,
"the personal, subjective, imaginative *durée*, the private time created
by the unfolding of the 'self.' The latter identity of *time* and *self* constitutes the foundation of modernist culture."[12] Satie, as we will continue
to see, constituted this sense of self by mocking bourgeois normativity:

his description of his rigid schedule is a jab at high society's pretensions, a society that was—to take liberty with Satie's own metaphors—just as white as the composer's diet.

In what follows, I will focus less on the theme of humor (though in any responsible discussion of Satie, this theme is unavoidable) and more on Satie and Bergson's mutual fascination with the mysteries of temporality, since it is objectifiable, socially measurable time that is the main target of Satie's disparagement in this short memoire and of Bergson's (much more rigorous) scrutiny in *Time and Free Will*. Perhaps more so than Debussy, Ravel, Fauré, or any of his better-known contemporaries, Satie used rhythmic repetition—the ostinato—as a structural and poetic crux throughout his career. The composer shared the philosopher's feeling of wonder at the magical effects of music's repetitive rhythms, the illusion that music lets us dive in, sensitizing us, allowing the subjective experience of time to accelerate, slow, or cease.

This chapter examines a transition that occurred as Satie, increasingly cynical after 1910, disavowed certain mystical influences that had shaped his musical style and artistic persona during the 1890s and as the twentieth century received Bergson's ideas about time. While the composer and philosopher began their careers inspired by music's profound illusions, their respective legacies bespeak a movement toward disillusion, and specifically toward ontology, that characterizes present-day studies of sound. Beginning from his experiences with sound art, for example, Christoph Cox theorizes "sonic flux" as an invisible and supra-audible field that remains, somewhat like white noise or electromagnetic frequencies, beneath and beyond what we can sense. Taking cues from (the Bergsonian) Gilles Deleuze, Cox casts sonic flux as something virtual; it exists prior to audibility, the ontological ground out of which any sound, any music, may be actualized.[13] By going back in time to Bergson—the philosopher who set the stage for Deleuze, and, obliquely, for latter-day Deleuzians for whom sound as vibrant matter is always beyond the human, shaping us before we have a chance to sing—I contend that to make an ontology out of artistic sounds is perhaps the ultimate "paradox" of the ineffable, really a failure of the ineffable. This chapter describes one possible byway through which we may understand how sound became Sound today, between sound studies

and musicology. For sound was not always "ontological"; it took time
to become so.

In the first section below, I read Bergson's writings about time and
listen to Satie's early music, briefly sketching Bergson's reception in
music studies to suggest that the "mystico-liturgical" musical style that
Satie forged during his early years well embodies the kinds of temporal illusions and quasi-mystical effects that fascinated Bergson. I examine Satie in Paris of the *fin de siècle*, where he encountered Joséphin
Péladan, the mystic and novelist perhaps best known for his Salons of
the Rose+Cross, gatherings at which symbolist painters and poets displayed their works and enjoyed music—including music that Satie, for
a short time the chapel composer of Péladan's Order of the Rose+Cross
of the Temple and the Grail, composed to accompany Péladan's mystical meanderings. From our perspective, Satie's music and Bergson's
ideas about time are inseparable from their Parisian world of occultism,
clinical experimentation, and exoticism—the otherness exposed at the
limits of reason. In section two I will suggest that Bergson's observations
of aberrant psychological phenomena formed the basis of his theory of
virtual memory, and in section three I will focus on Deleuze's *Bergsonism* to describe a transition that occurred as Bergson's twentieth-
century receivers took up his ideas. For Deleuze especially, and to a
lesser degree for Vladimir Jankélévitch and the musicologist Pierre
Souvtchinsky, Bergson's duration became the basis for a theory of ontological time that was avowedly depersonalized, "anti-psychological,"
hence real, and, to apply a modish anachronism, "posthuman." Duration became static and illusion fell by the wayside. To forge an ontology
is to efface otherness.

A similar transition, from "illusion" to "reality," characterizes Satie's
legacy. Though obscure during most of his own life, Satie would later
be hailed as a forefather of various twentieth-century movements. His
use of humor and love of the musical fragment would be understood
to anticipate the aesthetics of Dadaism or surrealism; his circling ostinati would be heard to prefigure minimalism and Muzak; and Cage
triumphantly hailed Satie as an anti-Beethoven, composing (as Cage
did) according to intervals of time rather than by following the narcissistic emotional telos of tonal harmony.[14] This posthumous canon-

ization is perhaps owed to Satie's disavowal, later during his life, of his early mystical influences, and the fourth and final section below will describe the composer's late style, taking recourse to Wassily Kandinsky, Jankélévitch, and Souvtchinsky to examine Satie's endeavor to strip music bare of its illusions. He quipped to Jean Cocteau in 1917 that "'Furniture Music' creates vibrations; it has no other aims; it fulfils the same role as light, heat and *comfort* in all its forms."[15] This half-winking gag, typical of Satie, speaks to the composer's endeavor to banalize his music and to think of sound as something impersonal, inexpressive, and hence more real. Always with a veil of irony and an air of sarcasm, Satie sought the "ontological" conditions, vibrations and fluxes, that rumbled under his *Furniture Music*.

Apropos to Satie, we end with an irony. The scholarly endeavor to dig sonic ontology out from under music's sensory illusions is usually inspired, after all, by actual experiences with music or sound art—that is, by the illusions that an artist might conjure. "Illusion" and "the real" are inextricable. However, to base an ontology on the ineffable, to make a *logos* out of something that cannot be spoken, is to dispel illusion. Ultimately, to dispel illusion is also to dispel the real. We are left instead with a pile of words—though we, unlike Satie, tend to forget our sense of humor.

A PENDULUM SWINGS: BERGSONIAN TIME AND SATIE IN MYSTICAL MONTMARTRE

With Bergson's notion of temporal accumulation in view, Satie's subtle play with repetitive rhythm in the *Première Gymnopédie* can be heard as a kind of aural transformation: a musical illusion. Fillerup describes this illusion as an effect educed in the listener as musical phrases that seem, on their face, to stay the same through many repetitions nevertheless create a feeling of propulsion.[16] In Satie, the left-hand ostinato and the slow transition from major to minor allow for an illusion of forward movement while, conversely, it is during moments when we *should* move—as when the major tonality suddenly breaks—that we might feel the mysterious pause, the sigh. Stasis paradoxically allows for a sense of motion while abrupt changes in harmony or feeling might beckon for certain moments to linger.

Bergson's notion of duration is a philosophical lens through which to understand such temporal illusions. When one is truly alive, he claims, one does not organize one's present state as a node in a progression of other neatly separable states: instead, one "forms both the past and the present states into an organic whole, as happens when we recall the notes of a tune, melting, so to speak, into one another."[17] Bergson evokes musical experience to put his reader in touch, once again, with this temporal reality: if time may seem to slow or speed up, and if these illusions may occur coterminously, then time is multiple and we are multiple too. Whence comes the oft-quoted line from *Time and Free Will*: "pure duration is the form which the succession of our conscious states assumes when our ego lets itself *live*, when it refrains from separating its present state from its former states."[18]

This temporal play is already familiar to those who play music. In *Matter and Memory*, Bergson recalls how "each note of a tune learned by heart seems," as one listens to or plays a melody, "to lean over the next to watch its execution."[19] The notes of a melody take place *in*, not after, the melody notes that precede, since music is a multi-temporal flow in which "the part virtually contains the whole." Describing melody allowed Bergson to attend to the concrete qualitative experience of the passing present. Whereas language seems to impose a set of demands and limits regarding the form that thought can take, to think in music is to move more quickly—intuitively—from tonal color to melodic line, and to compare, as if looking at a landscape, the recollection of the opening chords of the *Première Gymnopédie* with the feeling left over after the eventual turn towards melancholy minor. Consciousness for Bergson was inherently musical: this multi-temporal play makes us who we are. As he later stated in *Duration and Simultaneity* (1922), "when we are seated on the bank of a river, the flowing of the water, the gliding of a boat or the flight of a bird, [and] the ceaseless murmur of our life's deeps are for us three separate things or only one, *as we choose*."[20] Human free will—choice—comes by virtue of the indeterminacy of our temporal experience, and by the intervention of the soul that synthesizes and projects our many pasts toward an unknown future.

For Bergson, temporal experience seemed fundamentally as open-ended as musical experience, hence music scholarship that invokes the philosopher tends to wield his ideas to affirm the self-creative magic of musical time. Keith Salley and Arved Mark Ashby, for instance, suggest that however fixed and predictable music can seem, certain moments escape the familiar context in which they are situated. Salley pairs Bergson's sense of pure duration with Arnold Schoenberg's notion of "developing variation" to outline a mode of listening in which the lines between author, listener, and sound become blurred. Disavowing the idea of "an unchanging listener-as-subject who recognizes the development of a musical object," Salley claims that "[d]uration invites us to consider an inverted scenario where apparent changes to a musical object actually represent the attempts of a listener-subject to remember a basic idea within an infinitely variable flux of interpenetrating conscious states."[21] The musical object (or idea) changes us and changes with us; thus we move from a solid, singular "I" to a dispersed subjectivity. This partly accounts, in Ashby's view, for why even the most rigidly inscribed forms of musical reproduction—whether Beethoven's scores, the grooves of the long-playing record, or the mp3 file—may nevertheless allow for what Bergson termed a "free action": a spontaneous and unrepeatable act of free will. In any number of "Beethoven moments," Ashby writes, whether "the six-bar, fermata-ridden cadential delay that threatens to derail the very end of the Fourth Symphony, the delightful diminished-seventh aporia of the E-flat Piano Sonata, op. 31, no. 3, or the disruptively avant-garde *piano* chords in the opening movement of the first 'Razumovsky' quartet," the effects of these special moments "somehow escape again and again from multiple enforcements of linearity." "Each of these Beethoven moments—and there are many more—persists as a 'free action.'"[22] In other words, though we listen to the same tracks over and over again, it is always possible to sigh. Each of these moments involves an abrupt change in rhythm (a fermata in the Fourth Symphony, a cadenza in opus 31, and a series of discrete chords bouncing antiphonally between the low and high strings in the Razumovsky) that might have struck Bergson (if ever he listened to these examples) as evidence of music's power to expand and contract the flow of time.

Ashby's "Beethoven moments," like my own sense of Satie's sigh, affirm that musical repetition allows the listener to take the plunge into the ambiguous space opened between the oscillations of a pianist's left hand, as time stretches, seeming almost to stop. What I have called Satie's sigh is a marginal, subtle moment, and discerning readers may be wary of the kind of interpretation indulged here. It would be difficult (and rather silly) to try and locate other sigh moments in Satie's music; the sigh is not a strange Satiean topic. Rather, by listening through Bergson's words, that is, by opening oneself to what Steven Rings termed the deictic power of philosophical language, I would suggest that simple singsong melodies like the *Gymnopédies* may become vehicles for possible Bergsonian experience. Rings defines this deictic power as the "attention-directing (or 'pointing') character" of language about music, noting that Jankélévitch's descriptions of the music of Ravel or of Fauré, for instance, may sway a reader's apprehension of this music. Philosophical writing is not simply descriptive; it is also transformative.[23] Bergson not only described temporal experience but also hoped to shape how his readers would apprehend time.

The young Satie structured his musical language around contrasts like that between the flowing melody and swaying left-hand ostinato of his *Trois Gymnopédies*, and through the late 1880s and 1890s the composer continued to use melodic and rhythmic repetition to sensitize his listeners to sudden moments of rupture or concordance between opposing musical features. In Bergson's terms, these contrasting features correspond to distinct qualitative experiences of temporality that may be brought into relation, and in works of Satie's "Rosicrucian" phase, as he became involved with Péladan and the Order of the Rose+Cross, the composer's endeavor to lull listeners into a more sensitive state took shape as Satie forged what he would call a "mystico-liturgical" style.[24]

During the late 1880s and early 90s, Satie relied on a poetics of opposition, casting contrasting musical features as different characters that one may imagine, considering the influence Satie is known to have drawn from the café scene, as personae in a shadow play. Pitching his *Quatre Ogives* (1889) to the Chat Noir crowd, Satie described "a suite of melodies conceived in the mystico-liturgical genre that the author idolizes," which he "suggestively titled *Les Ogives*" (a term for Gothic arches).[25] Each of the four *Ogives* begins with a simple subdued melody sung by two voices each an octave apart in the manner of a medieval plainchant, and upon its repetition in the next system, chordal harmony explodes to accompany the melody. In the following sample of Satie's score, the reader may notice that the melody notated on the top staff (the first system) has the same contour as the lower system: it is the same melody, repeated. Satie "thickens" the melody during its repetition by adding other voices (i.e., triadic harmonization) between and beyond the original two voices (Figure 3).

Quiet monophony (i.e., the use of a single melody without other "voices") gives way to grand church homophony (i.e., big chords under a melody): each *Ogive* develops from monastic restraint to ecstasy. One can understand the sudden break into homophony as another musical illusion akin to the moan of sadness described by Bergson. The monophonic opening of the second *Ogive* establishes one kind of duration, static and subdued, recalling a chanting voice, and upon the melody's repetition in chorale, the melody (quite literally) becomes multiple. This change of voicing allows for what Fillerup terms a "transformative ascent": the illusion of an eye-opening spiritual shift that Satie figured in the music, and, by implication, sought to elicit in his listener's inner self.[26] It is as if the listener, at first called to follow the contour of the single line, perhaps to imagine oneself singing, suddenly awakens surrounded by a choir—a simple, faceless chant explodes into a qualitative multiplicity.

FIGURE 3. The opening of Satie's second *Ogive* (1889).

Before Satie met Péladan in the Chat Noir or some other Montmartre den around 1890, the young mystic had published a series of bestselling novels titled *La Décadence latine*, which Satie read (as Steven Moore
Whiting suggests) even before his convalescence from bronchitis—and
thus even before he composed the *Gymnopédies*.²⁷ Telling the tales of
(fictional) sages walking a fetid path of sin on the way to mage-hood,
Péladan invoked his own poetics of opposition, a dualism of body and
spirit that took form through a mixture of medieval austerity, religious
devotion, and adolescent licentiousness. Satie's invocations of chant
and his use of repetitive, hypnotic rhythm is best understood in the
context of Péladan's visions. *La Vice suprême*, the first novel in *La Décadence latine*, for instance, opens with a vignette of a princess lying
lonely in her boudoir:

> She is alone.
>
> Full of languid shadow and lulling silence, closed off from
> the light, closed off from the noise, the circular boudoir has the
> dreamy reverence, the gentle somnolence, of an Italian chapel
> during siesta hours; *buen retiro*, resembling the floor of a round
> tower, without a bay in its elliptical walls, or studded with silver
> at the folds, the heraldic purple calm, in a violet satin full of red,
> its royal bereavement and its sad magnificence. . . .
>
> On its Parmesan forms, the purple silk robe has creases similar
> to pouting lips, to timid and light caresses. One arm denuded
> by the fall of a sleeve encircles her head with heavy red hair, the
> other hangs down with the nimbleness of a vine, the suppleness
> of ivy, and the backs of pointed fingers touch the short plush of
> the carpet.
>
> A gap in the fabric reveals the throat, accented by azure veins.
> The breasts, laying well apart, arc above; the scuff slippers rest
> down below; the bare feet have the spread-toed appearance of
> statues that wear the bands of cothurnus: and after a bath this
> Primaticean ephebism softens with cozy dullness. One would say
> she is the Anadyomene of these primitives who, with a still mys-
> tical brush, try their hand at a resurgent paganism, a Botticelli
> where the saint, undressed and revealed to be a nymph, guards
> against awkwardness with the perversity of a plastic stupor: a

mad virgin of Durer, born under the Italian sky, and made elegant by a mixture of Florentine thinness where there is no bone and Lombard flesh where there is no fat.

The eyelid half-closed on a glimpsed vision, the gaze lost in the horizon of dreams, the nostril caressed by subtle scents, the mouth half-open as for a kiss—she dreams. . . .

She dreams of nothing, not of anyone, not even of herself.

This absence of all thought enamors her eyes and parts her thin lips with a happy smile.

She is totally lost in the exquisite pleasure of this moment of pure instinct in which thought, the anxious and always-moving pendulum of life, comes to a halt; in which the perception of passing time ceases while the solitary living body blossoms in an inexpressible well-being of its limbs. Her nerves at rest, she only perceives the sensation of her lush, supple, willing flesh; she enjoys the ecstasy of beasts, of [Paulus] Potter's cows hunched over in the tall grass, sated, and reflecting a paradisiacal peace in their large blinking eyes.[28]

Péladan's pulpy prose is as overly ornamented as the scene it describes; pornographic suggestiveness couples with visions of Pre-Raphaelite "Primaticean ephebism" (i.e., primitive youthfulness) to create a rather gaudy *effet du réel*. The misogynism of Péladan's Rosicrucianism is glaring: the princess's empty-headedness and garish sensuousness seem at once to be an overstated adolescent fantasy and a serious bid toward the pure. As Péladan advises in his 1892 *How to Become a Mage*, a work addressed to young men that had, like he, attended Catholic boys' school (and who had, like he, been almost completely isolated from women):

[t]o become beautiful, astralize your instinct; to become gentle, spiritualize your emotions; to grow toward the Absolute, develop abstraction in yourself. . . . Regard the sexual act as a very inferior thing, and political acts at that same level.[29]

Péladan expresses a will to truth by conquering that which is other: the princess (almost too obviously) represents "pure instinct," the "absence of all thought" that results when one is—thanks perhaps to the oscillating rhythm of a hypnotist's pendulum (or absinthe)—lulled into dreamy reverence, gentle somnolence, the cozy dullness of a horizon of dreams.

In the popular imagination of Satie and Bergson's day, to invoke hypnosis was most often to invoke a caricature of feminine docility and the beastly ecstasy of the unconscious. Péladan's vision of the princess, in fact, well depicts the problematic underside of Bergson's own lofty ambition to rescue free will. Péladan activates themes that are already familiar from *Time and Free Will*: when we are lulled into a state of perfect docility and hypersensitivity, the always-swaying pendulum of time and thought may seem to cease. Whoever holds the pendulum may exert a tremendous influence over whomever allows themselves to be quelled into bovine bliss.

Such a woman, in Péladan's view, is at once a plaything and a *tabula rasa* for the male disciple's encompassing and self-transcending gaze. This play of mastery, of spiritual elevation through pulp, defines Péladan's poetics of opposition, and while the princess's somnolent stupor represents an "awakening of immortal being," another figure, the Rabbi Sichem, appears toward the end of *Le Vice* as a caricature of Hebraic otherness, seeking immortal being through fire and brimstone. Lamenting the "metaphysical inertia [that] intoxicates the West," an inertia brought on through the supreme vice of greed for flesh or money, Sichem imagines that sin can be burned like a heretic at the stake. "When I contemplate the modern world with its theological indifference, focusing only on industrial activity, I, the Jew, miss the stake."[30] He goes on to imagine "the auto da-fé" as the ultimate proof of a society's faith, analogous to the mage's inner quest. "Passion is a spinning wheel, sinking into evil," he concluded: "It must be turned to good."[31]

Perhaps the moments of ecstasy figured in Satie's *Ogives* were the composer's effort to turn the spinning wheel, and his own poetics of opposition can be heard as a musical transposition of the tension between passion and purification that ran through Péladan's novels. While the *Ogives* enact this transformative ascent through melodic repetition, in other works Satie employs the kind of repetitive accompanying rhythm already familiar from the *Gymnopédies*.

After he became the chapel composer of Péladan's Order of the Rose+Cross of the Temple and Grail in 1891, Satie composed a series of short piano works written as ceremonial music for meetings of Péladan's Order. His *Air de l'Ordre*, the first of his *Sonneries de la Rose Croix*, begins with a long series of steady, brief chords (marked "slow and detached without dryness"), a plodding ostinato, and at various intervals the repetitive chords pause as Satie's right hand plays a longer, flowing melody (a legato "connected song") (Figure 4).

One can imagine these contrasting musical features as opposing characters in a Chat Noir-style shadow play—in which up to a dozen technicians would use zinc figures interlaced with hand-painted glass sheets to cast shadows on a screen, depicting dramas, satires, and fairy tales in the Chat Noir's third-floor shadow theater. The regular pulsing rhythmic ostinato can be heard as the marching forward of an occult order, while the chant-like melody might depict a lone vocalist, an individual standing apart from—and perhaps above—the faceless procession. Eventually these opposing characters meet, the plodding chords

FIGURE 4. The discreet, steady quarter notes contrast with chant-like melody in the *Air de l'Ordre*, the first part of Satie's *Sonneries de la Rose Croix* (1891).

lending a regular pulse to the connected song. Once joined with the steady ostinato, the flowing melody conveys the unity of an imagined order, the lone chanting voice connecting the procession's steps. The joining of these two forces depicts a kind of mystic transformation.

However, there was always an inner tension in Satie's aesthetic position and persona. One may not feel charmed: if, when listening to the *Première Gymnopédie*, one refuses to move to and fro and indulge in the nuances of French color, one is left with a simple—if not simplistic—café song. And if, following the same logic, one refuses to take works from Satie's Rosicrucian phase seriously, the ecstasy or mysticism figured in the composer's scores might backfire. While the contrasts between a lone chanting voice and ecstatic choir in the *Ogives* or between a uniform procession and soaring melody in the *Air de l'Ordre* seem to beckon for a listener to imagine these features as opposing characters in a shadow play, Satie is almost too successful. Satie's *Ogives* or his *Sonneries* are perhaps too "pure" to trust: there was always something satirical (*Satierikal*?) in the composer's treatment of his various musical themes. I would suggest that attending to Satie allows one to see that Péladan's mysticism—like Satie's own musical aesthetic—was as much a gag and a publicity stunt as it was a sincere effort to aestheticize Latin decadence. Crucially, I would suggest that attending to Satie's cynical wit also allows us to see the other side of Bergson's own avowals about the seeming magic of artistic aesthesia. For if we refuse to oscillate with musical rhythm and refuse the magical sighs evoked through musical sympathy, we are left with a rather boring scene. What could be more banal, after all, than the bare ticking of a clock? These opposing stances, part serious and part ironic, define Satie's earlier style as he developed a public persona.

Thousands of Parisians—including Émile Zola, Paul Verlaine, Pierre Puvis de Chauvannes, and Gustave Moreau—attended Péladan's first salon held at the Galerie Durand-Ruel during March of 1892.[32] The exhibited works depicted a set of themes already familiar from Péladan's writings: one drawing in particular, Jean Delville's (1867–1953) *The Idol of Perversity* (*L'Idole de la perversité*), depicts the duality of vice and purification, of eroticism and spiritism, familiar from *La Décadence latine*. Delville depicts a nude woman from the waist up, facing the viewer; a snake crawls between her outward-pointed breasts and disappears around her neck; she wears a crown and looks toward the viewer with partially closed, sedated eyes circled in darkness; dozens of small snakes gather in her curled hair, poking their heads outward around the idol's face, forming a halo.

The milieu assembled around Péladan enjoyed a pared-down neo-medievalist aesthetic as much as they delighted in pulpifying the sacred, and when Péladan gave Satie his first major public premiere on 22 March 1892 during an opening gala, the composer responded by producing an appropriately austere score. Originally a three-act drama, at the first salon Satie premiered only the instrumental preludes to each act of *Les Fils des étoiles*, the first prelude beginning with chords like Greek columns, marked "white and immovable" in Satie's score. These chordal "columns" move homophonically in a repeating rhythm, short-short-short-long (Figure 5).

The Greekishly medieval primitivism of *Les Fils des étoiles* made Satie's music particularly appealing to Péladan, an adamant Wagnerite who wanted the music of his salons to resound with the kinds of aesthetic-religious fervor that he had experienced during a trip to Bayreuth.[33] The reception at the salon, however, was lackluster, con-

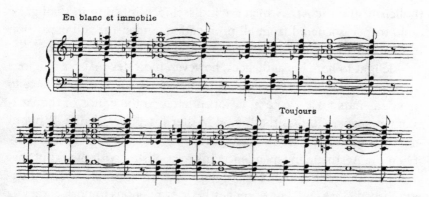

FIGURE 5. The opening of *Les Fils des étoiles* (1892). Two perfect fourths a tritone apart comprise each of these chordal columns, and one can hear a medieval austerity mixed with a mock-Greek flavor as fourths and major sevenths move crudely in parallel along a pentatonic pattern.

firming what a listener might already intuit: the composer delighted to irritate as much as to mystify. One of Satie's opponents, the music critic Willy (aka Henry Gauthier-Villars) claimed, as Whiting relates, that *Les Fils* "gave me but mediocre Satiesfaction," while critic Francisque Sarcey wrote that the music compelled "a slumber that the angels would have envied": according to biographer Pierre-Daniel Templier, "the music proved to be far above [the audience's] heads and was met by an icy silence."[34] Despite the paucity of evidence regarding what it was really like in the room during Satie's premiere, it seems reasonable to presume that Satie's cynicism had a political edge to it: *Les Fils* was his bid at an anti-Wagnerian Wagnerism. Complex chordal colors waft and wane ambiguously, creating an atmosphere of austere medieval grandeur, yet Satie staunchly rejected the long-developing harmonic drive of a *Tristan und Isolde* or the thematically driven musical narratives of *Der Ring des Nibelungen*.

This apparent conflict within Satie's style and persona, a deliberate tactic, also came to the fore in his writings. In an 1893 "Epistle" to Catholic artists, the composer parroted Péladan's orotundity to lament the decadence of western artistic expression and spirit. Since "Western society, daughter of the Apostolic Roman Catholic Church, is invaded by the shades of ungodliness," Satie envisaged a new "temple worthy of the Saviour, LEADER and redeemer of peoples," a "refuge where Catholicism, and the Arts which are indissolubly linked to it, shall grow and prosper, sheltered from all profanation, and at the full expansion of their purity, which the efforts of the Evil One cannot sully."[35] Satie's delight to bore his audiences, however, indicates that his religious rhetoric was likely parodic even as he appropriated Péladan's image to make his name. He wrote in an open letter to the editor of the Parisian newspaper *Gil Blas* that "good Master Joséphin Péladan, Whom I greatly respect and hold in deference, has in no wise exercised authority on my Aesthetic independence; his relationship with me is not that of my master, but of my collaborator."[36] Refusing to follow any then-established "LEADER" of either aesthetic or religious import, Satie was only willing to lead himself, though he closed his letter of independence with more lofty religious rhetoric, "[swearing] before the Fathers of the Holy Catholic Church" that he did not mean to offend Péladan, calling himself "a poor man with thought for nothing but his Art."[37]

Aping Péladan, the bestselling novelist, was a sensible move for an unknown café pianist who wanted to draw the public's attention and defend against certain critics. Whiting describes Satie and Gauthier-Villars's battles in the Parisian press in detail, noting that Willy sometimes asked his friends at various presses to respond to Satie the grandiose smart-ass in his stead. In May 1895 Satie, though very much undergunned, tried to play the same game. He took it upon himself to produce and publish the *Cartulaire*, a journal filled with declarative articles, which Satie signed with his own name and with pen names. One statement, signed by a François de Paule, Lord of the Marches of Savoy, reads:

I've gotten word about those who dare to murmur against Those who care to defend Catholic Art and Faith. It is madness. The madmen that drive the revolt to this point of aberration are the impious, the heretics, the apostates, the deicides, the affiliates of the odious Masonic sect, the mercenaries of Art, the evasive writers. Let them be silent, those who live in human corruption; they have no right to speak before their judges. Because the world allows itself to be guided by Evil, they have made themselves the propagators of abomination. They have driven God from earth, troubled the simple, defiled the splendid soul of Childhood, destroyed the holy institutions of centuries of grandeur. They have made art the source of the most guilty pleasures.

The time of their domination is at an end. They must be confounded and know the supreme punishment. The Christian world abjures weakness, dire complacency and human respect. God wished Us to be tested in affliction, to strengthen Our souls for the combat which shall give rise to the Regeneration of Western society. We rise to perform this task.[38]

Satie's conspicuous mention of the "evasive writers" seems to make his real target obvious. Reading this passage, one may assume that the "Evil One" that Satie lambasted in his earlier "Epistle," like the "madmen" whom he castigates here, refers to Willy. Satie established a clever middle position between Péladan and his nemesis in the press, using the same rhetoric as either a shield or a weapon, at his convenience.[39]

However, one may also get the sense from Satie's overblown rhetoric that his motivations were not entirely satirical. Why, during a moment in his life during which the composer was all but broke, would he spend his last pennies producing the *Cartulaire* if his aim was simply to make fun of Péladan, Willy, or the church? The composer's devotional rhetoric and his efforts to infuse his early music with a kind of spiritual aura may very well have been a smoke screen, a way of posturing himself to establish a presence in the press. Yet the screen seems, in my view, rather thin. There is little reason to doubt that Satie and Péladan saw the same problem: the decadence of "the West," a decay in genuine feeling that various artists depicted during Satie and Péladan's day. One need only think of Edgar Degas's *L'Absinthe* (1875–76), a painting that epitomizes the kind of estranged desolation and frightening vacuity wrought by modern urbanity. As tongue-in-cheek as certain of his statements were, and as cynical as he is known to have been, all evidence suggests at very least that Satie (and Péladan) shared a genuine commitment to the transformative power of new art—satirical, mystical, or symbolist—whether transformation would come about through some kind of immersive reverie, through humor, or through aversion to boredom. After all, why use chant motifs? Why spend so much effort to self-mysticize?[40]

Just as the young bohemian lacked the commitment necessary to be seriously religious, he lacked the pedigree (and work ethic) necessary to join the serious musical establishment. Thrice rejected when he applied to positions at the Institut de France or the Académie Française, Satie locked himself away scribbling—with obsessively ornate penmanship— about a fantasied Church of Art of Jesus Christ the Leader, in which the composer alone was founder and high priest leading a sect of billions of people.[41] His attempts to compensate for his lack of formal study by filling his resume with fictional compositions, a grandiosity on par with his Catholic writings, failed to impress the Académie, just as his mystical meanderings failed to impress the public. He was neither a true adherent of a particular religious sect, preferring to imagine his own, nor a member of the musical elite, imagining himself as his own elite.

Satie was alone. Two months after the publication of Satie's *Cartulaires* lambasting heretics (and Willy), he ran out of money. He moved to a tiny apartment, known in Satie literature as his *placard*, at 6 Rue Cortot in Paris. In 1897, the Chat Noir closed its doors, and by 1898 Satie ran out of money yet again, asking for his brother Conrad's aid to move, finally, to the unheated dingy abode in Arcueil-Cachan. He would return from time to time to Montmartre to accompany songs and see friends, but then would disappear again on an hours-long nighttime walk back to his lonely lodging, a manuscript in one hand and a cane or hammer for self-defense in the other. We are not sure what Satie did in his apartment in "Arcachan" (as he called it), other than drink, play piano, and continue to scrawl upon his manuscript, but I imagine he asked himself certain "ontological" questions. What is the point of being, after all? His answer, upon his re-emergence after the turn of the century and the beginnings of his fame, was to kill profundity and thus to move away from music's profound illusions.

· · ·

Just as Satie's "mystico-liturgical" style may be heard as either a serious bid to recreate Péladanian mysticism in musical form or as a gag, one may choose to experience musical repetition as a vehicle for a possible Bergsonian experience . . . or not. A tension between illusory experience and the invoked "reality," between mystery and banality, seems to characterize Satie's style and persona, and is an apt metaphor, too, for how a scholar might think of Bergson. The philosopher was, during the first decade of the twentieth century, worshipped as something of a philosopher-mystic at the same time that detractors such as Bertrand Russell called him a poet rather than a philosopher. There are stories of his followers making pilgrimages to Bergson's summer home in Switzerland, where they collected locks of his hair left at the local barbershop; of women fainting during his lectures, delivered in an overpacked auditorium at the Collège de France; of students crowding outside the doors and infiltrating windows to listen to Bergson's rapturous monologues every Friday at 5 pm.[42] Some believed that he revealed truth while others held that he missed it completely. From our perspective, Satie and Bergson may be seen to have allowed for quite different reactions in face of a similar temporal illusion. Now we oscillate and plunge into mystery; now we wake up and soberly listen to a simple and banal mechanism—either way, back and forth, back and forth we go. Bergson believed there *must* be something more than the dull churning of mechanism, insisting that the seeming magic of sensory experience affirms our freedom in face of whatever might limit it.

Though charmed by Péladan's mysticism, Satie does not seem to have made up his mind too clearly about what kind of experience his music was to evoke. This seeming inconsistency, as I have suggested, was the heart of Satie's aesthetic, an internal conflict that might lead one to think of the composer as having two faces, one looking upward toward mysterious ineffable heights, and the other sneering, daring to bore or to annoy with meaningless loops, harmonic colors that go nowhere, and musical ambience that just . . . vibrates. While each of his faces was present from the start, the jeering and mocking face won by the end.

Satie was, of course, not alone in escaping the Parisian scene during the *fin-de-siècle* period to seek inspiration elsewhere. Péladan and the symbolists in his circle sought this "elsewhere" in faraway religious states, just as Paul Gauguin, who had ventured to Tahiti beginning in 1890, sought refuge in the tropics where he developed a different way of depicting (and mastering) primitive femininity (Figure 6). What Gauguin's well-known paintings of Tahitian natives share with Delville's *Idol of Perversity*—aside from the obvious fascination with otherness (coupled with an inherent misogynism) and an anti-modern or anti-rational mode of artistic engagement—is a deeper sense of these artists' discontent with Euro-centered aesthetic ideals. Gauguin declared in an 1890 letter to his friend, Vincent Van Gogh, that "art is a business regulated in advance by cold calculations"—a business he despised. In quasi-mystical fashion, he imagined that living "with a gentle, moneyless tribe that lives from the soil" would allow him to create a "studio of the tropics" that would "perhaps form the St. John the Baptist of the painting of the future, re-immersed there in a more natural, more primitive and above all less putrefied life."[43]

Austere occult renunciation in Paris was therefore matched by a quite literal renunciation of all modern conveniences outside Paris. Keeping in view the work of Péladan and his Montmartre circle, Gauguin's vision of a simple hut-studio in the tropics, and Satie's self-cloister in Arcachan, one might speculate that for these artists, illusion *was* the other: that which allures the spirit toward another path, hinting of something truer and deeper beneath cold western calculation.

As the next section will suggest, for Bergson this realm of other-

FIGURE 6. Paul Gauguin, "Apple Picking," a portion of *Where Do We Come From? What Are We? Where Are We Going?* (1897–98), oil on canvas.

ness was to be found in the liminal states exposed through hypnotic practices. While Satie ventured on his nighttime walks, the philosopher drew inspiration from hypnotics, catatonics, hysterics, and other aberrant personalities in Parisian clinics. As we will see, however, Bergson's writings, which were inspired by actual experience, nevertheless laid the groundwork for his twentieth-century followers to forge an ontological understanding of time that went beyond any specific experience. Just as the pendulum swung, by the end of Satie's life, away from mystery and toward banality, Bergson's legacy suggests that the mystery and sensationalism of Paris's *fin de siècle* has been occluded from our own memory of this philosopher of time. There is always otherness concealed within an ontology.

BERGSON'S ILLUSIONS

Let us try to remember a moment of the past, something distant that we do not often recall. At first this moment is indistinct; we seem to leave the present in order to grasp whatever event or image we seek, yet we cannot at first find it. Then, slowly, the past begins to take form. Bergson led the reader through an internal contemplation. When we attempt to remember, he suggested, "we detach ourselves from the present in order to replace ourselves, first in the past in general, then in a certain region of the past—a work of adjustment, something like the focusing of a camera."[44] Observing this difference between "the past in general" and a "specific region" requires a certain sensitivity. Slowly the features of the memory come into focus, but before the picture takes shape "our recollection still remains virtual; we simply prepare ourselves to receive it by adopting the appropriate attitude." This attitude of openness or receptivity to something indeterminate is already familiar: it is akin to the sensitive state one must adopt in order to be moved to sadness by the musical imitation of a groan. This state is like a pause, a moment between breaths. "Little by little [the memory] comes into view like a condensing cloud," Bergson continued; "from the virtual state it passes into the actual."[45]

In *Matter and Memory*, Bergson visualized this play between past and present in the form of a cone (Figure 7). The point "S" signifies the present moment, and each curve moving upward from the point represents moments of the past receding further and further backward in time. The entire past is therefore always with us, an invisible and unconscious infinity that Deleuze would call a "virtual coexistence."[46] The "now" moment results from the downward pull of these many-layered pasts into the present. The self connects with the past anew in each moment; this is the self-creative power of the human being, what Bergson termed in *Creative Evolution* (1907) as the *élan vital*.

The curious thing about Bergson's memory cone is that the highest and widest part of the cone, the most distant layer of the past, is represented as much larger than the present moment. The further "up" the cone one travels, reaching further backward in time, the larger "the past in general" becomes. We are *not sensitive enough* to ever be fully aware of how strong a hold the virtual past has on us since we can only ever stand on the tip of the cone. Though the past is not actual, it is never really absent either—far from it. Beyond the specific feelings, moments, or images that we might recall or actualize, the very act of remembering indicates that a virtual past exists beyond the individual

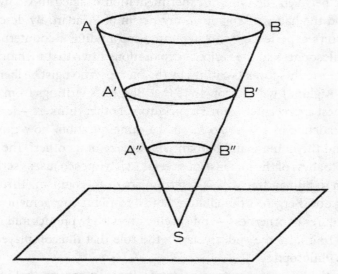

FIGURE 7. Henri Bergson's memory cone. From *Matière et Mémoire: Essai sur la relation du corps à l'esprit* (Paris: F. Alcan, 1896).

psyche. As Deleuze observed in *Bergsonism*, this virtual past is, in a sense, "identical with being in itself," and hence when we try to remember, "*we leap into ontology.*"[47]

In *fin-de-siècle* Paris, it did not require a "leap into ontology" to understand that the past is always present and tangible. Anyone who experimented with hypnosis could have felt this, since the hypnotic effects that Bergson found so compelling had a brutal real-world counterpoint in Parisian clinics. Beginning in 1877, Jean-Martin Charcot had used magnets and doses of amyl nitrate, colored images, and tuning forks on female patients at the Hôpital Universitaire la Pitié-Salpêtrière to provoke gestural responses that corresponded with his patients' mental states.[48] Charcot's well-known images of cataleptic faces and contorted physiognomies suggested that the conscious self was subject to an unconscious that, precisely because it was not there—not present—could exert a frightening influence.[49]

My purpose in this section is to suggest, first, that when Bergson wrote of the mysterious effects of rhythm and meter, of heightened sensitivity and virtual memory, he took cues from the same strange Parisian world into which Satie plunged—though, of course, there was a marked difference between the kind of experimentation enacted in Charcot's clinics and the half-winking, lurid mysticism of Péladan. By describing Bergson's experiences with hypnosis, and finding a counterpoint to the philosopher's (quite serious) explorations of virtual memory in (only purportedly serious) writings by the "parapsychologist" Albert de Rochas d'Aiglun, I will demonstrate that Bergson's writings from this time are best appreciated against a backdrop of other thinkers—serious or not, academic or not—who faced the same question: how can we understand the human, and human will, in face of its other? The unfathomable abyss of the unconscious seems to have posed just as serious a problem to human free will as determinism or mechanism. Through exploring how Bergson's thought developed from his engagement with various figures of otherness—and specifically with hypnotics and neuropaths—I aim, by the end, to clarify the role that illusion played in Bergson's philosophy.

Charcot's clinic represents one side of a Parisian context that introduced Bergson to hypnosis, while the other side was more sensationalistic, along the lines of Satie's Péladan. A particularly outlandish caricature of *fin-de-siècle* mysticism—and, for our purposes, an apt counterpoint to Bergson's (quite serious) exploration of virtual memory—hit the Parisian presses during the next decade when Rochas d'Aiglun, a military engineer who dubbed himself a parapsychologist, insisted that certain kinds of musical rhythm could put female somnambulists in touch with their astral self. Rochas claimed to have found a medium—really an actress that he called Lina—who, when hypnotized, would not only disrobe provocatively before Rochas's camera but would also mimic a number of folk dances that would have been "materially impossible for her to know."[50] Lina's dances included a Javanese dance to a newly composed tune, Spanish and Arabic dances, and a few French and Polish folk jigs—a *bourrée auvergnate,* a *danse brétonne,* and an "ancient provincial polonaise." Each of these dances, according to Rochas, Lina "recalled without hesitation, with all the characteristic gestures," and with the Javanese dance in particular, "she reproduced the very particular movements of the hands with extraordinary clearness."[51]

We might think of Rochas's musings about Lina as the misogynistic caricature of Bergson's own notion of virtual memory. The deep dark space of mysterium that the philosopher visualized as a cone was, for Rochas (or Charcot), a deep dark space of otherness, whether of aberrant femininity or of non-western cultural expressions that would spring suddenly, like the reflexes of a hysteric, from a world of half-dreams. It is as if that moment of heightened receptivity expanded infinitely, linking Rochas's Lina back to primitive and non-European dances.[52] Though Bergson likely would have balked at Rochas's sensationalism, he was nevertheless open to the idea that the curves of the memory cone might reach far, far back. He sought answers to questions that readers of Charcot's medical articles and of Rochas's theosophical rags also asked: between catatonia and astrologia, what is the human after all? Charcot's images were frightening portrayals of a kind of biologism—a radical disavowal of the conscious mind—while for Rochas hypnosis was a gateway to magic, an indication of astral bodies and other spiritualist myths. Each involved an emptying-out of conscious thought, as if "real conditions" could be revealed through the transparent medium of a docile woman.[53]

The proliferation of images of catatonic women—whether serious or farcical—may explain why, when Bergson wrote of the hypnotic effects of the arts during the opening of *Time and Free Will*, he emphasized that "the processes of art" allow us to "find, in a weakened form, a refined and in some sense *spiritualized* version of the processes commonly used to induce the state of hypnosis."[54] The process is spiritualized because art does not simply hollow us out into mindless shells, but rather allows for a heightened sensitivity to sense data. The philosopher believed that such heightened sensitivity might be the saving grace of philosophy, and before he wrote *Time and Free Will*, he had observed moments of heightened sensitivity quite directly.

Hyperaesthesia was the subject of Bergson's first published philosophical essay in 1886. Describing an experiment at the Académie de Clermont in which he and a colleague (a M. Robinet) induced a hypnotic trance in four fifteen- to seventeen-year-olds (apparently through prolonged eye contact and the placing of hands upon the participant's heads), Bergson stated that the teenagers "[plunged] instantly into a state of stupor that characterizes the most pronounced hypnotism: the eyes [remained] disproportionately open and fixed, the physiognomy losing all intelligent expression." This trance state was accompanied by "all the usual cataleptic phenomena: general insensitivity, obstinacy to retain the attitudes suggested by the magnetist."[55] By "general insensitivity," Bergson seems to have referred to a general absence of intervention by the representing mind—the mind that forms experience into an abstraction that is useful for instrumental ends (naming, reasoning, calculating, and working toward a practical end). That the teenagers became "insensitive" suggests that they were suddenly open to whatever happened to be there, refraining from normal conscious processes. As a result, they gained a whole other kind of sensitivity. Seated in front of Robinet, who had before him an opened book, the hypnotized teenagers were able to discern the page numbers and various phrases from the text. Despite the appearance that magic had occurred, Bergson did not take the teenagers' ability to read bits of Robinet's text as evidence of mind transference, but rather attributed this feat to heightened sensitivity induced by the hypnotism, which allowed the teenagers to discern parts of the text as reflected in Robinet's eyes. A "general insensitivity" to their physical surroundings was thus coupled with a superhuman sensitivity; once the conscious mind was subdued, vision was enhanced.

When Bergson wrote of the effects of musical rhythm in *Time and Free Will*, he surely had this hypersensitive state in mind. He did not believe that such a state allowed access to an otherworldly realm, but rather that human perceptions were mystical enough. Profound truth was not to be found in the *au-delà*, but rather in the usually obscured reality of actual experience. As art historian Todd Cronan has put it, "Bergson's claim is not that the artist produces sensations in the beholder's mind and body, as in traditional accounts of 'suggestion,' but rather that those emotions are *already there* in the beholder's self but buried beneath the 'normal flow' of conscious intent."[56] To argue for his belief that something is already there in the human being, Bergson smoothly integrated the lessons that he learned from observing the teenagers at Clermont with his discussion of musical aesthesia.

Studying hypersensitive psychological states allowed the philosopher to extrapolate truths about sensory experience in general. During a section of *Time and Free Will* devoted to the sensation of tone, for instance, Bergson remarks that "some neuropaths cannot be present at a conversation without moving their lips." Such individuals cannot help sympathizing with the speech uttered around them, mimicking the voices of others just as we might sigh at the musical imitation of a groan—after all, "this is only an exaggeration of what takes place in the case of every one of us." A phantom identification occurs as "we repeat to ourselves the sounds heard, so as to carry ourselves back into the psychic state out of which they emerged." In the same breath, Bergson then explains the "suggestive power of music" by writing of a certain motion and attitude that "sound imparts [on] our body," suggesting that we repeat musical sounds to ourselves in order to link these sounds to "original states."[57] This inner repetition of vocal or musical sound is a deeper, more introspective form of repetition than what Bergson previously described when he invoked the oscillations of a hypnotists' pendulum or of musical rhythm and meter; but whether we speak or we sing, the effect is the same. This movement is not an oscillation, but rather an instant psychic echo that establishes a sympathetic connection between an individual's present state and certain states inhabited in the past; in other words, we carry ourselves back into the virtual past, immediately, constantly. The connection cultivated through interior repetition between a sound (musical or vocal) and a memory reveals, once again, the actual temporal play of becoming. The past and present blur.

Beginning from his experiences observing hyperaesthesia and other sympathetic states, Bergson tried to see beyond the tip of the cone. To take some liberty with Bergson's diagram, it is almost as if the effects of hypnosis or musical aesthesia had the power to invert the memory cone (Figure 8). Suddenly point "S," the present, collapses with the distant past and it becomes possible to sense how profoundly the past shapes the present. It is as if one may step outside time, through a leap, a flip of the cone, to see the whole play of virtual and actual, and thus to apprehend what Bergson called "the *turn* of experience." Illustrating this turn as a "faint light" that "[illuminates] the passage from the *immediate* to the *useful*," Bergson contended that the real curve of experience, which "[stretches] out into the darkness behind us," is anterior to the conscious mind's intervention.[58] Just before the mind transforms our experience into a representation that is useful for our survival or for our life in society, the real curve moves in the dark.

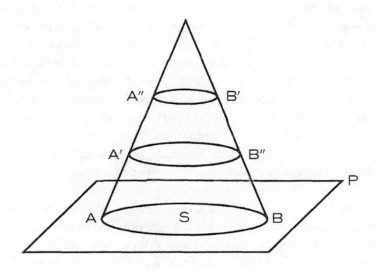

FIGURE 8. An inverted memory cone.

• • •

This real curve of experience, a peculiar poetic image, is only thinkable if one imagines oneself in a state like the teenagers at Clermont,
suddenly sensitive to a condition that consciousness would normally
ignore. This is the power, Suzanne Guerlac asserts, of Bergson's endeavor
to invoke the concrete reality of lived time as against the abstractions
upon which philosophy ordinarily relies. "What is so thrilling about
reading Bergson is that he undertakes to do the impossible, namely to
treat philosophically what thought has suppressed: the radical force of
time as becoming."[59] I would add that this figure of the real curve is further evidence that illusory experience was central in Bergson's thought.
For what is a real curve if not a profound philosophical kind of illusion?
It is not merely a literary trope or an abstract figure that Bergson fabricated. The real curve *is something to be experienced*; it has to do with
actual sensations that a reader may recall and rethink. This curve is
graspable only if one is willing to take the plunge, so to speak, to pass
one's actual experiences through the medium of Bergsonian intuition.
It takes a kind of trick of perception, a trick worked as one follows Bergson's thought and imagines oneself peering behind the abstractions of
conscious life into the very instability of the "now," the always-fleeting
moment that music well embodies. A deeper reality can be discursively
apprehended, and a distinction made, in Bergson's own words, between
"properly *human* experience" and experience beyond the turn.[60]

This integration of psychological and artistic experience, dual sides
of a philosophy meant to engage directly with temporal life, allows one
to confront the dual role of illusion in Bergson's thought. On one hand,
a kind of psychological illusion ensues when we make time into a representation imbued with space, when we confuse quality with quantity.
To quote Deleuze:

> Bergson borrows an idea from Kant although he completely
> transforms it: It was Kant who showed that reason deep within
> itself engenders not mistakes but *inevitable* illusions, only the
> effect of which could be warded off.[61]

According to the well-known Kantian notion, human understanding is
an *a priori* faculty that works like computer hardware, determining the
rules and limits of our subjective experience. The mind is both the tran-

scendental creator and supreme judge of all our experiences, and it sets the stage on which these experiences may take place.[62] In *Kant's Critical Philosophy*, Deleuze contends that the knowing subject, in Kant, is "deeply tormented by the ambition to make things in themselves known to us."[63] Human understanding can only grasp truth when it stays in the realm of appearances; but the understanding becomes greedy, seeking to overstep its capacity to apply the rules of subjective certainty to things in themselves. In this way, the subject cannot avoid creating what Deleuze elsewhere termed "simulacra of belief," and in *Bergsonism*, Deleuze implies that Bergson adjusts Kant's thesis, demonstrating that we produce simulacra of belief not because we try to understand that which is unknowable, but rather because we do not take the time to really understand our experience in the first place.[64]

"*Intuition*," in Deleuze's words, "is the method of Bergsonism": intuition is the method through which Bergson sorts out the inevitable category errors we make when we perceive only differences in quantity when in fact our experience is always composed of interpenetrating states and sensations that differ in kind. For Bergson, in Guerlac's words, "we make contact with duration by considering how time happens in us—how we feel it pass—and we do this by attending to the workings of our own consciousness."[65] It is along this route of correction, of intuitive reorientation, that we may sense that aesthetic illusion played a positive role in Bergson's thought, since the arts allowed the philosopher to make contact—or to put his readers in contact—with how time happens in us.

Bergson's description of the mysterious musical groan of sadness or the multi-temporal flow through which a melody proceeds recalls a familiar dichotomy between aesthetic appearance or semblance (*Schein*) and deeper reality from Nietzsche's *The Birth of Tragedy* (1872, 1886). As is well known, Nietzsche described the philosophical basis of the arts by way of a distinction between Apollo, the god of dreams who presides over the world of appearances with an air of detachment and mastery, and Dionysus, Apollo's obverse, who plunges headlong into appearances by way of intoxication. Describing the Apollonian spirit, Nietzsche drew heavily on the idea of illusion:

The beautiful illusion of the dream worlds is the prerequisite of all plastic art. . . . [Artists, like] philosophical men have a presentiment that the reality in which we live and have our being is also mere appearance, and that another, quite different reality lies beneath it.[66]

While the Apollonian artist strives toward the perfection of visible forms, the Dionysian seeks a raw experience of truth, an "intoxicated reality [that] seeks to destroy the individual and redeem him by a mystic feeling of oneness."[67] Bergson's mysterious groan was, along these lines, an illusory intoxication. Unlike Nietzsche, however, who invoked the notion of illusion or *Schein* as he described spiritual archetypes, Bergson trained his gaze toward the concrete truths (and illusions) of aesthetic experience—that is, toward sensation.

In the section of *Time and Free Will* devoted to the sensation of tone, Bergson urges his reader to consciously dissociate the sensation of sound from the physical effort necessary to sing. Since a pitch sung in the extreme high register requires extra vocal tension, resounding from the throat and nasal cavities, we tend to represent these pitches as greater in quantity and higher in space than the lower sounds produced when we sing from the chest or the belly. The temporal life of a sensation gets confused with a spatial representation. "I grant that a sharper sound calls up the picture of a higher position in space. But does it follow from this that the notes of the scale, as auditory sensations, differ otherwise than in quality?"[68] With his implied "no," Bergson insists that there is nothing inherently high or low about sound: physical sensations differ in kind from the sounds we hear. He asks the reader to

take away the shock, the well-marked vibration, which you sometimes feel in your head or even throughout your body: take away the clash which takes place between sounds heard simultaneously: what will be left except an indefinable quality of the sound which is heard?[69]

When one grasps a sound as pure sensation, one can then ascertain pure quality distinct from any representation of quantity.

This orientation toward the senses led Bergson to develop a position on aesthetic illusion that distinguishes him from Nietzsche—since, to recall Fillerup, an illusion is not something dreamed up, it is a trick of perception that involves actual sensory data—and that also sets Bergson off from the nascent phenomenological tradition. It is curious, on one hand, that with his instruction to "take away the shock" and "the clash which takes place between sounds heard simultaneously" in order to apprehend "an indefinable quality of the sound" perceived, Bergson seems to anticipate the *epoché* or reduction characteristic of Edmund Husserl's phenomenology.[70] He asks his reader to bracket out certain external sensory perceptions in order to grasp phenomena as intentional objects of the mind. One may point out various similarities between Bergson and Husserl, noting, for instance, that Bergson would seem to affirm that the "waking now" is, in Husserl's words, "infinitely alive," stretching out in both directions toward "its unalive past and future":

> When consciously awake, I find myself at all times, and without my ever being able to change this, set in relation to a world which, through its constant changes, remains one and ever the same. It is continually "present" for me, and I myself am a member of it.[71]

Bergson upheld a basic belief characteristic of Husserl's phenomenology that the soul is in some sense always coherent, able to discover and rediscover itself in the form of the "living present" (*der lebendige Gegenwart*). But, on the other hand, since Bergson insisted that sensation occurs (like everything else) in time, he would not have believed in the final analysis that phenomena can be adequately represented as intentional objects, since the "now" moment is in fact an intermingling of many coterminous states.

While on one hand the kind of illusion that ensues when we confuse quality with quantity presents a profound problem for the mind, on the other hand, Bergson's description of the sensation of tone, as well as his invocations of other artistic experiences, suggests that aesthetic illusion played a redemptive role in the philosopher's thought. The strange tricks of perception by which time seems to slow or cease; the hyperaesthesia inspired by rhythm and measure in music or poetry; the meditative experience of observing oneself recalling a long-lost memory; the inner psychic echo through which we associate a sound with a psychic state: these moments in Bergson allow one to see that aesthetic illusion offers a kind of corrective, an imaginative detour by which we might put ourselves back into duration.

TOWARD THE VIRTUAL: DELEUZE'S BERGSON

As Bergson's twentieth-century readers took up his ideas, however, the profound temporal illusions that so compelled the philosopher fell out of focus. Whereas Bergson took cues from the arts or from hypnotism to affirm the self-creative power of the "soul"—a word that Bergson frequently used in *Time and Free Will*—Deleuze was less interested in these illusions. In place of duration as a qualitative experience of lived time, Deleuze substituted "the virtual," a kind of impersonal, absolute, and ultimately abstract ground for all possible experience. This change in focus makes clear a central thread of Deleuze's *Bergsonism*: namely, his conviction that Bergson "develops the notion of the *virtual* to its highest degree and bases a whole philosophy of memory and life on it."[72] The virtual is somewhat like a non-actual or a negative time, which is not to say that the virtual is fictive—far from it: Deleuze is adamant that the virtual "*possesses a reality.*"[73] In other words, the virtual is not an illusion; it is not of the order of illusion. The virtual, instead, is an integral reality, crucial to defining how consciousness works.[74]

In *Bergsonism*, Deleuze reads Bergson's description (quoted earlier) of the act of trying to remember. Foregrounding Bergson's sense that following the process of recollection makes us "conscious of an act *sui generis*," Deleuze draws out the implications of this act. He cautions:

one must avoid an overly psychological interpretation of the text. Bergson does indeed speak of a psychological act; but if this act is "*sui generis*," this is because it has made a genuine *leap*. We place ourselves *at once* in the past; we leap into the past as into a proper element. . . . There is therefore a "past in general" that is not the particular past of a particular present but that is like an onto-logical element, a past that is eternal and for all time, the condition of the "passage" of every particular present. It is the past in general that makes possible all pasts. According to Bergson, we first put ourselves back into the past in general: He describes in this way the *leap into ontology*. We really leap into being, into being-in-itself, into the being in itself of the past. It is a case of leaving psychology altogether. It is a case of an immemorial or ontological Memory. It is only then, once the leap has been made, that recollection will gradually take on a psychological existence: "from the virtual it passes into the actual state. . . ." We have had to search at the place where it is, in impassive Being, and gradually we give it an embodiment, a "psychologization."[75]

Bergson never used the phrase "leap into ontology": here and elsewhere, Deleuze emphasizes the "extra-psychological range" of Bergson's thought, drawing out the implications of a difference that Bergson described between perception and recollection.

Common sense might suggest that time is linear, that the past disappears with each successive moment of the present never to be recovered in its fullness. No matter how vivid it may seem, a memory can only be a hollowed-out representation of a presence that has already dwindled like a cloud; only the present is alive to the mind. For Bergson, in Deleuze's view, to think of the difference between present perception and the recollection of the past in these terms—as more or less alive, more or less present—is to fall into another (inevitable yet) dangerous psychological illusion. We make time into a representation imbued with space yet again, conceiving present and past as nodes in a succession, which is to misunderstand the relation between present and past in terms of degrees of intensity or vividness when in fact there is a difference in kind between them. Perception attends to whatever is present to consciousness—sense data and mental images—whereas recollection involves making the past present and constituting the past *in* the present. In other words, perception has more to do with matter whereas memory involves a complex and always-present ontological condition that Deleuze aims to clarify, drawing from Bergson and even reaching beyond what Bergson seems to have intended.

Deleuze calls the theory of memory "one of the most profound, but perhaps also one of the least understood, aspects of Bergsonism."[76] In his explication, Deleuze shows common sense to be wrong: the temporal succession between past, present, and future is broken—or, at least, shown to be too simple, a misrepresentation. If the past in general makes possible all pasts, it is because the past endures; it is a general form that makes the whole play of perception and recollection possible. "We have great difficulty in understanding a survival of the past in itself because we believe that the past is no longer, that is has ceased to be." When we think in terms of differences in degree and think of the past as the absent shadow of our colorful, living present, we tend to think that whatever we perceive *is*, that only the present exists. "We have thus confused Being with being-present": in fact, "the present *is not*; rather, it is pure becoming, always outside itself. It *is* not, but it acts." This is a familiar situation: the performed presence of music is always already gone; the present is always shot through with traces of a present that no longer *is*. However, whereas Derrida (as I described in the Prelude) would illustrate this kind of temporal movement as a play of traces, Deleuze understands this always-vanishing nature of the present as a "pure becoming": the "proper element" of the present "is not being but the active or the useful." Whereas the present is best understood as something active and useful,

> [t]he past, on the other hand, has ceased to be active or useful. But it has not ceased to be. Useless and inactive, impassive, it IS, in the full sense of the word: It is identical with being in itself. It should not be said that it "was," since it is the in-itself of being, and the form under which being is preserved in itself (in opposition to the present, the form under which being is consummated and places itself outside of itself). At the limit, the ordinary determinations are reversed: of the present, we must say at every instant that it "was," and of the past, that it "is," that it is eternally, for all time.[77]

The past is the eternal condition for the passage of any present, a general "form under which" the in-itself of Being is preserved, and under which being places itself outside of itself. In Fann's words, "[t]his is, of course, an ontological talk. In plain English: we have replaced or misplaced ideas (words) with realities. Reality is a continuity of flow. Derrida calls it a chain of 'traces'; Bergson calls it 'pure becoming.'"[78]

The difference between Derrida and Deleuze's takes on this continuity of flow would be that the always-vanishing nature of the present destabilizes, in Derrida's view, any possibility that we might envision being-in-itself "eternally, for all time," whereas Deleuze believes that the past survives, that it IS ontologically. Once again, there are at least two ways of apprehending what appears to be the same temporal situation, the always-vanishing present. Bergson, as we have seen, sought stability for the soul, training his gaze toward the psychological experience of temporality to affirm our self-creative power, while in Deleuze this self-creative power fades into relief. In the final analysis, *Bergsonism* casts Bergson as an ontologist, a thinker of absolute conditions abstracted from any concrete real.

The difference between these two Bergsons, between Henri himself and Bergson*ism*, might be summed up, following Deleuze's caution, as one between a "psychologically" oriented inquiry and an "ontologically" oriented inquiry, and this distinction will become, through what remains of this chapter, something of a foil for our current thought about sound. This dichotomy between "illusion" and "the real," which runs through Bergson's own thought and characterizes part of his reception, is perhaps at the heart of what music, in the broadest sense, *is*. As I have endeavored to demonstrate, for both Bergson and Satie there was something magical about music's repeating rhythms. The state of artistic absorption, like the sleepy state of hypnosis, indicated to Bergson that consciousness depends upon a virtual realm beyond itself, which is a philosophical way of saying what artists in Satie's milieu already knew. As Deleuze took up Bergson's notion of memory, however, and even as Satie conceived of *Furniture Music*, these thinkers trained their gazes—one quite seriously, the other ironically—toward the non-psychological conditions undergirding any such mystical experience. The Deleuzian notion of virtuality casts Bergson and Satie's respective "mysticisms" in sharp relief. By following Satie and Bergson's respective twentieth-century legacies, from Satie's later phase to our own late-Bergsonian moment, one may understand how, and perhaps why, we have moved away from aesthetic illusion and toward "ontology."

To explain "the virtual," Deleuze carried Bergson's own effort to distinguish the qualitative from the quantitative further, though toward a distinct end. "'Object' and 'objective' denote [a] quantitative multiplicity," he wrote, whereas the subject or "the subjective" has to do with qualitative or non-numerical multiplicities. To understand the former, we can think of numbers, which "[have] only differences in degree, [hence their] differences, whether realized *or not*, are always actual in [them]."[79] Whether realized *or not*: this is the key phrase, since the number one hundred, for instance, is the aggregate of ten groups of ten and is also the sum of many smaller numbers that we may not "realize"; that is, we do not think of "ten tens." Yet these smaller numbers are always already there—always actual—within the bigger number. The "objective" in Bergson therefore referred to that which differs only in degree. A quantitative multiplicity is like a big mass of the same stuff— everything is in the open, so to speak; we can add, subtract, or multiply without changing the nature of numbers themselves. The same reasoning applies when we impose numerical values on an experience: notes are high or low, loud or soft, yet are still notes; sounds *are represented as* being of the same kind, ignoring subtler differences in quality. By contrast, in a qualitative multiplicity different *kinds* of phenomena become mixed. We cannot count how many different feelings are contained within a feeling of melancholy, for example, especially since our feeling of melancholy changes as soon as we attend to it.[80]

Virtuality is therefore the condition of complex aggregate psychological states. Aesthetic experience is symphonic: we blend different feelings or conscious states just as a listener hears different and layered instrumental voices, pushing some notes aside in order to dwell upon others. This process creates what might be termed a *multiplicity of virtuals*. Consciousness parries with related states—like envy and depression, for instance, two emotions that are different in kind; one state might form the background and the other the foreground, or vice-versa. Certain states are therefore virtual, others actual, and conscious life is a kind of constant oscillation between virtual and actual.

However, whereas Bergson may have preferred to think of this play as evidence supporting an inherently human capacity, ultimately affirming the soul, in *Bergsonism* Deleuze used Bergson's observations about consciousness to point toward something entirely beyond the human. Reading the passage from *Duration and Simultaneity* that I quoted earlier—Bergson's Walter Pater-esque description of sitting on a bank of a river and listening to his life's deeps—Deleuze writes: "The flowing of the water, the flight of the bird, the murmur of my life form three *fluxes*." *Flux replaces the soul*: "my duration is one of them"—the water, the bird, or the murmur, as I choose—"and also the element that contains the two others," containing them virtually. A bird's flight and an inner murmur are different in kind and uniting them into one duration, my duration, implies subsuming multiple fluxes into one.[81] The play of actual*izing* certain qualitative perceptions while leaving others unactualized, continues; we divide, unify, and divide again continuously.

While Bergson affirmed that the soul may indeed fly like a bird, with all the poetic and symbolic weight that such an image might carry, Deleuze emphasized the non-psychological, non-individual—in a word: absolute—nature of this self-creative power.[82] If there is anything special about the human being, it is only that it forms a locus of different fluxes reaching backward into the virtual past while also flowing forward. *This movement is pure ontology*, as if a person is merely a node linking many warps and wefts weaving through a timeless Time. "It could be said that in man, and only in man, the actual becomes adequate to the virtual"; only "man is capable of rediscovering all the levels . . . that coexist in the virtual Whole."[83] Psychological states, on this view, are mere epiphenomena of a fundamental time, an *ontological time* that flows beneath what we can actualize. We are always too limited, stuck on the tip of the cone; the flux is beyond us.

Perhaps the ontological flux vibrates like *Furniture Music*. In the next and final section of this chapter, I will describe other receivers of Bergson who conceived time as a kind of non-psychological flow, positioning Satie as a strange precursor to theories of "ontological" musical temporality. While Bergson philosophized about time in prose, from our perspective, Satie can be seen to have philosophized about temporality in his music. The composer made his own kind of ontological inquiry into the nature of sound—always, of course, with the familiar wink. His growing love of the musical fragment made possible a different poetics of repetition, more grating and less nuanced than the dancing and sighing melodies that echoed from the Chat Noir. By ousting his early mystical influences, the composer anticipated later endeavors to dig "real" sound out from under the baggage of musical metaphysics. The idea now current in a certain Deleuzian branch of sound studies— that our actual sonic experience derives from, and is owed to, a supra-audible virtual realm of fluxes and vibrations—owes something to that odd Arcachan cynic.

FINALE: ONTOLOGICAL TIME IN SATIE AND BERGSONISM

After he emerged from isolation and finally gained fame, Satie envisioned a *Furniture Music* that would pulse, somewhat like a flux, somewhere beneath conscious attention. Fernand Léger recounted a walk he had with Satie in which the composer imagined a "music [that] would be part of the noises around it": a "tuneful" music that would "[soften] the noise of knives and forks without overpowering them or making itself obtrusive"; a music that "would banish the need [for table companions] to make banal conversation," while also "[neutralizing] street noises." It would be a functional music "responding to a need."[84] The stories of Satie's early forays into *Musique d'ameublement* are well-known. Darius Milhaud recounted that he and Satie premiered *Furniture Music* during the intermission of a 1920 concert of music by Les Six and Stravinsky as well as a play by Max Jacob. "A programme note warned the audience that it was not to pay any more attention to the ritornelles that would be played during the intervals than to the candelabra, the seats, or the balcony."[85] Once three scattered clarinetists, a trombonist, and a pianist (Marcelle Meyer) began to play from various corners of the auditorium, however, the audience returned to their seats to listen, much to Satie's dismay—"Go on talking!" he yelled: "Walk about! Don't listen!"[86] The composer had arranged short fragments derived from popular tunes and instructed the small band to repeat these fragments *ad nauseum*: he kept his penchant for repetition, in other words, but without the ecstasy.

By this point, Satie had begun to favor pastiche, as in his texted piano works like the *Embryons Desséchés* of 1913, desiccated embryos of eighteenth- and nineteenth-century pianistic motifs, or his series of short *Sports et divertissements* of 1914, each devoted to some charming banality of bourgeois life—picnics, yachting, golf, and tennis. Even in later works that recalled his earlier introspective mood like the *Cinq*

Nocturnes of 1919, Satie refrained from opposing legato melodies against steady ostinati. Instead, the melodies of the *Nocturnes* are "built in" to the ostinati. The melody does not soar above the repeated rhythms but seems to be collapsed with them. And each ostinato is an atomized bit—a bar or two at a time (marked with boxes in Figure 9)—that Satie strung together. If we take any one of these boxed bits, repeat it over and over again, *voilà*, we get *Furniture Music*. This is a process we cannot apply to Satie's early works, at least not without doing serious violence to them.

Satie readily applied this process of fragmentation and repetition when he composed other pieces, perhaps most obviously *Cinéma* (1924), which he wrote to accompany René Clair's *Entr'acte*, the cinematic interlude for the ballet *Rêlache*. Promoted in the Parisian press as a "ballet *instantanéiste* in two acts, with a cinematographic interlude, and Francis Picabia's dog Tail,"[87] *Rêlache* was a Ballet Suédois flop, provoking scorn from critics who balked at its seeming absence of plot. In

1er NOCTURNE

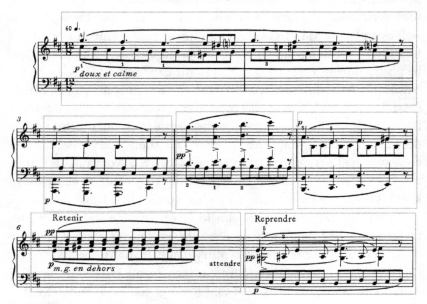

FIGURE 9. Satie's *Nocturne* no. 1 (1919).

front of a bleak set composed of metal discs, the ballet features a lone ballerina who smokes a cigarette and greets a series of suitors; gradually they all undress; she dons a beard, lies upon a stretcher, and pushes a wheelbarrow; a fireman pours water in a bucket; eventually they all disband into the audience. Francis Picabia's Dadaist aesthetic took form in the disjunct actions onstage as well as in the disjunct images of Clair's film. Beginning with slow-motion sequences of Clair and Satie jumping up and down next to a cannon (pointed at the viewer), *Entr'acte* proceeds through a hodgepodge of images, disparate signs that signify nobody-knows-what. Chimneys of Paris filmed upside down are perhaps a mock-marker of bourgeois society; the chess pieces on Marcel Duchamp's board perhaps are symbols of reason washed away as a fire hose douses Duchamp and Man Ray's chess game.

Composed of a series of short (usually one-measure-long) phrases repeated to fill up various sequences, Satie's *Cinéma* is devoid of sighs. His grating ostinati churn in ceaseless annoyance as the film moves through a loose narrative arc: a man shot dead in a hunting accident is given a funeral procession (led by a camel) that turns into a mad dash through the streets of Paris and down a rollercoaster as the coffin takes off on wheels, landing eventually in a field, opening as a magician emerges to conjure away his pursuers. Especially in the context of a ballet, Satie's musical loops recall a Stravinskian score for the Ballets Russes, though unlike the layered dissonance and polytonality of *Le Sacre du printemps*, Satie employs constant consonance and purposeful lack of orchestral finesse as tactics of aggravation. With simplistic counterpoint, *Cinéma* opens with a main "motif" (which does not really function like a motif; i.e., it never develops, is never re-cast or recontextualized alongside new musical features as the piece progresses): a bumbling bassline posed clumsily against shrill woodwinds, churning in mock-marching rhythm. Compared to the pendulum-like movement of the *Gymnopédies*, the ostinati of *Cinéma* circle and circle. Shrill monophonic wind instruments dip down and up against an ever-quickening two-step rhythm between a bass drum and cymbal—a crude mimesis of the rolling coffin wheels.

It was repetition devoid of mysticism, without long arching melodies, without sighs and moans of inimitable sadness. Whereas the *Première*

Gymnopédie featured lengthy melodic phases, *Cinéma* featured only
the barest traces of melody, a few notes in stepwise motion here, a frac-
tion of a fanfare there; instead of complex chordal colors, bare octaves
and fourths moving simplistically in parallel; instead of a poetic arc
leading from major to minor, the blunt restatement of *Cinéma*'s main
"motif" at various points hardly constituted a progression or narrative
arc. *Cinéma* is a musical collage, as if Satie fragmented items from the
everyday musical context—a march rhythm, a fanfare, a scale. No arc,
only loops; no depth, only surface. We are done with the magical effects
of induction. Late Satie, it seems, had little need for such illusions.

. . .

What happened? I take this change in Satie's style to suggest that the
composer was after a more real condition of sound, which he sought by
banalizing his music. When a composer refuses the "drastic," even as
a conceit, one is left with a bare reality, as when one refuses to take the
plunge into hypnosis, one is left sitting in front of a swinging pendulum, clock-like and mechanical. Satie's refusal of the sigh, of the poetic
illusions that characterize his earlier music, is reminiscent of the kind
of renunciation of artistic representation that Wassily Kandinsky had
theorized in 1912, claiming that abstract art, precisely because it no
longer imitates objects of the visual world, plunges deeper into the reality of line, figure, and color.

The dichotomy between the "Great Abstraction" and the "Great Realism" that structures Kandinsky's essay "On the Question of Form,"
published in Munich as part of the *Blaue Reiter Almanac*, is, despite
Kandinsky's distance from Satie's immediate context, an apt foil for the
internal conflict I have observed in Satie: namely, the clash between
his two "faces," mystical and cynical. Kandinsky provides a way to
see this opposition as dual sides of an artistic quest for the real, or, to
be more precise, for what Kandinsky would term the "inner sound"
of the medium. He explains the "Great Realism," for instance, as "a
desire to exclude from the picture the externally artistic [element] and
to embody the content of the work of art by means of the simple ('in-
artistic') rendering of the simple, hard object."[88] The "Great Realism" is
an ideal type, a style of painting in which the things of the world are

depicted plainly and simply.[89] The kind of stripped-bare simplicity and refusal of profound illusions that we can hear in *Cinéma* or even in Satie's *Nocturnes*, from this perspective, amount to the "exclusion of accustomed, importunate beauty": in other words, to a reduction of the "'artistic' element to a minimum," a refusal of embellishment, of elaborate textures and other painterly effects.

Conspicuously, for Kandinsky this reduction of the "artistic" element would allow, conversely, for "the inner sound of the thing" to ring: "the soul of the object sounds forth most strongly from within this outer shell, because external, palatable beauty can no longer distract us."[90] Satie certainly disdained the distraction of external beauty, and if we take seriously (a dangerous move) his words to Cocteau about *Musique d'ameublement* that I quoted earlier—that *Furniture Music* would create vibration for vibration's sake, like light, heat, or comfort in any form—then we might think of this banalized music as an absurdist kind of "Great Realism." *Furniture Music*, a music that refuses narrative, that proceeds through loops and through blunt restatement without development, hardly presents something "objective" in Kandinsky's sense. There is no *mise en scène*, no symphonic or operatic plot (the musicological hermeneut has no room to wax).

However, in describing the "Great Abstraction," Kandinsky invoked precisely this kind of refusal of representation, which allowed him, paradoxically, to claim that abstraction, by "[excluding] completely the objective (real) element and [embodying] the content of the work of art in 'nonmaterial' forms," accomplishes a higher kind of realism. I read "objective (real) element" to connote illusory experience: the sense that visual art (and, by extension, music) presents something beyond itself, recalling an image, drawing the audience in. Instead, the poetics of a work like *Furniture Music* hinges on "nonmaterial" forms, a phrase that Kandinsky puts in scare quotes, I think, because he does not wish to imply that the "materials" of painting are any less important in abstraction than in realism. Quite the contrary: through the use of lines, colors, and abstract shapes, which foreground the very materiality of paint on canvas, the painter would make it possible, "as in the case of realism," "to hear the whole world just as it is, without objective interpretation." The interpreter's words are useless; meaning goes silent; we hear the "inner sound" directly. This conflation of the aims of abstraction and realism allows Kandinsky, in a final moment, to synthesize the "Great Abstraction" and the "Great Realism," arguing that the former manifests *in* the latter, and vice versa:

> in their ultimate basis (= goal) these two poles equal one another. Between these two antipodes can be put an = sign:
> Realism = Abstraction
> Abstraction = Realism
> The greatest external dissimilarity becomes the greatest internal similarity.[91]

It is "objective interpretation" that is the problem for Kandinsky, since seeing an object in a painting (or perhaps hearing the musical imitation of a groan in a composition) detracts the viewer's or listener's attention away from this inner sound.[92] The inner sound is only audible once art's representational qualities are toned down in favor of color, line, and shape. Regardless of how serious Satie was, or how seriously one might take him, it is tenable that that composer was also after the "inner sound" of music—or the inner vibrations of sound—treating sound both as a "simple, hard object" in Kandinsky's sense and also as figureless material with its own life. In other words, when Satie wrote *Furniture Music*—or any of its offshoots like *Cinéma*—stubborn repetition was a kind of medium specificity: the "Great Realism" of sound. The composer's well-known quips (from his *Memoires of an Amnesiac*) that "[f]rom the beginning of my career I immediately classified myself as a phonometrographer" and not a musician—"[m]y works are of pure phonometrography"—are perhaps best understood in this light. Whatever "inner sound" Satie found may have been measurable by a *caléidophone-enregisteur*, a recording device he claimed to have used to write his *Pieces froides* of 1897 ("It took seven minutes. I called my servant to have him hear them"), or perhaps this inner sound could have been cleansed of external superfluous beauty (or "objective interpretation") through *phonotechnique*, Satie's process of "cleaning sounds" ("It is a rather dirty business").[93]

The more art refuses to imitate or represent, the closer it gets to a real element: for Satie, a rather banal reality of inert vibrating matter, hence his words to Cocteau. While Satie's cynical wit does not make an interpreter's job very easy, I doubt, contra Jillian C. Rogers's suggestion, that the composer *really* cared a great deal about the science or significance of vibration during his day.[94] Though Satie surely was aware of earlier experiments in resonance conducted, for instance, by Hermann von Helmholtz, his use of the term "phonometrographer" was most likely a winking parody of the scientific seriousness that characterized contemporary attitudes toward sound.[95] Satie's sense of vibration was as two-faced as the "Realism" that Kandinsky described. The precarious self-positioning that we encountered earlier in Satie's writings about Péladan recur in his later phase as he apes scientific ideas for avowedly *Satierik* ends, allowing himself to be read as *both* serious *and* a parodist of science's "Great Realism."

Though Satie the cynic often denied that Art embodies a single Truth, his late style, and specifically the manner in which he looped short musical fragments to create larger works, anticipated an understanding of musical *durée* that the musicologist Pierre Souvtchinsky, undoubtedly influenced by Bergson, theorized in a 1939 article for the *Revue Musicale* titled "The Notion of Time in Music: Reflections on the Typology of Musical Creation." A composer, in Souvtchinsky's view, seeks first of all to express "a complex of inner intuitions, based before all on the specifically musical *experience of time—of Chronos*—in relation to which music, properly speaking, only plays the role of functional director."[96] Souvtchinsky claims that different mental states—"suspense, anguish, pain, suffering, fear, contemplation, sensuousness"—seem to pass at different tempos, yet "all this variety of types and modifications of *psychological time* would be elusive if, at the base of all this complexity, we could not discover the *primary sensation*—often unconscious—*of real time, ontological time.*"[97]

Soutchinsky's typology includes two kinds of music: "a-chronometric music" proceeds by way of "a secondary notation of primary emotive impulsions." This form of music, dynamic and expressive, is guided by psychological time. By contrast, "chronometric music" allows the listener to experience the flow of musical time in the same manner as the composer. It "is characterized by the absence of emotional and psychological reflexes" and "evokes a particular sentiment of dynamic calm":

this music is ontological in so far as it flows from, and according to, the impersonal rhythms of ontological time. This ontological time is not simply the obverse side of psychological time but is the very condition for any emotionally varied and dynamic experience of musical temporality. "The particularity of the musical notion of time," Souvtchinsky continued, "consists precisely in the fact that music arises and flows either *outside* the categories of psychological time, or *at the same time* as them": this calm, well-metered time flows outside or underneath the manifest sounds. The interplay between these two types of time "[permit] us to consider the musical experience as one of the purest forms of the ontological sensation of time."[98] In other words, music reveals the real ground of temporality: a Bergsonian refrain to which Souvtchinsky gives an ontological twist.

According to Bergson's student Jankélévitch, too, ontological time is the ground for the fleeting, ever-changing forms of psychological time that shape the surface of a musical work, since music, by its very nature, "imposes . . . the law of measure—which is the beat—on the disorder of measureless chaos" and also imposes "measured and stylized time . . . on unequal time, time by turns languishing and convulsive, fastidious and precipitous: the time of our daily life."[99] Once again, an impersonal flow runs beneath psychological time and is often masked by the many different flows (or durations) that music seems to portray. For Jankélévitch the music of certain modern French composers best embodies (i.e., does not simply exemplify but actually reveals) this underlying real time. The music of Fauré or Debussy, in his view, does not merely represent, but rather directly enacts things: in *La Mer*, "Debussy put a stethoscope to the ocean's chest, to the tide's lungs," thus "there is nothing [in the music] but the dialogue of the wind and the sea, which is moreover the monologue of the ocean, excluding all anthropomorphism, all reference to the subject."[100] Jankélévitch uses Debussy to counter the tendency among (nineteenth-century German) critics to turn music into an exemplar of truth; French music, to Jankélévitch's ears, *is* truth; it cuts below faulty representations, the impressions of psychological time, and presents the depersonalized, and hence more real, flow of ontological time.

As Jankélévitch championed composers like Debussy, Souvtchinsky championed Stravinsky as a composer who best exemplified this ontological time. This dualism between "psychological" and "ontological" time, however, had been present in Satie decades prior, figured in the opposition between the steady oscillations of an ostinato and the enchanting effects of legato melody. As in Souvtchinsky's theory, in Satie's practice by the end of his life, the real or ontological time superseded psychological time—or, as Jankélévitch averred, the "implacable chronometrics" of perfectly metered time "casts out all weakness and ignores human lassitude." After all, "a motor never feels sorry for itself."[101]

Perhaps the late Satie never felt sorry for himself either. At home, aging and sick, he never let anyone visit his Arcachan dwelling; onstage, with Picabia and Clair at the premiere of *Entr'acte*, he rode about in a toy car with a sign claiming himself the greatest composer of all time. Self-mocking, maybe self-loathing, Satie's late music certainly "ignored human lassitude" and wiped out "all reference to the subject." But it is in this game of hide and seek, of self-effacing and self-aggrandizing, that one can see that Satie's bid for *Furniture Music*, a music of vibrating matter, was a Great Musical Abstraction leading to higher Great Realism—always with a wink. It is as if Satie's repetitive and depersonalized late style echoed in Jankélévitch's ears when the philosopher wrote that "all of music is in essence allegory and alibi—since a succession of sounds is, in itself, something entirely different from an emotion." The "great truth" that ontological time seems to have conveyed for Jankélévitch is the truth that music is always a lie, and further, that "the subject" itself is a kind of illusion: "acoustic vibrations are of an entirely different order than psychological facts."[102] A higher realism becomes possible when a composer shows the whole realm of psychological experience, his own and that of others, to be nothing but a big gag, a deceptive appearance under which one may sense a deeper lasting truth—of ontological time or of bare vibrating matter.

• • •

From our standpoint, Satie and Bergson can be said to represent two historiographical lineages that wind around their respective biographies, extending from the *fin de siècle* to our own day. One lineage leads from the Montmartre café toward the depersonalized churnings of minimalism and silence. The other leads from Parisian clinics like Charcot's toward Deleuzian ontology. What gets lost along the way, as I have tried to show, is illusion or illusory experience, that which in music beckons, through transient sensory effects, toward enduring meaning. Satie is something of an ironic foil, then, for a recent trend in studies of sound that peer through the screen of art toward a deeper vibrating realm. In other words, while Satie was never *too* serious about vibration, some of us are.

It may seem counter-intuitive to implicate Bergson in a historical shift away from music's illusions toward enduring "truth" since for Bergson the act of thought, as we have seen, always occurs in time, hence words prove inadequate to explain the "real curve." There is one loaded sentence in Deleuze's *Bergsonism*, however, that fittingly sums up the legacy that Bergson left for the twentieth century, and that made Deleuze's own picture of Bergson possible:

> The two major aspects of [Bergson's] evolution are the following: Duration seemed to him to be less and less reducible to a psychological experience and became instead the variable essence of things, providing the theme of a complex ontology.[103]

Duration appears at first to connote a mode of experience, but through the work of philosophy, temporality becomes more and more a matter of absolute, non-psychological conditions. Deleuze attributes these contrasting understandings of duration to Bergson himself, implying that Bergson's thought shifted from a psychological orientation toward an ontological inquiry. This is not without precedence. There is evidence in Bergson's texts that the philosopher aimed (as philosophers generally do) to go beyond psycho-sensual experience toward general conditions of being; he wrote in *Creative Evolution*, for example, of "a duration immanent to the whole of the universe."[104] But as we have seen, it was Deleuze who emphasized the notion of virtuality in Bergson beyond what Bergson seems to have intended. This transition that Deleuze finds in Bergson—from duration as psychological experience toward duration as "complex ontology"—says more about *Bergsonism* than it does about Henri. Since illusion involves plays of sensation—deceptive appearances; groans of sadness—it is fair to say that from a Deleuzian standpoint illusion would be merely of the psychological order, whereas philosophy aims to uncover the "complex ontology" of fluxes moving always beneath us.

It is conspicuous that these fluxes continue to move through sound studies. For Cox, "works of art are never representations and never signify" because art is "[fundamentally independent] from the world of subjects, objects, and states of affairs."[105] Fundamentally unrepresentable, a work of art is more than a piece of music, a sculpture, or something fashioned by a human: it is a condensation of various already-existing elements, percepts and affects. Cox focuses on sound art in particular, claiming that this art

> detaches sensations from objects and subjects, presenting [sensations] as pure intensive forces that inhere in things but are not reducible to them, having the power to act and affect as sensations independently of the subjects and objects who might bare or undergo them.[106]

I would call this way of describing the effects of sound art a *sonological mysticism*: sound art holds essentially the same potential for Cox that hypnosis held for Bergson. We, as viewers and listeners, are subject to a much larger virtual world of affects and intensities that we can never master. We merely actualize parts of an infinite virtual storehouse in the act of making and experiencing art, and therefore art is, once again, an illusion through which one can discursively grasp a deeper truth. This truth is the sonic flux, which Cox theorizes as a "materialist aesthetics" based on an immemorial material flow that goes beyond and beneath the sounds, feelings, and memories that one actualizes when one encounters the sonic arts. Music's rhythms die away; the sonic flux, the condition of actual sonic experience, always endures.

Bergson, as we have seen, would surely have agreed that art can reveal something about immaterial and invisible flows, since the human being is always limited and there is a larger domain beyond us. Yet Bergson and Cox are not only separated by a century: the former believed that the illusions of art fundamentally affirm the human being's free will, the inherent power of the soul to self-create, while the latter, taking his cue from Deleuze, seems not to care about our souls at all. It hardly seems necessary to point out the similarities between Cox's sense that art goes "below representation and signification," "[revealing] . . . forces, intensities, sensations, and affects" and nineteenth-century romantic beliefs about music's power to embody the will or to take the listener out of the everyday and into the realm of the infinite, to paraphrase E. T. A. Hoffmann's words about Beethoven.

But the sonic flux smells of bleach. Yearning, longing, and divinity matter about as little as human agency in Cox's understanding of the ontology of sound, since it is "noise" that is the ground, "the continuous acoustic flow," that "provides the condition of possibility for every articulate sound." "[A]ll speech, music, and signal emerge" from the sonic flux, and it is the sonic flux "to which they return."[107] While human acts might nudge this flow in one direction or another, ultimately this flow exists independently of any actual human. Sound art, in short, allows one to "leap into ontology," to return to Deleuze's phrase. The sound artists that Cox describes, on this view—whether Alvin Lucier or Brandon LaBelle—are merely human vehicles for a ~~divine~~ ontological truth that dwarfs and subsumes all of us.

"*We leap into ontology*" is an elusive phrase. Taken literally, a "leap into ontology" would mean a leap into a discourse, a *logos* about Being. As if one "leaps" into the pages of philosophy rather than into Being itself (or perhaps Being is only ever a figment of philosophical writing anyway). This is not what Deleuze meant, but is, I would suggest, effectively where we end after untangling the ontological notions in *Bergsonism*, or, for that matter, in Cox's *Sonic Flux*. By leaping into ontology, we make absolute conditions legible—*we leap into writing*. Sonic flux represents a kind of Deleuzian perversion of Bergson's ideas, since ontology is a metaphysics bleached of illusion.

Gone are the oscillating rhythms and sighs of sadness, the "properly human" experiences that inspired Bergson's inquiry. Effaced are the aberrant psyches of Charcot's hysterics or the astral bodies that Lina brought to earth as she danced before Rochas's camera. Absent are the Tahitian natives, the occult fantasies of medieval Catholicism, Péladan's princess or the idol of perversity, and the Greekish primitivism that formed the background—not the virtual background, but the *actual* historical context—for Nietzsche's clash of godly archetypes or for Satie's poetics of opposition. Now we are lulled into trance; now we awaken toward banality: the real and the illusory play and play, and this play *is* art. Through an ontological lens, however, these feminine interiors and these dark mysteries, this purity and pulp—all of this becomes derivative with regard to a play of fluxes that is adamantly *not* of the order of illusion but of the order of the virtual. Ontology is a *logos* of sublimation, a white science that whitewashes: an Absolute Bleach. Grappling with, penetrating, and blotting out that which is other than Being, ontology has its way with Reality, perpetuating the ultimate western illusion (perhaps the illusion *of* "the West").

But if we move beyond the turn in human experience, where do we go? When Bergson searched for the conditions of real experience, illusion and reality shared equal parts in the play. Cox, by contrast, underwrites the delusion (*Deleuzion*?) that the virtual overcomes and sublimates the whole play of illusion and reality by creating a different kind of real. This real, however, does not appear in miniature as a hypnotist heightens our senses; nor can we feel it as music lulls our consciousness away. Even if we do sense something beyond the turn, we are never adequate to the play of fluxes. We can only ever understand this reality of fluxes by taking a leap, not into life's deeps, but into the space of the text.

Two

ONTOLOGICAL MACHINES

Varèse and Bataille

> The only salvation: that some creators possess interior ears—
> Beethoven is the prototype—and I think his deafness to the sound
> of the world was for him a blessing—and the source of new concepts
> of sound.[1]

— EDGARD VARÈSE

••• Edgard Victor Achille Charles Varèse (1883–1965) surely knew, when he wrote to his student André Jolivet of Beethoven's deafness, that he was invoking Wagner. The latter once likened the deaf genius to "the blinded *Seer*" who, no longer troubled by "life's uproar," gains the "power to [shape] the unfathomable, the never-seen, the [never] experienced." As is the case with a blind clairvoyant, "the [deaf] musician's eye [grows] bright within."[2] For decades scholars of Varèse have tried to see the light inside the composer's mind.[3] Like Wagner, Varèse took Beethoven's deafness as a metaphor for his own musical vision, but even as he invoked the German musical tradition that the Beethoven–Wagner dyad well represents, he often publicly posed himself against certain of its features.[4] In a 1936 lecture delivered in Santa Fe, Varèse called for the disavowal of the "incidental, anecdotal, sensual or picturesque" use of "color or timbre," seeking instead to conceive sound as an "agent of delineation like the different colors on a map separating different areas."[5] This "liberation of sound" (Varèse's famous phrase) took form as the composer strove to oust the representational function that generations of past composers and critics had attached to certain European musical conventions: the anecdotal or the picturesque. Sound would become even less bound to the external world, functioning neither as a mime nor a mimic. However, despite Varèse's pronouncements about his music, he never entirely ousted musical representation; if anything, he sought a maximally intense and direct form of it.

This chapter will suggest that despite Varèse's forward-looking pronouncements, and despite his critical image as an oracle of musical modernism, he was perhaps the most regressive composer of the twentieth century: regressive because he took on a very old, very "ontological" view according to which an enduring reality might be uncovered, through a discursive process, from beneath the faulty world of appearances, or, to use a musical metaphor, that real sound could be revealed beneath the appearance of traditional musical syntax—harmony, form, and narrative. In his pronouncements, he rebuked the conventions of nineteenth-century European concert music, casting sound as a pure force in itself, as if sound had been waiting for centuries for just the right composer, just the right medium, to set its essence free. Varèse believed that certain kinds of sound had the ability to shape musical form, and he built a musical language on the conceit that we can, through his works, hear and experience sound as such.

Though Varèse's music is supposedly "about" sound, I will suggest that his music is actually about power. Power has a dual sense in what follows, referring to the power of sound on the senses, as Varèse deploys a brigade of brass against a battery of percussion, for instance, and also to the power of a modern individual mustering all the strength of his technique, leveraging his persona, and utilizing his connections—in a word, forging a "discourse," a term that I will use to connote what Varèse said about what he was doing and also what he did, the very writerly language of his compositions—all in an endeavor to envision a new order. During his early years in New York, he re-figured the sounds of the cityscape as a form of sonic primitivism, and during a visit back to Paris during the early 1930s, trained his gaze on certain representations of the non-European primitive. But in either case, Varèse's goal was to remediate "primitive" sounds in order to reveal something of the nature of sound itself.

My primary contention will be that Varèse was a *sonic ontologist*, and to get a sense of how Varèse envisioned sound ontologically—as a being in itself—the first section below will attend to Varèse's compositional practice, his actual methods of approaching sound. I will focus on three specific aspects of Varèse's discourse: (1) his concept of "the purity of sound"; (2) his spatial approach to sound—as in his conception of "sound masses" or "harmonic planes"; and (3) his poetics of intensity—that is, his obsession with combining sound masses to produce ever-more intense climax moments, a central structural feature of all of his works. Through describing Varèse's music, however, my ultimate endeavor is to suggest that the composer may best be understood as a species of the Modern Man (*l'homme*) that once preoccupied a certain Foucault: "an incredible and ultimately unworkable idea of a being . . . whose very finitude allows him to take the place of God."[6] Dreaming of an electronic music studio before electronic music existed; imagining new forms of musical writing akin to the curves of a seismograph; calling for "new dynamics far beyond the present human-powered orchestra," and new "[units] of measure or time which [are] humanly impossible to obtain": Varèse aimed to transcend the humanly possible to obtain the impossible.[7]

The second section will cast Varèse's compositions, as well as Varèse's discursive persona and authorial presence, as what Georges Bataille might have called "ontological machines," a pejorative phrase that the philosopher once used to describe the idealizing logic that had structured western thought at least since Hegel. In a 1930 essay in the collaborative Parisian journal *Documents*, "Base Materialism and Gnosticism," Bataille reproduced photos of various stone-carved icons dated to the first century CE, deities attributed to the early gnostic religions. As I will describe, Bataille dubbed these stone figures "base matter," that which cannot be taken up into rational processes like Hegel's dialectical idealism, the movement of sublimation by which whatever is "base" becomes subsumed within a higher form.[8] Bataille and Varèse shared a belief that certain archaic or non-European spiritual forms could productively resist the idealizing logic of the Hegelian dialectic or, perhaps, of the romantic symphony. While Bataille studied icons of gnostic *archontes*, Varèse read Miguel Angel Asturias's *Legendas de Guatemala* and wrote music inspired by fantasied images of ancient

Maya. For both, these figures of otherness amounted to "base matter," a phrase Bataille applied to expressive forms that would be "external and foreign to ideal human aspirations," "[refusing] to allow [themselves] to be reduced to the great ontological machines resulting from these aspirations."[9]

However, while Bataille wielded base matter to destabilize the founding concepts of western ontology, Varèse's compositions bespeak an even more absolute kind of idealizing logic. Section two follows the composer as he moved back to Paris in the late 1920s and conceived *Ecuatorial*, and I will use Bataille as a foil to distinguish Varèse the progressive from Varèse the regressive. While Bataille sought to undermine ontological thought—in a way that foreshadowed Derridean deconstruction—Varèse, though he shared certain aesthetic convictions with Bataille, held an ontological understanding of sound. Sound was, for the composer, an arcane ephemeron with its own life and power, and a vehicle, maybe a guise, for the composer's own egotism. Varèse's search for "pure" sound is best understood as a search for personal power and composerly authority, thus we might say that sound was Varèse's vehicle to rebuff metaphysics and declare his own myth—that is, an ontological myth.[10] Varèse's ontological machines are like musical Panzers, ready to blast through appearances to declare timeless sonic truth.

"THE PURITY OF SOUND AND HARMONY OF THE WORD": VARÈSE AND THE SOUNDS OF DADA

Fresh off the boat at age thirty-one, in 1915 the émigré Varèse sought refuge at the Breevort Hotel in Greenwich Village along with Marcel Duchamp, Francis Picabia, and a horde of Dadaists and Dada-esques. Prior to his emigration, he had attended the Schola Cantorum in 1904, a year before Satie would return to school to hone his skills in counterpoint.[11] Unlike his elder, however, Varèse did not take to the Schola: he dropped out, attended the Paris Conservatoire instead, but as legend has it, chafed under the compositional dogma of the moment. He was already something of a rugged individualist, refusing to become an acolyte of Vincent d'Indy, and found an answer to his frustrations through his interactions with poets and painters.[12] A portrait of Varèse by Clara Tice appeared in a 1917 issue of *The Blind Man*, the journal published by New York Dadaists that made Duchamp's *Fountain* famous, and Varèse is known to have frequented Walter and Louise Arensberg's exclusive avant-garde salon in lower Manhattan, where he encountered Tice, Duchamp, Man Ray, Joseph Stella, Arthur Cravan and Mina Loy, Albert Gleizes and Juliette Roche, Baroness Elsa von Freytag-Loringhoven, and others.[13]

There was something about the urgency with which a Dadaist poem composed of fragmented syllables could confront a reader that appealed to Varèse. Dadaist writing disavowed normative syntax in favor of the music of phonetics. In 1923 Varèse wrote:

> If certain new words, called barbarous by academic purists, live in spite of the science of etymology and of established grammatical conventions, it is because their only criterion is the *purity of sound and the harmony of the word*, their only law the law of phonetics. And it is this law that decides the fate of a new vocable, even in deforming it, without a thought for its etymology. The musical works of to-day make their appeal directly and uniquely to their listeners' ears.[14]

Sound poetry bolstered one of Varèse's own discursive leitmotifs: that sound is beholden to its own law. Though Varèse did not refer explicitly to Dadaism, his mention of the "purity of sound and harmony of the word" likely referred to the fragmented syllables and musicalized speech of poetry in the style of Kurt Schwitters, for instance, who composed his *Ursonate* (1921–32) by constructing a set of pronounceable syllables based off a sound poem by Raoul Hausmann.[15] Or, perhaps Varèse had in mind a work by Duchamp that called for a performer to compose a musical piece for three voices by pulling notes out of a hat. Calling his composition *La Mariée mise à nu par ses célibataires même. Erratum Musical*, Duchamp used a technique of chance to strip music bare, foregrounding the sounds of chance pitches. *Erratum Musical* also stripped bare the process of musical writing. Duchamp included a text from a dictionary defining "*imprimer*": "Faire une empreinte; marquer des traits; une figure sur une surface; imprimer un sceau sur cire" ("To make an imprint; mark the traits; a figure on a surface; impress a seal in wax").[16] Bare figures on a surface, the notes of *Erratum Musical* become like Duchampian readymades, each one picked with "visual indifference" and "the total absence of good or bad taste"—as Duchamp put it when he described the process of picking out a bicycle wheel, a broom handle, or a urinal for the gallery.[17]

Erratum Musical took form as notes, rendered inert like one of Duchamp's readymade artifacts, nevertheless posed a conceptual challenge to the meaning of sound.[18] Experiments like this form the context for Varèse's remark that new music works directly on listeners' ears: the harmony of phonetic utterance, rid of representational function, creates a "purity of sound," hence Varèse's later disavowal of the anecdotal and picturesque in music may be traced back to his early experiences with Dadaists. His endeavor to endow his works with sonic power, in other words, was already anecdotal, for he took cues from his comrades in New York and, as we shall see, from the city itself.

Between 1918 and 1922, as Varèse spent time at the Arensbergs', he composed his first (extant) large-scale work for orchestra. In *Amériques*, I suggest, one may hear the tension between the composer's affirmation of sonic purity and his reliance on the anecdotal and picturesque, a duplicity that is at the heart of Varèse's early musical language as the composer began establishing himself and forging a public persona. In *Amériques*, Varèse started from the sounds of the city, but then, in the manner of a Duchampian pulling notes out of a hat or a Dadaist cutting syllables from a newspaper, Varèse began to conceive his music visually: as an assemblage of "sound masses" that would occupy different spatial areas of the orchestra, establishing different layers of sound that would bump against one another, clashing and overlapping. This spatial approach to sound would characterize every work that was to follow and can be seen as the composer's own Dadaist approach to sound. By attending to *Amériques* as well as to the image of the composer that began to spread in the press—an image forged partly through this tension between sonic purity and musical representation—one can get a sense of how Varèse's discourse of musical power took shape.

Amériques begins with a melodic machine: a solo alto flute plays a brief repetitive motif that spans a wide range (or ambitus), composed

FIGURE 10. The opening of Varèse's *Amériques* (1918–22).
This musical quotation is drawn from: *Amériques,* music by Edgard Varèse, published by Casa Ricordi Srl, a division of Universal Music Publishing Group. *International Copyright Secured. All Rights Reserved.* Reprinted by permission of Hal Leonard Europe BV (Italy).

of three main pitches each a perfect fifth apart (Figure 10). Soft, unaccompanied, the alto flute sets the tone for the opening of what will be an epic twenty-minute exploration in tonal color.[19] By structuring the motif this way, Varèse created a rather open and neutral sound, neither major nor minor, consonant nor dissonant. The motif may be heard as a kind of shell or container: when two harps enter to accompany the flute, moving up and down repeatedly like the churning of an engine, and when a bassoon enters in its extreme upper register, playing its own repeated upward-climbing motif, it is conspicuous that the harps and bassoon fit neatly within the range set out by the flute. Varèse constructs a coherent "unit" of sound, limited to the register (or range) outlined by the flute.

On its face, the opening motif of *Amériques* recalls the famous opening phrase of *Le Sacre du printemps*. The use of a bassoon in its upper register and a repeated ostinato in the harp are direct references to the early, primitivist Stravinsky. The way Varèse uses these opening themes, however, distinguishes him from the Stravinskian lineage to which he alludes. The flute motif does not develop, nor does it give way to another theme in a similar style; instead, it remains faceless—mechanical—and, like the harp, resembles a building block, especially once Varèse layers other blocks on top of it.

After several repetitions of the opening flute phrase, its pace quickens. The accompanying harp ostinato slowly dies away, and one gets the sense that Varèse's orchestra will fade to silence. Out of the blue, however, a brigade of French horns enters supported by the bass (at about :40 in most commercial recordings), sounding a sudden fanfare: a rapid series of repeated notes with an intervallic leap, the kind of concise, brassy phrase one might hear from a trumpeter rushing alongside troops into battle. This call is quickly echoed by the trumpets and flutes, then by the other high winds—a sudden layering that occurs all in one measure (about three seconds in duration). After these fanfares, Varèse's percussion section enters with a richly textured counterpoint.

In Figure 11, the reader need not attend to the details of Varèse's orchestration. It suffices to note that three groups of instruments enter quickly one after another, and I have outlined each group using boxes in the score. Varèse would not have included such markings, of course, though according to various accounts of the composer's studio, he would often construct his scores by cutting and pasting different musical fragments and integrating them into the overall texture of the orchestra. At the drafting stage, his scores sometimes resembled collages. From a listener's standpoint, I suggest it is possible to *hear* this "collage" method at work in moments like this, as Varèse divides the sudden fanfare into three main groups. The horns form the first unit, and in some performances, may be positioned offstage; the trumpets, flutes, and high strings form a second (onstage) unit; and finally the piccolos and oboes form a third unit, screaming over the top.

The full effect of moments like this is not well conveyed in recordings: if we were to sit before an orchestra during a performance of *Amériques*, we may get the sense that each of these fanfare motifs occupies a distinct place onstage. The play with register is also a play with space—sound becomes "an agent of delineation, like the different colors on a map," delineating different registral areas that will come into conflict.[20]

The scene has exploded. The earlier ostinato may have led one to expect that *Amériques* would develop like a primitivist ballet, with sections conveying different moods, allowing for a longer narrative progression or even for dance. Now suddenly the range of the orchestra expands, like opening the blinds to a too-bright sun, as Varèse layers this abrasive theme (marked triple fortissimo in his score) via these different instrumental groups. The opening flute phrase and harp ostinato then re-commence accompanied this time by the percussion, which is

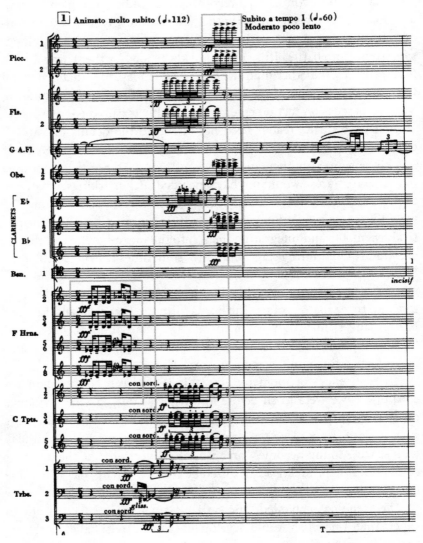

FIGURE 11. Musical Dadaism during the opening of *Amériques*. After the opening flute motif repeats many times, quickening, Varèse suddenly layers a fanfare theme across three instrumental groups (outlined here with boxes).

This musical quotation is drawn from: *Amériques,* music by Edgard Varèse, published by Casa Ricordi Srl, a division of Universal Music Publishing Group. *International Copyright Secured. All Rights Reserved.* Reprinted by permission of Hal Leonard Europe BV (Italy).

layered and cacophonous, disorienting any sense of a consistent tempo. The various percussion parts seem to play independently: a sleigh bell in counterpoint with a snare drum, two bass drums at odds with a triangle, a castanet, and a tambourine.

"As I worked in my Westside apartment . . . I could hear all the river sounds," Varèse wrote in a note about *Amériques*: "the lonely foghorns, the shrill peremptory whistles—the whole wonderful river symphony."[21] The composer invited his listeners to associate these distinct layers of sound, the voices of instruments and percussion, with various river flows, including the imagined river of people walking the Manhattan streets. Perhaps the offstage brass—which soon interrupts the percussion with static, drawn-out dissonant honks—alludes to these distant foghorns; or, perhaps the fanfare fragments were meant to convey the deafening shock that the young immigrant must have experienced from time to time amid the blaring of big city car and train horns. The Varèse of this early phase was apparently not opposed to the idea that instrumental music represents our external world: "the shrill voice of the trolley wires, . . . strange moanings of appeal from the tug boats,"[22] and so on. Already one gets the sense that there was an element of mythmaking in Varèse's later disavowal of the anecdotal or picturesque use of sound.

Over the next two minutes or so, Varèse introduces several new motifs that form a kind of dialogue across different areas of the stage: a series of long, drawn-out tones from the brass that center around the interval of a tritone; high-pitched chromatic flurries in the winds paired with sudden rolls and rapid spells in the percussion; harp glissandi echoed by upward-reaching violins and accented by sleigh bells; deep, dark, rumbling cascades in the low strings. The familiar alto flute motif also returns, paired with the up-and-down harp ostinato, and the percussion seems to play its own symphony throughout.[23] These opening moments of *Amériques* essentially lay out the tools and concepts of Varèse's mature style. It is a kind of aural jungle, as if the orchestra *becomes* the cityscape that Varèse heard outside his window.

The composer's sense of spatial sound is perhaps most clearly expressed during two early climactic moments. At about two-and-a-half minutes in to *Amériques* (rehearsal number 4 in Varèse's score), the high winds and trumpets join in a downward-stepping figure (a series of three-note chords moving in parallel), and the percussion, formerly a disparate jumble, becomes a unified front. A cymbal crashes as the winds and trumpets hold out a final pitch, the low brass enters with an abrupt upward leap, and an additional two trumpets blare a perfect fourth that clashes with the rest of the ensemble, adding dissonance on top of dissonance. The percussion section swells and intensifies—a cymbal, snare drum, and bass drum rolling while a siren screams.

The left side of Figure 12 shows the individual parts that Varèse wrote for various instruments whereas the right side shows a simpli-

FIGURE 12. Varèse's first punch: left, a reduced score; right, a reduction of Varèse's chords; bottom, the percussion. Note Varèse's inclusion of a siren (marked by an arrow).
This musical quotation is drawn from: *Amériques,* music by Edgard Varèse, published by Casa Ricordi Srl, a division of Universal Music Publishing Group. *International Copyright Secured. All Rights Reserved.* Reprinted by permission of Hal Leonard Europe BV (Italy).

fied, reduced score notated for a piano. Here, the reader may see, once again, how Varèse orchestrated *Amériques* by grouping distinct sound masses (in brackets). This moment gives credence to Varèse's account during a 1922 interview with Winthrop Tryon, one of the composer's early advocates in the New York press, that "we are working toward placing one harmonic plane against another and one volume of sound against another."[24] Varèse's poetics are built on passages like this, where themes build and bump against each other, preparing ground for certain extreme moments—in this case, a kind of aural punch.

From an interpreters' standpoint, there are at least two roads one may take to explain climactic moments like this. One could imagine this moment as another allusion to New York City, using Varèse's words about the sounds of the city to suggest that this moment is mimetic—maybe of a traffic jam. Varèse's inclusion of a siren is conspicuous: another marker of the New York cityscape, the siren makes a programmatic reading of *Amériques* even more tempting. Or, taking a music-theoretical tact (and looking at Varèse's score), one may describe the nuances of the composer's orchestration—noting, for instance, that the trombones span a minor ninth; that the perfect fourth played by trumpets 5 and 6 rubs against the rest of the section, a minor second or a minor ninth away from other voices; or, that when he constructs chord clusters in the high winds and brass, Varèse seems to favor placing the highest voices close to each other, often a minor second apart, like a dissonant cherry on top. However, these modes of interpretation—taking *Amériques* as a musical representation of a specific environment (the city) or as a "purely" formal music-theoretical exploration in orchestral color—seem only to tell part of the story. As Varèse commences with a second punch (Figure 13), the sheer force of the orchestra seems to challenge the hermeneutic strategy through which an interpreter might associate the siren, the clash of "harmonic planes," or the percussion barrage with the New York that Varèse heard through his apartment window.

After a cool-down period during which Varèse elaborates on the various thematic material already introduced—adding more dissonant brass; regular, abrupt repeated notes in the low winds and strings accompanied by the siren; upward-and-downward harp and low string cascades—the brass and winds suddenly erupt (shortly after 3:00 in

FIGURE 13. The second and even bigger punch in *Amériques*: left, a simplified reproduction of Varèse's score (excluding percussion and strings); right, an even more simplified reduction of Varèse's chords (taking much liberty with register).

This musical quotation is drawn from: *Amériques,* music by Edgard Varèse, published by Casa Ricordi Srl, a division of Universal Music Publishing Group. *International Copyright Secured. All Rights Reserved.* Reprinted by permission of Hal Leonard Europe BV (Italy).

most commercial recordings). It is another aural punch: one does not need to use the language of music theory to sense that Varèse seems to jam every available pitch together across every possible register (in the score, one may see that the composer stacks minor ninths in the horns and bassoons while the highest winds scream a minor second). The whole ensemble joins in during the following measures: the winds, brass, and high strings sustain their dissonant color, building, growing, meanwhile the percussion churns away and the familiar siren sings. The trumpets soon commence with the downward-stepping motif from the first punch, adding another sound mass to the whole before another crescendo, another percussion roll, another big crash.

I would take Varèse's words about the Manhattan soundscape literally up to this point; *Amériques*, in a sense, *is* this soundscape. But the spatial understanding of sound to which Varèse alludes in his program note seems to take on its own life during this moment, pointing us elsewhere. When the Philadelphia Orchestra premiered *Amériques* in 1926, with a whopping 140 players on (and off)stage, this climactic moment must have felt like an assault (it feels so even through headphones today). The hermeneutic game of linking Varèsean sound to the city, or the music-theoretical game of taking apart tone clusters, analyzing intervallic structures, and so on, seems to fall short. The former is too literal, the latter too boring.

For Varèse, theory and practice were in constant tension—a tension that perhaps *defines* his discourse. There was always a slippage between music-as-mimesis and sound-as-violence, between the real-world associations that one may make between Varèse's sounds and the world in which he lived, on one hand, and the sheer visceral impact of his sound masses on the other. Through this brute force of sound, the siren takes on something of the autonomous quality that Varèse claimed to hear during certain interviews. "What we want is an instrument that will give us continuous sound at any pitch," Varèse explained to Tryon; "the composer and the electrician will perhaps have to labor together to get it."[25] The siren is a marker of a particular place and time, in other words, but also suggests the possibility of hearing beyond a particular time—as if one may hear another world created in sound. "I studied Helmholtz," Varèse recounted in an interview from the late 1950s, describing his fascination with certain scientific

experiments with sirens. . . . Later I made some modest experiments of my own and found that I could obtain beautiful parabolic and hyperbolic curves of sound, which seemed to me equivalent to the parabolas and hyperbolas in the visual domain.[26]

Varèse certainly took Helmholtz's experiments with resonance more seriously than his winking predecessor Satie; there is no reason to doubt that he thought about the sound of the siren in visual terms. But there is also reason to suspect that his words to Tryon about hyperbolas were hyperbolic: Varèse invoked the language of a scientist to explain something that was, in the first place, hardly scientific at all. This is the inconsistency, and also perhaps the allure, of Varèse's self-positioning; he was both an "art-scientist" (his own term) and a dramatist, both a formalist who thought in purely musical terms and a stage director of a sort, turning the orchestra into a sonic cityscape.

"We should write today . . . in a telegraphic style," Varèse continued in his 1922 conversation with Tryon: "[w]e should not hint at situations and emotions; . . . we should discard . . . material which is not purely musical and should try for expression in the simplest way."[27] In listening to *Amériques*, his adjective "telegraphic" seems like an empty signifier if by this Varèse meant that music would somehow be neutral, pulsing like a patterned electrical signal, spanning distance and affecting listeners without alluding to "situations and emotions." If he felt charmed as he listened to the sounds of the city through his window, then there is no reason for Varèse to have disavowed "situations and emotions." When his acolyte and biographer Fernand Ouellette remarked "it was necessary to have known [Varèse] a long time to be able to tell *when* in his replies he was telling the truth," Ouellette allowed—perhaps unwittingly—for critical suspicion of his master's many oft-quoted aperçus.[28] One could therefore ask: when Varèse famously dreamed of his liberation of sound, when he declared in 1917 that "[m]usic, which should pulsate with life, needs new means of expression, and science alone can infuse it with youthful vigor,"[29] when he avowed in the Santa Fe lecture that "the new notation will probably be seismographic," and when he imagined (in 1939) a kind of musical "machine" (a proto-synthesizer? multiple loudspeakers?) that would liberate music from "the arbitrary, paralyzing tempered system," allowing for "a sense of sound projection in space"[30]—how much of this talk of an "art-science" of music was true and how much amounted to self-posturing?

The question only seems meaningful if one takes Varèse (as he may have wished) as the main authority when it comes to his music. But rhetoric aside, what *is* going on with these various sonic punches? An aural assault; a musical Panzer: Olivia Mattis opened her doctoral dissertation about Varèse with a quote from another of the composer's painter friends, Juliette Roche, who described Varèse's torturous "desire to strangle someone, anyone, at random."[31] It is easy to imagine that his audience in Philadelphia would have felt stifled or strangled by this wall of sound in *Amériques*. Even if one lacked the sense of hearing, the bombardment of 140 players may have felt like a vibrational assault, just as a rapidly approaching train that blares its horn provokes a visceral response, gooseflesh by reflex.

It does not follow, however, that these sounds, by virtue of their violence, completely transcend representation. Music critic Paul Rosenfeld fell right in line with Varèse's own call for the "purely musical" when he wrote (in a 1925 review of *Integrales*) that "Varèse never has imitated the sounds of the city, as he is frequently supposed to do, or supposed to have been said to do by critical writers. His work is much more the penetration." Mythopoeia through crude metaphor: Rosenfeld celebrates the "genuine feeling of power" evoked through the "pulsating swing" of "brass and steel" as Varèse "thrusts" sounds upward in the air, "masses of . . . impenetrable bodies in collision."[32] Bodies in collision? Penetration? Strangulation? (Perhaps Varèse's music would have been a better candidate for Susan McClary's rape whistle than Beethoven's.[33]) What Varèse termed the "purely musical" was something of a mythology, for his sonic punches are about as "pure" as his fantasies of strangling someone, anyone, at random. Purity, power, and penetration (*on my!*): it does not take much of an intuitive leap to sense a deep connection between Varèse's call for musical purity, or the "genuine feeling of power" that Rosenfeld felt in his music, and the composer's desire to strangle.

• • •

After the Philadelphia premiere of *Amériques* in 1926, Varèse got to work on *Arcana* for the next season, retaining his spatial approach to sound but foregrounding even more his poetics of intensity—what he would later call his work with "zones of intensities": "zones . . . differentiated by various timbres or colors and different loudnesses."[34] Though in *Arcana* Varèse abandoned the siren, and did not pitch the work as an embodiment of a particular soundscape, the title as well as the addition of an epigraph from Paracelsus signal what the piece was meant to convey:

> One star exists, higher than all the rest. This is the apocalyptic star. The second star is that of the ascendant. The third star is that of the elements—of these there are four, so that six stars are established. Besides these there is still another star, imagination, which begets a new star and a new heaven.[35]

Apparently Varèse wanted to add another spatial metaphor to his repertoire, and a more literal one: space travel.

In the opening bars of *Amériques*, Varèse took the quiet approach; *Arcana*, by contrast, opens with a repetitive upward-climbing three-note motif in the low winds, brass, and strings, accented by the timpani, conveying urgency and grandeur from the very beginning. Colorful blaring dissonances quickly ring out in the high winds and brass before the three-note bass motif continues to bumble belligerently along. This dialogue between the low and high voices structures the opening of *Arcana*, the low orchestral instruments playing repetitive motifs and the high ones blaring away with various abrupt intervallic leaps and sustained pitches. A minute or so into *Arcana*, however, Varèse introduces a new tactic. We encounter another of the composer's sonic pile-ups, more extended than any in *Amériques*, but with an obvious climb upward toward the cosmos.

A blaring low drone (on an E flat) in the low brass, basses, and finally bassoons is a conspicuous moment in the piece that sets the ground for another play of registral layers. Another fanfare-like figure rings out from the horns, a rapid succession (of staccato E naturals, forming a minor ninth with the droning bass). Over the following measures, at least three other "zones of intensity" come into play while the drone—or some variation of the drone—continues. The bass clarinet, four horns, and cellos commence with a leaping melodic line; another four horns, an English horn, and other winds play a variation of the fanfare figure, elongated this time, culminating in two immense leaps upward; and finally, the trumpets enter, recapitulating the earlier sharply attacked repeated-note figure. Each of these themes has a distinct character—a drone, a phrase defined by intervallic leaps, and a longer fanfare—as well as a distinct registral identity. But specifics aside, anyone can hear that Varèse is leading us up, up, up . . .

These two motifs, one resembling a fanfare and the other based on intervallic leaps, travel up the orchestra and culminate with the strings, who enter following the high brass to carry the ensemble ever upward, moving by step to the highest possible range of the orchestra. The brass enter again, restating the fanfare motif, and the lowest voices and percussion interject with sharp jabs and violent crashes. The strings form a kind of "ceiling," and with the epigraph in mind, it is difficult not to hear this gradual ascent as an allusion to ascent into space, and hard not the hear the soaring strings as a figuration of Paracelsus's firmament.

"One star exists, higher than all the rest. This is the apocalyptic star." This opening ascent in *Arcana* is perhaps the highest-reaching moment in Varèse's *oeuvre* up to this point, or at least a moment that foregrounds ascent, the push ever upwards, more so than any comparable moment in *Amériques*. The Paracelsus epigraph mentions seven stars: it is almost too easy to interpret Varèse's play with register as a literal representation of the space described in this obscure text (Varèse ascends at least seven octaves). The constellation of stars and their symbology—the apocalypse, the elements, the ascendent, and life-giving imagination—all add up to complete the picture of *Arcana*: indeed, a picture of the arcane.

In interviews, however, Varèse denied any representational impulse, insisting on his music's abstract qualities. "The title of my composition, Arcana, and the epigraph from Paracelsus have nothing to do with the actual composition of the work," Varèse bluffed in an undated statement collected by Louise Varèse and published in 1976: "My titles are never descriptive."[36] In light of this dizzying musical ascent, the composer's disavowal has an almost comical effect. This music *is* space travel, the accumulation of intensities pushing ever upward—and in performance, the effect is so intense that the listener may feel the sensation of departing from the external world.

Amériques and *Arcana* are vehicles for a possible, and maximally intense, experience of sound. Through examining his spatial conception of sound as well as his work with "zones of intensities," we might grasp on an experiential level what sound or sonic liberation meant to the composer. Varèse began from city sounds, from river flows or sirens, or perhaps from the imagined sounds of outer space, and aimed to arrest these fleeting presences, to solidify—or, to play on one of his own terms, to *crystallize*—these sounds into new musical units or sound objects. He sought to create a new musical order from the play of sound masses rather than counterpoint; the clash of sound planes rather than tonal harmony; a sonic drama rather than musical dramaturgy.

It is precisely through the discursive rub between what Varèse said and what he did—his denial, on one hand, of the link between his music and the external world (i.e., a city or outer space) and, on the other, the simple fact that anyone may hear that *in* the music, in the sonic drama and in Varèse's plays with register and spatial location onstage—that Varèse constructed his composerly persona, a pure art-scientist and also something of a painter in sound. I would contend that Varèse, rather than disavowing the possibility that abstract instrumental music may represent something beyond itself, played the representing game on a new level. Metaphor was a kind of convenience for him; *Amériques* is "about" a city, but one also gets the impression that Varèse wished sometimes for the association to be reversed: the alluring, fast-paced modern city—technologically advanced and future-bound—becomes a metaphor for new music, progressive and timely. Is *Arcana* "about" space travel, or is science fiction (the futural past of Paracelsian astronomy) merely a prop for musical autonomy?

As Varèse wrote his music, ripe as it is with powerful effects, another kind of power began to accumulate around this music as his critical image was born—an image perhaps advocated loudest by Rosenfeld:

Edgar Varèse follows in the steps of Wagner . . . and all of the young musicians not so much interested in the creation of beautiful objects as in the penetration [again?] and registration of the extant. He, too, is a kind of philosopher or sacred doctor, hearing the logic of things, the way the world is put together as other logicians may see or feel it; and his art is a sort of revelation, made through the manipulation of the musical medium. . . . [Varèse] is one of the conscious truth-seekers; and his music is a genuine declaration of things as they are; not the mere illustration of a system. . . . Varèse is to be placed entirely in the company of the composers who have actually philosophized in music.[37]

Rosenfeld seems to have delighted at invoking an old German Power. Varèse was a "philosopher or sacred doctor," registering "the extant," hearing deeper than others because he was not hindered by the trappings of the external world. As if Varèse could hear old Hegel's *Geist*, the Western Spirit that unfolds through violent clashes with its others, eventually attaining self-consciousness. This teleological narrative undergirds Rosenfeld's celebration of Varèse the conscious truth-seeker; the composer pushes, even further than Wagner before him, to uncover "things as they are." Or, at least to hear sound as it is.

It is in this sense that Varèse may be understood as a sonic ontologist, and his whole method and approach to sound an ontological approach: the composer aimed to seek a truer sense of sound, a sound that was ephemeral, fugitive, and contingent—to paraphrase Baudelaire's well-worn words about modernity—yet also eternal and immutable.[38] It was as if the Being of sound, its ontological status, needed the proper method in order to be uncovered. This is the context in which Varèse's oft-quoted statement from his first published interview in Manhattan is best understood:

> Our musical alphabet must be enriched. We also need new instruments very badly. In this respect Futurists (Marinetti and his *bruiteurs*) have made a serious mistake. New instruments must be able to lend varied combinations and must not simply remind us of things heard time and time again. Instruments, after all, must only be temporary means of expression. Musicians should take up this question in deep earnest with the help of machinery specialists. In my own work I have always felt the need of new mediums of expression. I refuse to limit myself to sounds that have already been heard. What I am looking for is new mechanical mediums which will lend themselves to every expression of thought and keep up with thought.[39]

Varèse wished for electronic means through which to express his inner sound, but not the sound that Luigi Russolo produced beginning in 1913 with his *intonarumori*, noise-generating machines constructed by attaching large horns to boxes containing metal plates, gears, and strings with which Russolo and other futurists would produce a symphony of noises. This was perhaps the first figuration of the "all-sound music of the future" that Cage would theorize over two decades later and that Varèse heard as something of an aberration. It would not suffice, in his view, to just produce noise; rather, sound needs a system of organization.

It is only by passing through the composer's inner ear—and, by extension, through his pen, his piano, and his orchestration—that sound would be truly liberated. The "Art of Noises" devised by Russolo as well as Filippo Marinetti's celebration, in his 1909 "Futurist Manifesto," of the "roaring motor car which seems to run on machine-gun fire," "the gliding flight of aeroplanes whose propeller sounds like the flapping of a flag and the applause of enthusiastic crowds"—a glorification of war, "militarism, patriotism, the destructive gesture of the anarchists"—all this futurist chest-banging missed the point in Varèse's view.[40] These sounds have already been heard; when new electronic instruments are able to keep up with thought, expressing the composer's imagination directly, only then may new sounds emanate from the inner world. Varèse, as we shall see in the next chapter, thus anticipated Pierre Boulez's own insistence that sound needs *écriture* to be music; noise is insufficient on its own and requires a medium—in Varèse's case, new instruments and means of writing—in order to be music. Organization, orchestration, form, technique and technology: only the media *écriture* might access—and make audible for the listener—the world of the composer's inner ear.

One may imagine Varèse as something of a sonic painter of modern life in the mold of Baudelaire's vision of the watercolor painter Constantin Guys, one who, in the poet's own words, transmutes the world as it appears into a new, idealized version, putting the "noises" of the world (so to speak) through the filter of the artistic medium.

And now, whilst others are sleeping, this man is leaning over his table, his steady gaze on a sheet of paper, exactly the same gaze as he directed just now at the things about him, brandishing his pencil, his pen, his brush, splashing water from the glass up to the ceiling, wiping his pen on his shirt, hurried, vigorous, active, as though he was afraid the images might escape him, quarrelsome though alone, and driving himself relentlessly on. And things seen are born again on the paper, natural and more than natural, beautiful and better than beautiful, strange and endowed with an enthusiastic life, like the soul of their creator. The weird pageant has been distilled from nature. All the materials, stored higgledy-piggledy by memory, are classified, ordered, harmonized, and undergo that deliberate idealization, which is the product of a childlike perceptiveness, in other words a perceptiveness that is acute and magical by its very ingenuousness.[41]

To invoke Baudelaire's description of the modernist artist is to suggest that Varèse, despite the composer's rhetoric of transcending tradition—or, at least, of purifying music of its representational effects—was very much a part of a tradition. Like Baudelaire's painter, Varèse possessed a "will to 'heroize' the present," as Foucault had it, a will to intervene on the present to forge the eternal and immutable out of the transient. The composer possessed what Jürgen Habermas termed, drawing from Foucault, an "intractable will to knowledge and ever more knowledge": Modern Man, or the modern knowing subject, expresses a "unique dynamism of a *will to truth*," which is "the key to the internal nexus of knowledge and power."[42] Knowledge and power: we can think of Varèse's ambition to go beyond the human-powered orchestra, or his will to push ever upward (metaphorically) in his music, to reach unseen, unheard heights technically and conceptually, as a "will to truth," or a will toward total mastery of a newly discovered sound world: a world made of the purity of sound and the harmony of the word.

During the late 1960s, (the Bataille acolyte) Foucault put forward his well-known contention that this figure of the Modern Man was an affordance of a new configuration of knowledge that all in all effaced the metaphysical presuppositions of the Classical Age (the seventeenth and eighteenth centuries). This Modern Man, who was a uniquely western (European) product fabricated "less than two hundred years ago" by "the demiurge of knowledge," would soon crumble like a sand painting on the edge of the sea.[43] Through the next section, we may come to see that this Foucauldian narrative of the creation and disintegration of the figure of *l'homme* took up something of Bataille's restive recalcitrance in the face of modern western reason. This Modern Man, like Varèse, was possessed by a sheer will to cognitive self-mastery.[44]

The next section begins with the observation that Varèse and Bataille shared similar tastes: the philosopher certainly loved the profound "punches" of avant-garde art, and he took such extreme experiences to indicate that beneath the façade of western reason and faith, there exists a certain excess that undermines the philosophical double bind of idealism and materialism—two sides, in his view, of the same ontological coin. By casting Varèse's "punches" as endeavors in musical "base matter," I will show that Varèse shared something with the renegade surrealist Bataille—they were both stranglers eager to wield the visceral presence of avant-garde art against traditional western aesthetics—but also will use Bataille as a yardstick to measure Varèse's own latent German Power. For by the end, one may find that the Hegelianism—or, more precisely, Hegelian Idealism—that Bataille vehemently opposed was in fact the core of Varèse's sonic philosophy. This is, I think, what drew the composer to Wagner and also to another Wagner fan, the leader of the Third Reich: as if Hegel's *Geist* took sonic form.

SONIC BASE MATTER: VARÈSE THROUGH BATAILLE

> What a mixture, this mélange of torrid nature, jumbled botany, indigenous magic, and Salamancan theology, where the Volcano, the friars, the poppy man, the merchant of precious jewels, the "flocks of parakeets in their Sunday best," the "master-magicians who throughout the cities and countryside would teach cloth-making, the value of zero" are the stuff of the most delirious dreams.[45]
>
> —PAUL VALÉRY

Reading Guatemalan writer Miguel Angel Asturias's breakthrough novella of 1930, *Legendas de Guatemala*, Paul Valéry found images of a primordial earth, naked natives, licentious gods, spirits of the heavens, and eternal temples juxtaposed through constantly shifting narrative modes. Asturias posed images, places, and peoples long gone against

incantatory passages of prayer and surrealistic jumbles of short utterances, native cries, erupting volcanoes, and percussion music. The
Legendas won Asturias literary fame: as Valéry exclaimed in his above-
quoted letter to the French translator of the *Legendas*, Asturias's legends were "story-dream-poems."

In 1934 Varèse premiered a work of story-dream-music, *Ecuatorial*,
for orchestra, two electronic instruments (designed by Léon Theremin),
and bass voice. Taking a passage from Asturias's *Legendas* as his text,
Varèse explored the incantatory depths of vocal color. Shocking New
York's Town Hall in 1934 as bass Chase Boromeo sang through a mega-
phone in front of Theremin's malfunctioning aerophones (which the
composer eventually replaced with ondes martenot), *Ecuatorial* would
not be performed again until the 1960s. However, the story of Varèse's
conception of this work in Paris between 1928 and 1933 indicates that
the composer shared a common urge with his contemporary Bataille to
seek a more immediate and visceral form of expression.

For Bataille, however, German power was a problem. The philosopher was enraged when, in 1933, Elizabeth Foerster attested to Hitler
that her brother, the late Friedrich Nietzsche, was devotedly anti-
Semitic. Debunking Foerster's words and rescuing Nietzsche from the
Nazis was the explicit topic of an issue of the journal *Acéphale*, a publication that served as the public face of a sect that Bataille otherwise
preferred to keep secret, the members bound in silence: periodically
Bataille and his comrades met at a "sacred" place near a tree struck
by lightning, meditated together on texts by Nietzsche, and—as Allan
Stoekl accounts—planned to carry out a human sacrifice that was never
fulfilled.

> The Acéphale group was . . . outside the mainstream of political
> life: subversive yet not intended to lead an organized mass move-
> ment . . . its main goals were the rebirth of myth and the touching
> off in society of an explosion of the primitive communal drives
> leading to sacrifice.[46]

It is unclear who attended the secret meetings, but we know who
contributed to Bataille's journal: Michel Leiris, Roger Caillois, Pierre
Klossowski, Jean Wahl, and others. Bataille, of course, was their ring-

leader, declaring with contempt that "[t]he Jew Judas betrayed Jesus for a small sum of money":

> after that he hanged himself. The betrayal carried out by those close to Nietzsche does not have the brutal consequences of Judas's, but it sums up and makes intolerable all the betrayals that deform the teachings of Nietzsche (betrayals that put him on the level of the most shortsighted of current enthusiasms).

Bataille dubbed Nietzsche's sister "Elisabeth Judas-Förster" and called her betrayal "even more vulgar than Judas's deal."[47] Beyond the fact that Nietzsche was *not* anti-Semitic, at stake for Bataille was the conviction that philosophy ought to seek an elsewhere, a mode of thought and of experience that runs counter to the mainstream of western philosophical and theological thinking.

Base matter was Bataille's means to destabilize what he saw as the basic premises of an ontological tradition always divided between idealism and materialism. While on one hand idealists like Hegel viewed all of history as the gradual progression of "Spirit," which overcomes everything that would mar it from self-realization (i.e., religious devotion, the master–slave dialectic, or unhappy consciousness), eventually overcoming and subsuming otherness within itself, on the other hand modern science progressed through the study of "dead matter." In a short and gnomic text for *Documents* entitled "Materialism," Bataille stated that materialists, though they claim to move away from abstract ideals toward the concrete real, tend to "situate dead matter at the summit of a conventional hierarchy of diverse facts." Materialists wind up "[obsessed] with the *ideal* form of matter": "what matter *should be*": materialism is therefore no different than idealism. Whereas an idealist answers profound questions about the nature of being by recourse to abstract spiritual truths, materialists simply substitute dead matter for abstract truth. Science wields dead matter the same way that theology wields God: materialism answers "the question of the essence of things, precisely of the *idea* by which things become intelligible." "Materialism is a senile idealism."[48]

If materialism and idealism represent dual aspects of the same western ontological machine—that is, if all western science and rationalism is structured around a fictive binary opposition—then there must be a third term of a sort, something structuring the opposition, allowing it to be set in motion. Bataille's "base materialism" can be understood as a way of comprehending the condition of possibility for this fictive (yet powerful and long-entrenched) western dualism: Bataille thus anticipated the Derridean notion of the supplement or the trace.[49] In the days of the Acéphale group's secret meetings and meditations on expenditure, sexuality, and death, this third term (i.e., "base matter") was avowedly of the order of avant-garde strangling—the performed presence of the most extreme new art—and also could be experienced, in Bataille's view, through the alterity of certain non-western artifacts. "When the word *materialism* is used, it is time to designate the direct interpretation, *excluding all idealism*, of raw phenomena, and not a system founded on the fragmentary elements of an ideological analysis, elaborated under the sign of religious relations." To Bataille, there is always otherness caught up within an ontology, the perverse or profane elements that he aimed to foreground in order to resist "the West's" great ontological machines. "The existence of a sect of *licentious Gnostics*," he wrote in "Base Materialism and Gnosticism," with their "love of darkness, a monstrous taste for obscene and lawless *archontes*, fulfills this obscure demand for a baseness that would not be reducible, which would be owed the most indecent respect."[50] The demand was not too obscure; it was Bataille's own demand for a baseness that would be irreducible to ontology, whence came his call for a "base matter . . . external and foreign to ideal human aspirations," refusing to allow itself to be taken up by "the great ontological machines."

How much Bataille actually knew (or cared to know, or was able to know) about the various early religious sects that developed during the first century CE, and which are classed as gnostic today, seems beside the point (for him, if not for us).[51] His essential view, which he articulated repeatedly throughout his career, was that the third term—the excess, accursed share, or base matter—belongs neither to God's kingdom nor to the realm of ontological truth. Whether in non-reproductive sexual practices (especially perverse ones) or in banal violent modern spectacles like sporting events, a certain non-instrumental excess is produced, an expenditure without return.[52] In "Base Materialism," he reproduced pictures of various stone-carved icons—humanoid figures with duck heads; animals surrounded by planets; and a god with the legs of a man, the body of a serpent, and the head of a rooster—as symbols of this profane excess that resists idealism. These objects were not interesting as ethnological artifacts per se, but rather as poetic devices for an avant-garde puncher. That Bataille packed a punch is confirmed by the particular allure that the "solar ass," another humanoid figure with the head of a donkey, exerted on him. Calling "the ass . . . the most hideously comical animal, and at the same time the most humanly virile," he imagined its "comic and desperate braying [as] the signal for a shameless revolt against idealism in power."[53]

In Sylvère Lotringer's words, "[r]eclaiming Nietzsche from the Nazis was . . . a way of validating his [Bataille's] own fascination for violence and fanaticism, a 'fundamental aspiration of humanity,' he said, that the fascists misappropriated."[54] It is conspicuous, for our purposes, that Bataille voiced his rage against the Nazi machine just before Varèse, as Mattis accounts, wrote "Heil to Hitler" to end a 1937 letter to the American painter Will Shuster. The composer also griped in 1934 (to Jolivet) about a Jewish acquaintance, suggesting that Hitler's hatred may have been justified, and in a 1928 profile published in Le Figaro, the composer exclaimed "Jazz is not America. It's a Negro product, exploited by the Jews."[55] While his "Heil" cannot be explained away as the misplaced aggression of a restive youth, Varèse seems to have had complicated and inconsistent views on both race and power. He was never an official member of the Nazi Party, nor did he publicly endorse the Third Reich. He also changed his mind about jazz by the 1950s (if not well before), collaborating with Charles Mingus during a series of improvisation sessions at the Greenwich House, and he certainly was neither a stranger nor an adversary to critics of Jewish descent like Paul Rosenfeld.[56] I would presume that when he wrote "Heil" in his letter to Shuster, Varèse was drawing on Hitler's power to undergird his own view of his world and his art. In other words, his "Heil" bespeaks a kind of ontological suprematism, a belief in the supreme power of a specifically western approach to Being.

Varèse and Bataille's specific political allegiances are less important for the present discussion than what such allegiances betray about these thinker's ontological convictions—this is the primary distinction between them that I wish to foreground in the remainder of this chapter. In "Base Materialism and Gnosticism," Bataille railed against the western notion of ontology, making a characteristically bold and sweeping claim that Christian theology as well as Hegel's philosophy, as twin monoliths of western dualism, both "proceeded from very ancient metaphysical conceptions" like those developed by the gnostics.[57] Hegel's system and Christian tradition hinged on a tension between "an abstract God . . . and abstract matter; the chief guard and the prison walls" of the western metaphysical prison house.[58] Bataille positioned gnostic religion as an archaic development phase for western dualism, believing that certain gnostic icons expose the "sinister love of darkness, a monstrous taste for obscene and lawless *archontes*" that is actually the bedrock of Hegelian or Christian metaphysics.[59] By thus returning to origins, the philosopher could imagine an epoch in which matter and spirit existed in a dualist relationship that was not dialectical—that is, a dualist relationship that would neither be defined by nor would develop according to the teleological battle of thesis-antithesis-synthesis.

On the surface—and this is precisely how Bataille and Varèse each understood the sources from which they drew: as surfaces, primitive expressions that can be read at their face—the philosopher and the composer played the same anti-western avant-garde game. Bataille's *archontes* embodied the perversions at the heart of western idealism, while for Varèse the primitivist imagery conveyed in Asturias's *Legendas* resonated with a dark sound echoing somewhere under the façade of western musical meaning. As if through surrealist prose or surreal music we may go back to origins—however vague these origins are.

But nobody has ever accused Bataille of seeking the pure. It is Varèse's obsession with the purity of sound that most clearly distinguishes the composer from his philosopher contemporary. It is time now to listen to *Ecuatorial* while reading the source text, Asturias's *Legends of Guatemala*, as I believe we may come to understand the philosophical basis of Varèse's efforts through his career to liberate sound by examining the sound world he imagined during his years in Paris. *Ecuatorial* is unique among Varèse's *oeuvre* because its text setting refers so explicitly to something outside the music: Varèse could not have denied the representational function of his sounds even if he wanted to do so. While the composer employed various techniques that will be familiar—sound masses and zones of intensity, the interplay of distinct registral areas that build in dissonant cacophony—it is in his treatment of the Asturias text that one may hear the purity of sound and harmony of the word that drew Varèse to Dada, and that also aligns Varèse with a very old, very western metaphysical view according to which speech is an ideal sonic medium that transcends materiality, joining the voice with the soul through the breath.

From the standpoint of Bataille's base materialism, *Ecuatorial* may be heard as Varèse's endeavor to leverage an archaic source to create a sonic form of "base matter." His text includes a prayer to an imagined deity: "Hail, beauty of the day / Givers of yellow, of green . . . . Give life, existence / to my children, to my offspring," exclaims Varèse's bass singer in a passage that cherishes "Your power, Your sorcery," the power of mythic beings who bestow and protect life. In 1930, the ex-surrealist Robert Desnos introduced Varèse to Asturias, who had traveled to Paris during the early 20s to study jurisprudence and who stayed to translate the Mayan *Popul Vuh* with French religious studies scholar Georges Raynaud. Asurias had just released his *Legendas*, which Varèse quickly came to love: as Ernst Lichtenhahn accounts, Varèse's papers (held at the Paul Sacher Foundation) include a copy of Asturias's text with the composer's scribbled annotations (including short sketches of vocal phrases).[60] The passage that Varèse chose from the *Legendas* to set as the text for *Ecuatorial* was one that Asturias borrowed and reworked from the *Popul Vuh*, a desperate plea for these great deities, "Givers of children, of daughters," to bestow life and prosperity on future generations.

This excerpt from Asturias derives from a chapter titled "Now That I Recall" in which an old hunter, Goldenhide, recounts a journey through a forest. He hears the sounds of the turquoise-browned motmot (in Asturias's original text: guardabarranco), a colorful bird of Central America that is able, according to Goldenhide, to cast spells. As the hunter walks into the forest, he hears the guardabarranco sing and associates its song with "the timeless soul of the stones and ageless soil of the fields." These birds are not the only sources of sound in this mythic world:

Within the jungle, the forest closes off path after path. The trees fall like flies into the spider web of impassable undergrowth. And at every step, echo's nimble hares run, bound, fly. In the loving depths of half-light, the doves cooing, the coyote howling, the elk running, the jaguar tracking, the kite winging, and my footsteps falling roused the echo of the wandering tribes that came from the sea.[61]

Ecuatorial begins with a downward-stepping motif in the piano and trumpet, a quiet, gentle opening comparable in mood to the flute solo at the start of *Amériques*.[62] Unlike the mechanistic repetition that characterizes Varèse's New York soundscape, however, *Ecuatorial* may be described as organic. Descending motifs and static, prolonged pitches fill the sparse space in Varèse's ensemble, and it is the absence of a clear meter and the slow, rubato unfolding of his themes that distinguishes the sound world of *Ecuatorial* from the repetitive, mechanistic churnings of *Amériques*. The first minute or so of *Ecuatorial* is composed solely of variations on a chromatic three-note descent; the piano and a trumpet finally sustain the same pitch, the former rapidly repeating it and the latter adding flutter-tongue while Varèse's percussion section enters with scattered, brief accents; Varèse then introduces an organ and his electronic instruments—originally etherphones—which ascend into the stratosphere and, along with the trumpets, sustain a high, shimmering pitch. Then comes brass blares, percussive stomping, and steely counterpoint between Varèse's etherphones.

It is tempting to cast the opening of *Ecuatorial* as a wholesale re-imagining of Asturias's Mayan forest. The fluttering repeated tones of Varèse's trumpet and piano can be heard as the pattering of nimble hares or cooing of doves; the scattered strikes in the percussion as panicked galloping hooves; the ascending etherphones as coyote howls; and perhaps the opening descending motif casts the eerie spell of the guard-abarranco. Of course, to associate Varèse's sounds in such a direct way with Asturias's soundscape is to indulge—in an admittedly opportunistic and even puerile way—in the game of hermeneutic conjoining. Abstract instrumental music becomes something of an aural cartoon depicting rabbits, coyotes, and a lurking jaguar. Varèse never claimed that *Ecuatorial* follows the narrative arc of Asutrias's text to the letter, and to associate Varèse's sounds with specific figures in Asturias's text would be to bracket the specificity of Varèse's medium. His sounds *are* abstract; his plays with sustained tones, instrumental articulation, and registral areas are a Varèsean language of timbre. And yet . . . no listener can deny that *Ecuatorial* depicts a landscape of a sort. Varèse creates another spatial environment in sound, beckoning his listener to enter a foreign aural land, and playing in the ambiguity between explicit musical representation and its other.

Ecuatorial and Asturias's narrative follow a similar arc. After Goldenhide's footsteps wake the sounds of "wandering tribes that came from the sea," and after Varèse introduces his various sonic characters—the downward-stepping motives, sustained pitches forming another sonic "ceiling" (in the manner of *Arcana*), organ runs and rapid percussive stabs—Asturias and Varèse seem to introduce human song at the same point in their respective stories. Asturias writes:

> Here was where their song began. Here was where their lives began. They began their lives with their soul in their hands. Amid the sun, the wind, and the earth they danced to the rhythm of their tears as the moon made ready to come out. Here under the cherimoya trees. Here on the capuli flowers . . .[63]

The prayer from the *Popul Vuh* then begins. In *Ecuatorial*, the bass voice erupts in song along with the whole ensemble—the brass, organ, and etherphones sustain a bold chord as the vocalist almost chants: "Oh, Oh, Oh, Oh!" The ensemble then quiets down as a solo etherphone follows the contour of the bass melody: "Constructores! Oh Formadores! Vosotros veis. Vosotros escucháis. No nos abandonáis, Espíritu del Cielo, Espíritu de la Tierra" ["O Builders, O Moulders! You see. You hear. Do not abandon us, Spirit of the Sky, Spirit of the Earth"].

During this bass and aerophone duet, the familiar downward-stepping motives in the piano and trumpet recur and the rest of the ensemble provides sparse accompaniment, occasional accents, and dissonant interjections between lines of text. The prayer, in Varèse's own translation, reads:

Give us our descendants, our posterity as long as there are days, as long as there are dawns. May green roads be many, the green paths you give us. Peaceful, very peaceful may the tribes be. . . . O Master Giant, Path of the Lightning, Falcon! Master-magi, Powers of the sky, Procreators, Begetters![64]

It is after the Asturias text invokes "Ancient Mystery," an "Ancient Sorceress, Ancestress of the Day, Ancestress of the Dawn"—a text that Varèse instructs his vocalist to sing with a "dark chest tone"—that the style of recitation changes, and Varèse begins to demand extended vocal technique. On "que la germinatión se haga, que el alba se haga" ["Let there be germination, let there be Dawn"], Varèse writes "*trés nasal— percutant*" ["very nasal—striking"] in his score, and in performance, the listener may find that this sudden transition from chest voice (i.e., traditional operatic singing) to coarse nasal grinding signals a change in narrative content. The bass vocalist has until this point recited a prayer; now, in the manner of a shaman, he will summon the spiritual forces beckoned by Asturias's re-working of the *Popul Vuh*. We will experience the harmony of the word.

The plea to the "Givers of daughters, of sons," soon follows, and must have been spoken, in Asturias's text, by an imagined Mayan native. In Varèse's setting, the bass voice veers between stammering recitation, arching melody, and nasally hummed incantation to invoke these deities' life-giving powers. The vocalist ascends a familiar melodic motif that had previously been stated by brass and organ, but, conspicuously, Varèse sets this moment of the vocal score to syllables that are not in Asturias's original text: "Hongh! Hengh whoo," which he marks "hummed—very nasal" (Figure 14). After a stammering, pattering recitation of the next line ("Hail beauties of the day, givers of yellow," etc.), the bass voice ascends with "ho ha," and Varèse instructs him to "*close mouth abruptly after attack.*" The quivering voice with harsh "h" syllables (a desperate braying?) gives way to the upward soaring voices of the etherphones, resounding as if a response from the gods. Hovering disembodied above strikes of a timpani, the two electronic instruments— ondes martenot in contemporary recordings—suspend time between vocal utterance and the denser orchestral passages that follow. The role

FIGURE 14. Excerpt from *Ecuatorial*. Note Varèse's use of harsh "h" syllables in the vocal part: "Hoo-Ha"; "Hongh! Hengh Whoo," which he marks in the score: "Hummed—very nasal."

This quotation from Varèse's score is drawn from: *Ecuatorial,* music by Edgard Varèse, published by Casa Ricordi Srl, a division of Universal Music Publishing Group. *International Copyright Secured. All Rights Reserved.* Reprinted by permission of Hal Leonard Europe BV (Italy).

that the two ondes play, however, is not at all new from the perspective of Varèse's poetics; they replace the winds and strings that soared into the high reaches of the orchestral "space" in *Arcana.* Finally the composer found an instrument that could produce the "pure" continuous artificial sound for which he had wished during the prior decade.

Text aside, much of the musical language during this incantatory moment of *Ecutaorial* is already familiar. Upward-reaching gestures reminiscent of the grand ascending passage from *Arcana* abound. Shortly after the vocalist cries "Héngh! Hengh whoo," for instance, and after an organ interlude, Varèse commences another upward climb from the orchestra's lowest register toward the high *vibratissimo* of the ondes, propelled by a series of staggered entrances each a minor ninth apart (perhaps the composer's favorite interval). Keeping the Asturias text in view, however, I would suggest that this Varèsean play with registral areas, his sound masses, takes on a distinct representational function in *Ecuatorial*. The pairing of scintillating, soaring electronic voices with a human voice rooted somewhere in the soil, singing of an ancient spirituality now lost, betrays something, I think, about what Varèse's sense of spatial sound and this poetics of intensity really meant all along. After writing *Ecuatorial*, the composer could never have claimed, as he did with *Arcana*, that the text is of no import to his sound world. In fact, hearing these familiar musical features paired with imagery of gods and a mythic living forest seems to confirm that these features *always were* representational—picturesque and anecdotal.

Two sides of the same coin, the near future and primordial past, scientific reason and primitive unreason, represented by the tension between the soaring ondes and phonetic bass, would together lend musical writing a renewed vigor in Varèse's aesthetic. "We are at a new primitive stage of music today," he claimed in the Santa Fe lecture, calling instruments like Theremin's etherphones "primitive electrical instruments," which demanded new methods of writing closer to the ideographic inscription for the medieval voice prior to the invention of the modern staff. He imagined that a distant past, what he called the "Mediaeval primitive," could serve "our own primitive era."[65] Musical writing needed to be freed from the rules of western music's twelve pitches in order to approximate the parabolas of the siren or the arches of hummed glissandi.

Varèse's jumble of sound masses can be heard as a musical embodiment of the jumble of sounds in the Mayan forest that Asturias describes a page lager when his hunter, wandering through the woods, hears natives in dance and prayer.

> Delirious night. Silence follows sound; desert follows sea. In the
> shadow of the forest my senses deceive me: I hear the cries of

mule drivers, marimbas, bells, steeds galloping down cobble-
stone streets.[66]

This delirious night is more than a metaphor for Varèse's sound masses:
the exotic elsewhere depicted in the *Legendas* is not a "scene" accompanying this music. It seems more appropriate to suggest—once again—
that this music *is* a delirious night. Varèse deconstructs sound, stripping
musical grammar bare just as Asturias deconstructs the sounds of marimbas and bells into free-floating syllables as the passage continues:

> Clasping one hand with the other, I dance to the rhythm of the
> vowels of a cry: *A-e-i-o-u!* *A-e-i-o-u!* And to the monotonous
> rhythm of the crickets.
>   A-e-i-o-u! Softer A-e-i-o-u! Softer! Nothing exists! I, who am
> dancing on one foot, do not exist! A-e-i-o-u! Softer! U-o-i-e-a!
> More! Chirp-chirp! More! Let my right hand pull at my left until
> I have split in two—aeiou—to go on dancing—uoiea—split down
> the middle—aeiuo, but joining hands—chirp . . . chirp![67]

Varèse's use of the harsh "h" in "Hongh! Hengh whoo" is a transposition of Asturias's play with these letters, an incantatory music of
phonetics. These vocal effects take on tremendous symbolic weight in
the *Legendas*: the dancer dances in two; words divide into their base
sounds. A native prays; the solar ass brays.

The syllable games that Varèse inserts into Asturias's version of the
Popul Vuh prayer, or the disjunct vowels that sound in Asturias's delirious night, become expressions of "pure sound" like the fragmented
syllables in works by the Dadaists with whom Varèse surrounded himself during his early New York phase. An aesthetics of collage bestowed
a kind of musical ambiguity on spoken and written utterances. "Their
only law the law of phonetics": stripped of semantic meaning, sound
has its own law. Varèse's sound masses, like the harsh syllables of his
bass vocalist, are a kind of musical base matter, bare building blocks
forged from a neo-primitivist will to take music down to its most basic
elements. In this sense, *parameterization*, a buzzword often associated
with Varèse and with modernists of his ilk, *is primitivism*, a return to
origins in the sense of a return to the basic components of musical language: timbre, register, and interval.

Bataille and Varèse's works are vehicles for a similar kind of experience. The former's pornographic prose works seem to perform the same profane violence against Christian tradition that the latter's sound masses perform against the hallowed norms of western music. The "solar ass" mentioned in "Base Materialism," for instance, is a recasting of "the solar anus" about which Bataille wrote a surrealist text in 1927 (that was later published with a set of André Masson's drawings). He explains volcanic eruption as the result of "the earth sometimes [jerking] off in a frenzy"; he likens "[c]ommunist workers" to "ugly and dirty . . . sexual organs" in the eyes of the bourgeoisie; and thus "the erotic revolutionary and volcanic deflagrations antagonize the heavens," an anti-bourgeois and anti-Christian refrain that culminates with the image of "the *solar annulus*," "the intact anus of her body at eighteen years to which nothing sufficiently blinding can be compared except the sun."[68] Pornographic surrealism and archaic mysticism were dual means for the philosopher to foreground the otherness at the heart of "the West's" various idealisms.

But, once again, nobody has ever accused Bataille of seeking the pure. The Varèse–Bataille dyad represents two divergent ways of giving form to and wielding base matter. While Bataille's base matter—whether the solar ass or solar anus—was a means to resist the great ontological machines, Varèse's musical base matter can be heard as the composer's means to construct a kind of *neo-ontology*. Sound poetry, sound masses, the voices of the forest, and the voices of soaring electronic instruments altogether bolstered one of the composer's discursive leitmotifs: that sound is a substance with life and power, beholden to a deeper truth, which the composer might uncover through new technologies and new methods of writing. As I have suggested, his obsession with the pure, with claiming an otherworldly status for liberated sound, constitutes the main difference between Varèse and his philosopher contemporary. Through the methods I have described—his work with sound masses, his poetics of intensity, and his obsession with purity—he constructed his own musical ontological machines, treating sound *as* other and then purifying sound into musical systems.

This process of idealization through subsumption is precisely what Bataille found so problematic about Hegelian Idealism. In "Base Materialism," he claimed that "Gnosticism, in its psychological process, is not so different from present-day materialism, I mean a materialism not implying an ontology, not implying matter is the thing-in-itself."[69] "Present-day materialism" refers to Bataille's own sense of base matter, a material that cannot be taken up and recast, through some dialectical magic, as merely the external appearance of a deeper and loftier ontological condition. If matter is a thing-in-itself, it therefore is not a thing for us; Bataille claimed that to "submit [oneself] entirely to what must be called matter"—that is, to attend to base matter—"is a question above all of *not* submitting oneself . . . to whatever is more elevated," to the higher realms of reason or "to whatever can give a borrowed authority to the being that I am."[70]

On the surface, it is *as if* Varèse, by seeking another world in sound, could have "submitted himself" to matter in Bataille's sense—to the brute force of vibration and to the unreason always cloaked inside the west's great ontological machines. But his musical systems seem, instead, to reaffirm in a different form the "ideal human aspirations" that would function, in Bataille's words, to efface base matter and assert a "borrowed authority" for "the being that I am"—or to the being that Varèse was.

CONCLUSION: "HEIL" ONTOLOGY

After his endeavors to explore the purity of sound and harmony of the word, Varèse's music lay dormant, performed a handful of times and then all but forgotten. Having failed to establish himself in Paris, he floundered, returning to New York in 1933, and for the rest of his life his music was not often heard in public. It was only recently—during the last half century—that many of his works were reactivated, edited, performed, and recorded, that doctoral theses and music-theoretical studies began to be published about him. Why does this long-muted music carry so much clout?

The lasting life of Varèse's music depends on a particular retrospective game. We *need* his words, his concepts, to untangle what this music meant and to understand what sound "is" according to the composer's method (a method that was taken up by many later "art-scientists," up to the spectralists and beyond). To play again on Varèse's own word, the life of his music depends on the listener's will to "crystallize" his sounds. While he used this term to describe a compositional process through which an initial musical idea "[expands] and [splits] into different shapes or groups of sound,"[71] I would prefer to use this term, contra Varèse's apparent intention, to describe the perceptual process through which the listener or scholar, by attending to Varèse's discourse (his scores and his words) learns how to hear his sound masses, to distinguish zones of intensity, and so on. Crystallization occurs in hindsight: we look back and see his sound blocks, and then we know how to engage with this music.

I end, therefore, with an aforementioned irony. Varèse's music *is* violent and powerful, yet even this music—the music that seems to be most clearly "about" presence, liveness, shock, and goosebumps—has only endured on account of Varèse's discursive power. Sound, for Varèse, amounts to a written being, the phrase that Derrida once used (filtering something from Bataille, no doubt) to suggest that ontology had only ever been "written in" to many philosophical texts—and beyond this, that the medium of phonetic writing, the writing of speech, grants a certain privilege to sound.

It seems hardly necessary to point out that the "purity of sound" Varèse envisioned was—at least when he used this phrase in print, referring to new poetry—a phonetic sound. Though the composer is known for his abstract instrumental music, and *Ecuatorial* is one of only a few works in which Varèse included a voice, the connection between Varèse's liberation of sound and avant-garde poetry—a connection born out as Varèse's bass singer articulates incantatory syllables like those that echoed in Asturias's imagined Mayan forest—suggests another deeper relation between Varèsean sound and a specifically western philosophical view of writing.

Varèse's avowals about liberating and purifying sound shared the spirit of Hegel's thought about writing. "Alphabetic writing expresses *sounds* which are themselves signs," in Hegel's words, "[i]t consists therefore of the signs of signs."[72] Hegel held a chauvinistic belief that phonetic writing is superior to non-western written forms because the breath transcends the material signifier; it is "the best writing, the mind's writing," to quote Derrida's synopsis of Hegel's view. Phonetic writing "respects the interiority of phonic signifiers"; it "sublimates space and sight" by uniting the material signifier with the voice, allowing "the infinite spirit [to relate] to itself in its discourse and its culture."[73] "The mind, distancing itself from the concrete sense-perceptible," in Hegel's words, "directs its attention on the more formal moment, the sonorous word and its abstract elements, and contributes essentially to the founding and purifying of the ground of interiority within the subject."[74]

It is conspicuous that Hegel's ideas about phonetic writing aligned with his view of musical tone: "in tone music forsakes the external form and its sensuous *visibility*"; hearing is "more ideal than sight" because "the ear [does not place] itself in a practical relation towards" whatever object vibrates, but rather "receives the result of that ideal vibration of material substance" directly. To forsake visibility is to forsake exteriority; it is necessarily to forsake the merely material form of writing. Musical tone is what Hegel termed a "twofold negation" since, by allowing us to perceive the inner vibration of an object, tone negates our practical relation to that object, and therefore negates any spatial relation to externality in general. Music is, to sound a Varèsean refrain, the renunciation of the external world: we plunge into the materiality of the vibrating object; "it is no longer the material object in its repose" that we hear, "but [rather] the first example of the more ideal activity of the soul itself which is apprehended."[75] If tone allows one to transcend externality and to lay ground for the interiority (i.e., self-presence) of the subject, then phonetic writing, which activates the tone of the voice, may allow for a similar transcendence.[76]

Hegel's words about musical tone and the ideality of western language offer us a final glimpse into what Varèse found so compelling about Beethoven's ear. Deaf to the external world, the composer hears the inner murmurings more clearly. With Bataille's vehement anti-Hegelian anti-idealism in view, it strikes me that Varèse—once again, while seeming always to share Bataille's anti-western avant-garde ethos—fell right in line with the old German when he echoed Wagner's avowal that certain geniuses possess a prophetic "inner ear." Varèse's affirmation about the purity of sound and harmony of the word uphold the privileged status that Hegel had granted to phonetic writing—a privilege that the whole western tradition had, in Derrida's view, granted to this writing of speech.

We may hear the poetics of *Ecuatorial*, the dualism of bass voice singing incantations of the earth and the electronic voices soaring ever upward, as an *allegory for the metaphysics of phonetic writing*. As if the metaphysical dualism of speech versus writing, the ideal versus the sensible, and interiority versus exteriority was figured into Varèse's musical poetics as the tension between the low rumbling phonetic bass and pure parabolas and hyperbolas of his electronic instruments. On one hand there is the dirt: the harsh incantatory syllables, the abrasive sounds of the city, the clashing dissonance of sound masses that accumulate and lead us upward, elsewhere, where we find—on the other hand—the realm of pure sound, scintillating like the ondes martenot or high strings, the pure and ideal domain of sound. Always there is tension in Varèse between the tendency of art to represent, to mimic, to reference something outside itself—to fall into exteriority—and the wish for personal autonomy through aesthetic autonomy, to leave the sensory exterior and seek the more ideal activity of the soul. Another world created in sound.

Three

ONTOLOGICAL APPROPRIATION

Boulez and Artaud

• • • In his 1963 article "Dire, jouer, chanter," Pierre Boulez (1925–2016) explained his use of certain exotic sounds in *Le Marteau sans maître.* "I chose this 'body' of instruments with the influence of extra-European civilizations," he wrote: "the xylophone transposes the African balafon, the vibraphone refers to the Balinese gender, and the guitar recalls the Japanese koto."[1] The composer insisted, however, that "neither the style nor the very use of these instruments is related in any way to the traditions of these different musical civilizations."[2] Boulez did not wish to represent the music of peoples outside Europe as an ethnologist might when organizing artifacts into a colonial exhibition. Rather, once purified of context, these sounds would "enrich the European sonic vocabulary through extra-European listening," and, Boulez hoped, have a refreshing and estranging effect on the listener accustomed to traditional western timbres. With this move, Boulez also hoped to sever his chosen sounds and harmonies from the historical baggage of the classical tradition, and thus to amplify the presence of music in its moment. In this endeavor he took a cue from the creator of the Theater of Cruelty. "Music should be collective hysteria and enchantment," wrote Boulez in 1947, "violently modern—following the direction of Antonin

Artaud, and not a simple ethnographic reconstruction in the image of civilizations more or less remote from us."[3]

What does it mean for a composer to take sounds from the ethnographic other without "reconstructing" the other? This chapter will argue that Boulez's endeavor to aestheticize the "hysteria" he perceived in the culture of the other was a moment of *ontological appropriation*, turning the other into sound. Boulez's aim was not to reconstruct a specific other. Rather, *sound* was the other: it emanated from someplace strange and primitive, carrying a visceral immediacy that could be leveraged to undermine western musical meaning. Boulez sought a compositional method that would, to use his own term, render sound "neutral": a sonic color rather than a musical sign; a pure quality rather than a representation.[4] I will argue that Boulez's compositional strategy prefigured recent claims on behalf of the ontology of sound: that sound can put us in touch with a world more real, or perhaps that sound simply *is* the real. This search for pure sound, a recurring refrain of twentieth-century musical modernism, is, and always has been, inherently ethnocentric. It is a process of *making sound ontological*.

While the question of otherness is seldom addressed in scholarship on Boulez, it is clear that his sense of sound developed as he reconstructed "extra-European" expressions in sonic form.[5] In the first section below, I use Artaud as a foil to explore how Boulez's idea of musical writing—or *écriture*, his medium to write sonic "hysteria"—took shape as he distilled and sublimated otherness. While Boulez credited Artaud with forging a style of expression that would recreate "collective hysteria and enchantment" without aspiring to realist ethnographic representation, the composer endeavored to push Artaud's expressive style beyond what even the theater guru had achieved. For Artaud often acknowledged the sources of his "delirium": he mimicked the rituals of the Rarámuri tribe of Mexico, infusing his performances with cries, gasps, and ululations, a style of vocal performance that well captured, as Boulez put it, "the basic preoccupations of music today."[6] Boulez's exoticism, by contrast, was more veiled: rather than follow Artaud to intensify the alterity of the other, Boulez sought instead to purify or occlude otherness, a stance that was continuous with certain aspects of surrealism propounded by André Breton (1896–1966).

The approach Boulez took to sound could be called ontological because he treated sound as something more real—more evocative and powerful—than anything that had been, or could be, expressed through the normative musical languages of the western tradition. In what follows, I will first suggest that Boulez's philosophy of writing hinged on an ideological distinction between "the West and the Rest," and then will follow the composer to South America with the Compagnie Renaud-Barrault to hear how he filtered sounds from an extra-European source that he never acknowledged outright: Afro-Bahian Candomblé. I will suggest that Boulez modeled the poetics of one movement of *Le Marteau sans maître*, the "Commentaire I de 'Bourreaux de solitude,'" on the ritual of spirit possession he witnessed in Bahia in the company of actor and director Jean-Louis Barrault (1910–1994). Unlike Barrault, who claimed that the Candomblé embodied the essence of Greek tragedy, Boulez neither wanted nor cared to turn the Candomblé into an allegory for an original western essence. The "delirium" of Candomblé practitioners in the throes of physical spasms and amid abrupt vocal utterances—the kinds of experiences that Artaud emulated directly—took sonic form in *Le Marteau*. As Boulez modeled the "Commentaire" on a fictive narrative of spirit possession, I suggest, sound became an allegory, a figure for an original essence and a kind of elemental force.

Boulez's sounds are still with us today. Following Christoph Cox or Nina Sun Eidsheim, one might argue that a supra-audible "sonic flux" or reality of vibrating matter exists beyond human perception, as a virtual ground for the sounds that we actualize when we make music.[7] The concluding section of this chapter suggests that every scholar who holds that sound is a link to the real, to a reality beyond or behind what we can know and represent, implicitly relies on a notion of sound as allegory—a notion that links sound studies to Boulez and a group of his contemporaries in France. This attitude toward sound, often touted as a way to think beyond entrenched west-versus-east and self-versus-other dualisms, risks reinscribing these dualisms on an ever-deeper level. The problem is not with thinking imaginatively about sound, but with the philosophical idea that guides scholars to take sound as an allegory for truth and reality: ontology.

The term "ontology" has enjoyed a resurgence of late as a marker of a kind of cultural relativism following the ontological turn in anthropology and as a substitute for aesthetic autonomy in sound studies. However, I am not convinced that the idea of ontology can be purged of its history as a "philosophy of power."[8] The very idea of ontology presupposes a relation between the knower and the known such that the known entity, by becoming an object of knowledge and a figure of western writing, loses its alterity.[9] Lévinas coined the term "ontological imperialism" to describe the greedy egotism through which "the West" constitutes itself by first imagining and then incorporating the other.[10] To the extent that Boulez attempted to transmute extra-European sounds into the realm of musical writing, he was an "ontological imperialist." He constituted an idea of sound, not by representing the other as other, but by subsuming the Other into the Same. Recent scholarship, too, treats sound as a figure of radical alterity, yet sonic allegory becomes a means to bolster scholarly authority.

BOULEZ, ARTAUD, AND THE ETHNOGRAPHIC OTHER

"By the time he was eighteen," biographer Joan Peyser writes,

> Boulez had turned against his father, his country, and everything else that had been held up to him as sacred. . . . He repudiated Catholicism, spouting Latin obscenities when he was drunk, . . . he never studied under any one man for any length of time, "detesting the father-son relationship."[11]

While this phase of Boulez's early life clearly had a strong Oedipal dimension, it was Boulez's defiance of the role of the religious Father in French society that made him so receptive to Artaud's cries, shouts, and profane challenges to God's judgment.

As Edward Campbell, Peter O'Hagan, and François Meïmoun recount, Boulez saw Artaud read his own texts at Paris's Galerie Loeb in the summer of 1947, witnessing the dramatist performing the kinds of vocal expressions that would be recorded by the Radiodiffusion Française (RDF) later that year.[12] The broadcast *Pour en finir avec le jugement de Dieu* (recorded in November 1947) documents Artaud during a period of rapid physical decay following a series of electroshock treatments administered against his will at the Rodez asylum (1943–1946).[13] The forty-minute broadcast consists of readings of Artaud's texts by the writer himself, his friend (and later literary executrix) Paule Thévenin, and the actors Maria Casarès and Roger Blin. Censored by the RDF just before its premiere in 1948 (due in large part to Artaud's inclusion of anti-American rhetoric, ill-timed in the wake of the war), *Pour en finir* allows us to hear the voice that Boulez experienced live that summer.[14]

In his opening unaccompanied monologue, Artaud shouts in his high register: "I learned yesterday . . . ," and then pauses. His pacing deliberate, his rasping voice swooping low, he describes "one of the most sensational official practices of public American schools": a "sperm test" in which all young boys are required to give sperm for the government to build an artificial army. America not only manufactured people, but also warships and plastic consumer products, inaugurating "le règne . . . de tous les faux produits fabriques" ("the reign of fake fabricated products") and replacing everything natural with "les ignobles ersatz synthétiques" ("awful ersatz synthetics"). These words come at the end of a series of short phrases in which Artaud crescendos, charging the text with belligerent vocal expressions. On "fabriques," his voice quivers as if a mocking laugh; on "les ignobles ersatz," he tightens his throat, pushing air with tremendous strength to produce a guttural growling; and before the final syllable of "synthétiques," he pauses as if out of breath, separating the last "-que," a percussive click, from the rest of the phrase. Artaud believed in the music of spoken utterance, in the voice's ability to create meaning through its own contours, sometimes bolstering the literal meaning of a text or—in this case—working against the meaning of the words ("fabriques," "synthétiques").[15] He rails against an ersatz, synthetic American war machine and then introduces a contrasting figure: "I love most the people who eat off the very earth the delirium from which they are born." His voice shivers; he blurs "la terre" (earth) to sound like "le délire" (delirium); he whispers: "I speak of the Tarahumaras. . . . Thus you will listen to the dance of the Tutuguri."[16]

The collective enchantment that enthralled Boulez was thus achieved through the rites of the Rarámuri of the Sierra Tarahumara, whose peyote rituals, Artaud claimed, revealed a primordial state of being. After a silence, the next section of *Pour en finir* begins as Artaud screams, a pair of drums and a gong accompanying his ululations as he soars into his extreme upper register. This crude "ethnographic reconstruction" (an avant-garde performance cloaked as a kind of sensationalistic re-imagining of a non-western practice) seems to account, in retrospect, for the stammering articulations and long-drawn-out pacing of the broadcast so far: Artaud speaks as if in a trance. Casarès then enters to read the "Dance of the Tutuguri" text, her enraptured voice vibrating as Artaud's shouts continue. This text describes a ritual in which six Rarámuri men, each symbolizing a sun, surround a seventh who races across a primordial land nude upon a horse. The dance culminates with the letting of blood and the ripping of Catholic crosses out of the Mexican soil.

For Boulez, Artaud's alternation of words with "shouts, noises, or rhythmic effects," and his effort to push vocal utterance beyond what any written text can convey, felt like an affirmation of the musical language that the composer was in the process of conceptualizing and putting into practice. "I am not qualified to discuss Antonin Artaud's use of language," he wrote,

> but I can observe in his writings the basic preoccupations of music today; hearing him read his own texts, accompanying them with shouts, noises, or rhythmic effects, has shown us how to affect a fusion of sound and word, how to make the phoneme burst forth when the word can no longer do so, in short how to organize delirium.[17]

Boulez's efforts to "take delirium and, yes, organize it," however, masked Artaud's explicit exoticism. Perhaps we can hear something of Artaud's "shouts, noises, and rhythmic effects" in the musical language that Boulez forged in his Piano Sonata no. 2 (1948), written after Boulez heard the raving dramatist in person.[18] During the climax of the fourth and final movement, Boulez prompts the performer to "pulverize the sound" in a short passage composed of a rapid-fire succession of quavers and semiquavers leaping between the extreme high and low registers of the piano—*rhythmic effects*. This harried back-and-forth motion culminates with abruptly attacked chordal clusters—*shouts*—before a series of connected pitches in the left hand (marked "Élargir rapidement": expanding quickly) winds upwards toward a group of descending dyads in the extreme high range—*noises*. Boulez commands the pianist to play "in a very strong shade," to sound "exasperated," commencing another phrase of leaps.

Boulez put little stock in verisimilitude, refusing musical "topics" that his listeners or critics could have taken to represent images or scenes in a narrative mode. But although he downplayed the representational function of music—just as he disdained "simple ethnographic reconstruction"—Boulez's musical gestures were often visceral, demanding an identification between his listeners and performers on a corporeal level. His early pianistic language might not represent, but certainly *presents* rapid leaps, sweeps, and chordal clusters, modes of attack that were part of the composer's endeavor to forge a new kind of musical experience—a pianism otherwise.

Boulez's concept of *écriture*, the French term that connotes not only literal inscription but also the symbolic reasoning behind it,[19] took shape through a compositional practice that consisted of creating contrasts like that between the leaping attacks of the Piano Sonata no. 2—in which pitches seem to be either isolated or slammed together—and moments in which successive notes are smoothly connected into lyrical fragments. Boulez's musical language consisted of opposing features like this, a dialectical approach to timbre and phrasing that Jonathan Goldman describes through various binaries: figure versus structure (i.e., part versus whole), chord-figure versus interval-scale ("chord" versus "scale," or vertical versus horizontal construction), and smooth versus striated time—the list goes on.[20] Boulez owed this approach in part to the voice that we can hear in *Pour en finir*: rasping and low in one moment, then quietly drawing breath; suddenly shouting and leaping into the falsetto; finally slowing, stuttering, gasping out of breath. This voice is a model also for the sonic palette of the *Livre pour quatuor* (1948–49, 1959–60).[21] With each movement structured around a contrast between longer resonant tones and short percussive attacks, the violent oppositions of vocal sounds echo in ever more abstract form.[22] The first four measures of movement 1b of the *Livre*, for instance, feature a series of intervallic leaps, starting in the viola and echoed by the violin, which sustain long tones in the upper register against a quiet cello attack below, pizzicato. After a fermata, the second short phrase is abrupt, the cello rushing upward to meet the trills and pitch clusters in the violins.

Scholarly writing on Boulez, which seldom addresses the question of otherness, is often caught in a hermeneutic double bind. By approaching the music as an object that requires laborious decoding (searching for the tone rows and tracing their genealogies, for example), one tends to miss some of its most striking qualities.[23] One does not need to listen "hermeneutically" to hear that the ethnographic other is *simply there* in the music; yet when one delves beneath the surface for compositional processes and deep structures, the other vanishes. This is a problem that seems to haunt studies of Boulez (and, more generally, of serialism): the rigorous methods employed in creating this music seem to demand decoding, as if there is always a hidden order behind every musical utterance. But precisely when we engage in decoding, the music's "otherness" is concealed.

This double position, I would like to suggest, was part of Boulez's distinctive mode of appropriation. In contrast with Artaud, who sought to present the extra-European *as* radically other, Boulez sought to occlude difference, and musical writing was his medium to do so. This mode of appropriation involved a specific attitude toward sound and writing that Boulez received partly through Artaud, but also through a larger movement of which Artaud was—at least initially—a part. It is worth pausing over the surrealist stance toward non-European expressions to see how surrealism set the tone for Boulez's engagement with sound.

Though he broke from the official surrealist group led by André Breton in or about 1926, Artaud retained something of the surrealist attitude toward cultural order and meaning. This attitude had to do with reassessing the west in relation to its newly exhibited others: as James Clifford has suggested, the artifacts imported from France's colonial possessions indicated to Breton and to other surrealists that "culture and its norms—beauty, truth, reality" were merely "artificial arrangements, susceptible to detached analysis and comparison with other possible dispositions."[24] Detached analysis and comparison were

central in the emerging "ethnographic surrealist" view of cultural order—a view according to which western culture is merely an arbitrary
collection of signs ready to be reconfigured and jumbled like objects on
display in an ethnographic museum.

The presence in Parisian museums and exhibition spaces of ethnographic artifacts motivated surrealists and ethnologists alike to
understand European culture as an assemblage of signs, an attitude
that Clifford has termed "ethnographic surrealism." Detached analysis and comparison were central to the surrealist quest: as Breton declared in his *Manifesto of Surrealism*, automatic writing (i.e., stream
of consciousness) would resolve the states of dream and reality "into a
kind of absolute reality, a *surreality*."[25] This quest implied two distinct
ways of grappling with society and its signs. In theory, surrealism was
self-consciously reflective: a poet or painter would engage with society's signs on a second-order level of observation, juxtaposing signs in
order to widen the gaps between signifiers and their signifieds. In practice, however, surrealist automatism demanded a renunciation of self-
conscious reflection, a headlong plunge into the murky unconscious
abyss that eventually drove Artaud toward Rodez.

Sound played a conspicuous—though largely unrecognized—role in
surrealism. Not only did Breton put tremendous weight on the voice,
claiming in his 1944 essay "Silence d'or" that surrealist poets best understand the "*tonal* value of words," since "great poets have been 'audi-
tives,' not visionaries," but he also claimed that music exemplified the
kind of direct communication that he sought through automatic writing.[26] He credited music for its "immediate, pervading, uncriticizable
communication of feeling," a kind of presence beyond representability.[27]
The poet, by freeing "a monologue spoken as rapidly as possible without any intervention on the part of the critical faculties," would endow
language with the direct communicative power of music, and hence *re*-
appropriate society's signs and symbols through the hodgepodge logic
of the dream.[28] Automatism was thus Breton's means to rescue the artist
from a more pervasive and negative form of appropriation, the "cold
and hostile irrationality" of capitalist commodification.[29] By liberating
the voice, surrealist automatic writing would allow "visual elements [to]
take their place *between the words* without ever duplicating them," and

it was "between the words" that Artaud inserted his shouts and cries.[30]

We might call the surrealist mode of appropriation, then, a *symbolic* mode, since the poet was to engage with society's signs on a second-order level of observation: fragmenting and re-assembling verbal signifiers in order to widen the gaps "between the words." Like Breton, Artaud wanted to re-associate viewers with a self that had been alienated from them, but rather than emphasize second-order reflection, Artaud took a different tact: the extra-European seems to have impelled him to intensify the first-order gut reactions one can have in the presence of performance. Artaud's mode of appropriation might best be termed an *affective* mode on account of the emphasis he placed on bodily immediacy: he sought to plunge headlong into the unconscious abyss that Breton's surrealism opened up "between the words."

"It is essential to put an end to the subjugation of the theater to the text," Artaud declared in his 1932 "Manifesto of the Theater of Cruelty," "and to recover the notion of a kind of unique language half-way between gesture and thought."[31] The sound of Artaud's voice, echoing in *Pour en finir*, gives us a sense of how this language was to work. Words *become* gesture through the act of enunciating them with sudden shouts, leaps, and screams—that is, by filling the gaps "between the words" with sound. The normative written systems of western theater were therefore inadequate to afford the kind of expression that Artaud sought to make available. The movements and utterances of Artaud's ideal theater would live only for a moment, beyond what could be written and repeated from reading a script: hence, "let us leave textual criticism to graduate students, formal criticism to esthetes," he exhorted, "and recognize that what has been said is not still to be said; . . . that all words, once spoken, are dead and function only at the moment when they are uttered." This is why "the theater is the only place in the world where a gesture, once made, can never be made the same way twice."[32]

At stake for Artaud was the contention that the culture of the west had been dominated by a theological metaphysics according to which life in the world—like the actions on a stage—are subordinate to an original presence, the Divine Word contained in the texts of the Bible, or the theatrical Word written in a phonetic script. "Cruelty" not only meant engulfing viewers in a sensory barrage—producing the kinds of visceral gestures that we can hear, for instance, when Boulez's pianist "pulverizes the sound"—but also demanded a commitment to staying as close as possible to the limit of representability.[33] Rather than confront society at the level of its representations, Artaud dreamed of a *pure presence*, an ideal of immediacy and un-representability. Hence the Theater of Cruelty, in Derrida's words, would be the art of "pure presence as pure difference": it would move like a language, carrying a signifying force, yet without forming iterable signs.[34] Producing an always-renewed effect of presence, a cruel theater would seek to elide the movement and mechanisms of re-presentation.

But, like Boulez, Artaud needed writing. As we have already seen, ethnographic reconstruction was a part of how the dramatist enacted his "pure presence," and he anticipated Boulez's own search for a new form of writing that would organize the delirium that Artaud imagined to emanate from Mexico or elsewhere. Artaud saw a vision of this new writing when he witnessed Balinese theater at the 1931 Exposition coloniale held in the forest of Vincennes outside Paris. There, the French government hosted groups of people from Africa, Oceania, West India, and other colonies to exhibit arts, to make food and crafts—including the Oceanic artifacts that fascinated Breton—and to perform music and dance like the Balinese spectacles that Artaud witnessed, claiming that the Balinese embodied "the idea of pure theater."[35] It is unclear (to us) what Artaud actually saw at the exposition, though he wrote of Balinese theater as if it was a collage of ritualistic movements, song and poetry, costume and other visual elements, all appearing before his eyes as a kind of hieroglyphic writing. These "spiritual signs," he declared, "[strike] us only intuitively but with enough violence to make useless any translation into logical discursive language."[36]

The non-phonetic writing of Artaud's ideal theater would arrange configurations of bodies and objects, mapping out events; it would therefore silence the voice of the absent author–creator, all in an endeavor to approximate the immediacy of "Chinese ideograms or Egyptian hieroglyphs." Rather than inscribe dialogue, this writing would directly deal "with objects . . . like images, like words, bringing them together and making them respond to each other."[37] However, while this new non-phonetic writing would bypass the written voice of the author, it would not silence the voice of the actor. Far from it: Artaud insisted that the hieroglyph would give a new place to voice, to the real embodied voice onstage, since vocal sounds would no longer be texted, reproducible and representable. He dreamed of a radically other voice.

Boulez stood at a distance from the symbolic and affective modes of appropriation that characterized Breton's surrealism and Artaudian cruelty, but, as I have suggested, Artaud's vocal sounds continued to echo under Boulez's pen. One can hear how Boulez entextualized the "delirium" that he heard in Artaud into an abstract musical language.[38] But while the composer aimed to produce sudden first-order gut reactions through musical violence, he also reflected—in published essays and later lectures—on the processes through which this violence would be produced. He sought a technique through which to build upon the "pure presence" of Artaudian expression, taking up Artaud's aesthetic ideal into an ideal musical writing.

With the emphasis he placed on writing and structure, Boulez positioned himself as part of a lineage of French artists and intellectuals leading from the ethnographic surrealist moment of Paris's interwar years toward the mid-century, in which tremendous theoretical weight became attached to the notion that culture is written. The surrealist conviction that Beauty, Truth, and Reality are mere products of symbolic arrangements laid the groundwork, as Clifford suggested, for the "semiotic" view of cultural order that one can read, for instance, in Roland Barthes's claim that "everything can be a myth, provided it is conveyed by a discourse." If culture is a collection of signs, then forms of discourse—"modes of writing or of representations; not only written discourse but also photography, cinema, reporting, sport, shows, publicity"—inevitably entwine themselves with power.[39] Artaud, in seeking a form of vocal utterance beyond the "mythical speech" that had upheld bourgeois normativity, gave a specific privilege to sound as a vehicle of transgression. This is the kind of sound we can hear in Boulez.

Boulez's stance toward sound was imminently surrealist since it was a musical response—albeit very abstract—to the transgressive aesthetic put forward during the surrealist years. As Clifford wrote, "the exotic [was] a prime court of appeal against the rational, the beautiful, the normal of the West," allowing thinkers in the surrealist camp such as Bataille to deconstruct the hallowed beliefs of western culture, claiming, for instance, that every cultural norm contains and conceals its obverse. Tonal harmony, on this view, is one European myth among others, tired and two-faced: confront tonal harmony with its other—dissonance—or confront good with evil, piety with perversion, and one can see that every norm contains the seeds of its own dissolution. This valorization of transgression, in Clifford's words, "[provides] an important continuity in the ongoing relation of cultural analysis and surrealism in France."[40]

Music and sound played a role in establishing this transgressive aesthetic—an aesthetic that links "the twenties context of surrealism proper to a later generation of radical critics."[41] The jumble of non-European signs presented at colonial exhibitions (and later housed in the Musée de l'Homme) not only prefigured the semiotic view of cultural order in vogue by Derrida's day, but also suggested that new and violent sounds—shouts, noises, and rhythmic effects—might echo from between the cracks in western cultural meaning. By liberating a stream of speech through surrealist automatic writing, or by shouting, stuttering, and speaking in tongues, sound became other: that which resounds beyond the norms of pictorial and linguistic representation, "between the words." Hence the free play of signs was not only Oriental but was specifically sonic. This is the Artaud that Boulez found so alluring:

> [B]y an altogether Oriental means of expression, this objective and concrete language of the theater can facilitate and ensnare the organs. It flows into the sensibility. Abandoning Occidental usages of speech, it turns words into incantations. It extends the voice. It utilizes the vibrations and qualities of the voice. It wildly tramples rhythms underfoot. It pile-drives sounds. . . . It ultimately breaks away from the intellectual subjugation of the language, by conveying the sense of a new and deeper intellectuality which hides itself beneath the gestures and signs, raised to the dignity of particular exorcisms.[42]

ONTOLOGICAL APPROPRIATION

In his disavowal of "ethnographic reconstruction," we can sense that Boulez distanced himself from Artaud even as he drew inspiration from the theater theorist. For Boulez, the ethnographic other did not offer a favorable alternative to western modes of artistic expression: re-creating the sounds of the other did not go far enough. Yet, Artaud and Boulez each participated in the mutual construction of "the West" as opposed to "the Rest," an opposition that undergirded each artist's essential views about their respective media—theater and music. Boulez's mode of appropriation was *ontological* because he aimed to reconstruct the "hysteria" of the other at an ontological remove from any specific people or place. He whitewashed extra-European sounds in an endeavor to create what he called "*pure sounds*—fundamentals and natural harmonics" that could be subsumed within a musical fabric.[43] This process of purification was always a part of Boulez's stance toward sound, part of his own transgressive modernist aesthetic. Yet, as this section will demonstrate, the search for a new form of *écriture* tied Boulez and Artaud to a much older, and explicitly ethnocentric, philosophy of writing.

In practice, Boulez's *écriture* was a medium to organize delirium, and in theory, too, *écriture* hinged on a distinction between individualized sound and neutral sound, itself a species of a more general dichotomy between a western self and the ethnographic other. "The more a sound has remarkable individual qualities, the less conformable it will be to other sounding phenomena," instead "[preserving] its own individual profile," stated Boulez in a 1994 lecture at the Collège de France.[44] In this he echoed a trope that he had voiced much earlier in a 1949 preface to John Cage's *Sonatas and Interludes*. Expressing a deep respect for Cage's use of "non-tempered sound spaces" as well as "sound complexes" in his experiments with the prepared piano, Boulez nevertheless suggested (rather subtly at the time) that his American correspondent was barking up the wrong tree.[45] Cage did not produce pure sound, relying instead on the individualized characteristics of sounds made from placing bits of metal, screws, and paper clips amid the piano strings. This endeavor, inspiring and fresh though it was for the young

Boulez, ultimately constituted a regression in musical thinking. In a 1972 conversation with Célestin Deliège well after Boulez and Cage parted ways, Boulez aligned Cage's use of individualized sounds with the twanging and buzzing of the African sanza (or mbira).

> In the music of some African peoples (not the most highly-developed from the musical point of view) we find an instrument, the sanza, that has vibrating blades [which] could make up a neutral universe—they form a scale that is fixed and modal, as all African scales are.[46]

Without the mutes and resonant rings that mbira players attach to the vibrating blades, the sounds of the blades "could" be neutral, just as the notes of a piano are neutral before a composer inserts debris between the strings.

Boulez's mention of an African instrument bespeaks the composer's interest in non-European instruments, an interest that he developed early in his musical life as he honed his composerly skills by transcribing musics from outside Europe—a practice that undoubtedly informed Boulez's view of individualized versus neutral sound. During the summer of 1945, while a student at the Paris Conservatoire, Boulez heard Balinese music in a class with Olivier Messiaen, and as he would later account, "dreamed, for a moment, of specializing in musicology: not in the study of texts, but in ethnomusicological investigation in connection with a department of the Musée de l'Homme or the Musée Guimet."[47] This was not just a dream: after listening to discs of various non-European musics, Boulez planned to go on an ethnological expedition to Cambodia and Laos hosted by the Musée Guimet in 1946, a voyage quickly cancelled as the First Indochina War broke out that winter.[48] In preparation, however, Boulez transcribed various songs including a "Laotian song of possession" for two voices.[49] This was an ethnographic reconstruction in the most literal sense: according to Luisa Bassetto, the composer likely jotted down this song—as well as others from Cambodia and Cameroon—quite quickly, perhaps as part of a dictation test prior to the ethnographic voyage.[50] Transcriptions like these are precisely what the Boulez of 1947 would renounce as Artaud's voice rang in his ears. Simply reconstructing (transcribing) the sounds of extra-European ritual or spiritual practice did not go far enough for the restive composer, who ultimately did not seek ethnomusicological knowledge for its own sake, but rather for the sake of expanding the timbral and rhythmic possibilities available in new music.

Boulez adopted (by default) a Eurocentric view according to which musical writing allows for a level of abstraction and sophistication unknown in cultures that lack a written musical system, and his transcriptions of these songs give us a hint about what neutral sound came to mean for him. While the recordings housed in ethnographic collections—including those of André Schaeffner, whom Boulez would meet in 1949 and with whom he would correspond for nearly two decades—exerted a particular allure for the composer, he was most interested in exploring what a song of spirit possession might become through the act of transcribing it and studying its written form. Cage (from Boulez's standpoint, anyway) perhaps would have believed that the specific characteristics of sounds—Laotian or otherwise—were interesting enough on their own; Boulez, by contrast, felt that merely letting sound be sound (to paraphrase a well-worn Cage-ism) was inadequate. Sound had to pass through the medium of *écriture*—Boulez's medium—to truly become music.

There is perhaps no better summation of Boulez's take on the difference between his and Cage's approaches to sounds—and, for our purposes, of Boulez's own sense of the difference between individual and neutral sounds—than his statement in the 1949 Cage essay: "Noise does indeed have a very great immediate physical effect, but utilizing this is dangerous, since its novelty rapidly wears off."[51] Noise can strike us powerfully, but only so many times. Buzzing and twanging are insufficient. In order to preserve the immediate physical effect of noise, perhaps to base a musical language on its visceral presence, a composer must put sound through *écriture*.[52] For Boulez, Cage's approach to sound was not only mistaken; it was primitive. "In *that* kind of musical civilization"—Africa—"and with an instrument of this sort"—the mbira—"the procedure has every justification": *those* civilizations are simple.[53] But it would be unjust and "contrary to the entire evolution of music" for a European composer "to delimit an instrument within highly typical and individualized characteristics, since we are moving more and more in the direction of relativity," that is, toward rendering sound neutral.[54] Only neutral sounds can be subsumed into a broader texture, allowing their true individuality to ring.

Boulez's essential view of sound and writing seems not to have changed throughout his career.[55] The term *écriture* not only connotes a compositional method (which may change through time) but also, more fundamentally, encompasses a philosophical view of writing premised on the difference, formally and ideologically, between individual (primitive) and neutral (written) sound. Like one of his early influences, Boris de Schloezer, Boulez believed that *écriture* allowed for an idealization of sound that was impossible in cultures that lack a written language. The same year he heard Artaud at the Galerie Loeb, Boulez studied Schloezer's newly published *Introduction à J.-S. Bach* (1947), in which the musicologist, anticipating Boulez's own attitude toward the mbira, claimed that non-western musical cultures were limited to the material conditions of their instruments. "The essential characteristic of the space elaborated by western musical culture," Schloezer wrote, "is its total independence from sonorous material."[56] Through the medium of writing, a composer takes a sound as a "number," not as a material element, amounting to a "dematerialization" of the sound space.[57]

It is through Schloezer's affirmation of the western composer's writerly authority—his claim that the "creative act of the artist is to embody this number, to charge it with a certain reality, to confer a qualitative value upon it"—that we can hear the echoes of an earlier philosophy of writing that, as I demonstrated in the previous chapter, also implicitly undergirded Varèse's aesthetic position.[58] By affirming that western phonetic writing is the *Aufhebung* or "sublation" of non-western forms of writing, Hegel performed the kind of "dematerialization" that characterized Schloezer's notion of the western sound space. "Intelligence expresses itself immediately and unconditionally through speech," Hegel proclaimed, affirming that hieroglyphic or pictographic scripts are merely material.[59] A pictogram creates meaning through the physical trace of a word, whereas phonetic writing activates the medium of voice, floating free of materiality.

Even as Artaud disdained the metaphysics of phonetic writing, he still relied implicitly on this metaphysics. According to this metaphysics—which Derrida termed "logocentrism"—the presence of voice, of vocal sound, grants western forms of writing a privileged ontological status. Though Artaud sought, in his own theory of the theater, to disavow the representational norms of theatrical writing in the west, the theater theorist's dream of a "hieroglyphic" writing hinged on the same east–west dualism that Derrida found in Hegel's philosophy. And even though Boulez's own musical writing was never, strictly speaking, "phonetic," *écriture* was his vehicle to subsume expressions drawn from sources outside of Europe. Thus, the distance between "us" and "them," between "the West and the Rest," was not only affirmed but also served as a basic premise of Boulez's musical language through the various stages of his development.

To hear how Boulez "dematerialized" the sounds of Europe's others in a slightly later phase, let us follow him to South America with the Compagnie Renaud-Barrault. In the period following his early encounter with Artaud, Boulez's quest for pure or neutral sound took shape as he heard the percussion of Afro-Bahian ritual, sounds that fueled his endeavor, as he later put it, to "absorb" non-European sounds into the abstract and ideal space of western music.

"A MAGICAL GREECE": BAHIAN RITUAL IN *LE MARTEAU SANS MAÎTRE*

> [This], for me, is very important: that we absorb other cultures not only by their content, but also by the way they are transmitted through sound.[60]
>
> —PIERRE BOULEZ, from a late interview

As the musical director of the Compagnie Renaud-Barrault (from approximately 1946–1956), Boulez encountered many extra-European sounds. "I am already back at work on Le 'Marteau sans maître,'" he wrote to Stockhausen in August 1954 while on a boat from Brazil to Dakar.[61] "I've brought back a haul of 'exotic' instruments: wooden bells, double bells made of iron [cloches doubles en fer], Indian flute, little Indian guitar, frame drum, bells [grelots], Jew's harp [birimbao] (a very curious instrument from Bahia, but of African origin)."[62] This curious collection supports Boulez's admission that the timbral palette of *Le Marteau sans maître* derived from sources beyond the borders of Europe, but the connection between *Le Marteau* and Brazil goes a step further.

While visiting Bahia during the Compagnie's tours of 1950 and 1954, Boulez and Barrault witnessed spiritual rituals that the composer dismissed as "ineffectual rites and cults" and that the actor championed as expressions of the essence of Greek tragedy.[63] "I saw macumba," Boulez stated—a term that refers to many varieties of Afro-Brazilian magico-ritual practice.[64] "Some absolutely incredible things occurred," he continued: "I remember now, for example, that there was a black man who weighed at least 110 kilos, huge"; after entering trance, "he spun like a spinning top, very quickly," and while "all of this . . . seemed very dangerous and violent at times, it ultimately was not at all, since you have kids from four- or five-years old in the middle of it all."[65] What Boulez and Barrault likely saw in Bahia was a Candomblé *xirê* or "liturgy." The term "Candomblé" connotes various religious practices of West African origin.[66] Once imported to Brazil beginning in the early nineteenth century, Candomblé became a complex syncretism of African and Catholic beliefs—still today, Yoruba and Fon deities (*orixás*) are often idolized as Catholic saints. In a later interview with O'Hagan, Boulez expressed awe at the percussion of the public Candomblé ceremony he witnessed, much like Barrault, who, in his 1959 *Nouvelles réflexions sur le théâtre*, described his obsession with the Candomblé after witnessing a man spinning about in trance.[67]

> The manner in which a being, whether black or Indian, suddenly finds himself struggling as the Spirit is transmitted to him; the manner in which the medium, after transmitting the Spirit to him, follows alongside this being; the manner in which trances are developed; the "purified" calm that follows; the ritual of these nocturnal ceremonies—all of this struck me, and, so to speak, bound me to these mysterious and endearing people.[68]

It may seem outlandish to suggest that any part of *Le Marteau sans maître*, a monolith of autonomous modern music, was in fact modeled after a Candomblé liturgy. While Boulez did not explicitly cite the Candomblé as a source for *Le Marteau*, by examining the "Commentaire I de 'Bourreaux de solitude'" alongside Barrault's account, we perhaps discern traces of spirit possession taking musical form.⁶⁹ Boulez finished the "Commentaire" in South America, mailing the first completed draft to his publisher, Universal Edition, during the 1954 tour⁷⁰—and he had already witnessed Candomblé at least once (if not several times) by this point. The poetic arc of the "Commentaire" follows that of the Candomblé *xirê*—or, at least, seems to follow the "ethnographic reconstruction" of a *xirê* that one can read in Barrault's *Nouvelles réflexions*, or see in another contemporaneous source, director Marcel Camus's film *Orfeu Negro* (1959). While Barrault and Camus each turned the Candomblé liturgy into an allegory for a kind of timeless (but ultimately western) spirituality, Boulez relocated the allegory from the level of representation to the level of sound, employing what might be called *sonic allegory*. Of course *Le Marteau* does not "sound like Brazil"; of course it is not a literal reconstruction. Boulez neither cited Aeschylus (like Barrault) nor the story of Orpheus (like Camus): instead, I suggest that Boulez's sounds became infused with mythical presence through an allegorical use of the Candomblé.

Figures of the Candomblé liturgy described in ethnographic sources align with the principal characters in Barrault's account. In his *Nouvelles réflexions*, Barrault describes entering a large gymnasium and watching a group of white-clothed initiates walk together toward their *pai de santo*, the main priest.⁷¹ Accompanied by the regular beat of a drum—presumably played by the master drummer, or *alabé*—the practitioners gather before their priest, who is seated next to an altar scattered with Catholic relics and a large statue of Christ. "The glance of the priest and his smile," writes Barrault, "the huge Christ's sorrow dominating the table, and the pervasive scent of the incense gave an unusual touch to this small-town cocktail-party."⁷²

The liturgy that Barrault describes unfolds with a specific pacing and a gradual increase in intensity—a kind of dramatic arc reminiscent of Boulez's "Commentaire." The opening bars produce a similarly meditative mood, complete with a subdued processional rhythm (Figure 15). Warming up with three leaps of a flute, a xylorimba and pizzicato viola playing short percussive attacks, the "Commentaire" is a rhythmically layered fabric supported by the irregular accents of a frame drum (like the one that Boulez brought home from Brazil). The score partakes of the cryptographic sublime: with many changing time signatures, the music seems to conceal an underlying order. Even without cracking the Boulez code, though, we can hear that the "Commentaire" shares a basic rhythmic feature with the Candomblé: a regular pulse—notated with vertical lines in the score—which will undergird a longer unfolding progression.

In Barrault's account, the regular drum rhythms accompany the practitioners as they sing a "canticle," and then, during an interval of silence, the main priest and practitioners begin smoking "cigars . . . that stimulate hallucination."[73] This moment of silence is crucial to the overall narrative arc of the ritual that Barrault describes, just as the insertion of a fermata (a lengthy pause) one third of the way through the "Commentaire" prepares ground for the tumultuous section to follow (Figure 16).

During the lull, as Barrault accounts, a medium elected by the high priest—perhaps the *babakekerê* or *pai pequeño* ("little priest")—begins to walk among the initiates. The drums start again; the practitioners sing; the medium wanders among them; and as the canticle becomes more intense, finally the medium provokes ecstasy. "All of a sudden one

FIGURE 15. Opening of Boulez's "Commentaire I de 'Bourreaux de Solitude.'"
This musical excerpt is reprinted with permission of Universal Edition (London) Ltd. and drawn from: Pierre Boulez, *Le Marteau sans maître,* © Copyright 1954 by Universal Edition (London) Ltd., London. Final Version: © Copyright 1957 by Universal Edition (London) Ltd., London / UE12450.

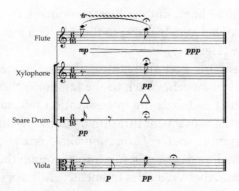

FIGURE 16. A fermata ends the first section of "Commentaire."
This musical excerpt is reprinted with permission of Universal Edition (London) Ltd. and drawn from: Pierre Boulez, *Le Marteau sans maître*, © Copyright 1954 by Universal Edition (London) Ltd., London. Final Version: © Copyright 1957 by Universal Edition (London) Ltd., London / UE12450.

of the choir singers was electrocuted by the medium. Like a wounded man he bent forward and moved inside the circle."[74] Following the motions of this initiate, Barrault begins to insert vocal utterances drawn from a much different source. "Let us follow the 'wounded' man. At first the others do not notice him. . . . He looks surprised: '*O to to toï.*' Something like a burning arrow has stuck in the middle of his heart," and with a grimace of pain, he cries "*Popoï da!*"[75] This "wounded man" begins to writhe, his movements

> reminiscent of sex or of nausea, of carnal trembling or of vomitous expulsing: his mouth is twisted, his eyes bulging out. "*Apollo! Apollo!*" . . . He begins to whirl round like a top . . . his face is completely deformed. . . . He sometimes seems to be in contact with the Spirit who clings to his neck and speaks to him; he lifts his eyelids and eyebrows to ask: "Apollo, god of voyages, where are you leading me?"[76]

After Boulez's fermata, an increase in tempo accompanies an intensification in timbre as the next section of the "Commentaire" commences. The xylorimba player switches to hard mallets and the tambour player to four bongos. Boulez notates the pulse with triangles and brackets rather than vertical lines, and he inserts momentary pauses: we can imagine the wounded man bending to the side for a moment before the spasms continue (Figure 17).

The "Commentaire" eventually calms, the original tempo returning as the bongo player switches back to the tambour; then decrescendo; then lull to a quiet end. It is the intensification midway through this movement, and the subsequent thrashing, jolting rhythms, that betray Boulez's ethnographic source. "The *candomblé* was . . . most impressive," he recounted, presenting "a mixture of sound: the excitement of the percussion, and then . . . a calm moment, . . . always with voice—the contrast between percussion-voice, like psalms."[77] The four instrumental voices in the "Commentaire" mirror the four main percussion voices in the *xirê*: the smallest drum (the *lê*), the middle-sized *rumpi*, and the bell (*agogô*) repeat their own distinctive patterns, while the largest drum, the *rum*, organizes the choreography. The *rum* player, according to Gerard Béhague, spurs practitioners to trance through techniques of *dobrar*—or diminution, "doubling" the frequency of repetitions—and *virar*, abruptly shifting to denser rhythmic patterns.[78] The intensifica-

FIGURE 17. A more intense section erupts after the fermata of "Commentaire." This musical excerpt is reprinted with permission of Universal Edition (London) Ltd. and drawn from: Pierre Boulez, *Le Marteau sans maître*, © Copyright 1954 by Universal Edition (London) Ltd., London. Final Version: © Copyright 1957 by Universal Edition (London) Ltd., London / UE12450.

tion midway through the "Commentaire," a kind of *virar* spurred as the tambour player switches to bongos and as the tempo increases, echoes the kind of rhythmic diminution and timbral intensification through which Candomblé drummers thrust practitioners into bouts of *santo bruto*—or "wild god," an especially exuberant form of spirit possession.

Barrault's description of spirit possession seems to pose certain questions of an anthropological bent about the Candomblé as a performed event (what is going on? how do practitioners understand what is happening?) and about the Candomblé's authenticity (does a practitioner really enter the trance state? does a god really possess her?). In the state of "wild god," according to Béhague, initiates appear to become "horses of the deities" (*exin orixá*). The "thought-image" of a particular deity comes down and "mounts" the devotee who enters *santo bruto*; through a divination game, the main priest interprets these acts of spirit possession to determine which *orixá* has mounted the initiate, who henceforth devotes him- or (more often) herself to this deity.[79] Boulez's observation that the *xirê* "seemed very dangerous and violent at times" but "ultimately was not at all," since children walk among the practitioners, had implications that the composer may not have intended. Candomblé is itself a kind of reconstruction, a deliberate and consciously practiced performance through which practitioners can enter another state of awareness, but always with an element of control. *Santo bruto* allows the illusion, as David Graeber has written with reference to certain African fetishes, that the apparent magic one witnesses is *both* a farce *and* an authentic spiritual transformation. Both positions seem to coexist, however impossibly: that the Candomblé is "mere show"—a god does not really mount its devotee—and that *santo bruto* is a genuine process of becoming. The writhing body is both an actor and also a god "in the process of construction."[80]

The seeming or real presence of gods—depending on one's perspective—has allowed the Candomblé to become an allegory for various kinds of spiritual experience. In Barrault's account, it became an allegory for an originally western theatrical essence, the "wounded man" embodying the spirit of Aeschylus's medium, Cassandra. In 1954 the Compagnie Renaud-Barrault adapted the Aeschylus trilogy *Or-esteia*, a production for which Boulez, eagerly at work on *Le Marteau*, would provide music. In Cassandra's opening utterance of the *Agamemnon*, "*Ototoi popoi da; Apollo, Apollo!,*" unintelligible, foreign syllables burst from her lungs as a choir sings, much as the Bahian chorus accompanies the wounded man's spasms. She calls out to Apollo as she prophesies Agamemnon's impending murder, soon to die with him. While sketches of the Compagnie's production of *L'Orestie* are scarce, and Boulez's music is incomplete and no longer performed, I wonder if Cassandra's ecstasies found their way into *Le Marteau*. According to his and Barrault's plan for the production, Cassandra's prophecy was to be accompanied by an extended percussion passage (in place of Aeschylus's choir), and one can imagine that this music would have sounded a lot like the "Commentaire."[81]

In any case, Barrault whitewashed the Candomblé as an expression of primordial Greek-ness. His account concludes with a vignette of himself, back home in Paris. He pulls his copy of Aeschylus's tragedy off the shelf and re-imagines Cassandra's prophetic bouts of hysteria as if she were a Bahian native, believing that the nameless wounded man's cries and spasms revealed a pure and timeless "true life."[82] A narcissistic projection indeed, the Bahian ritual reflected for Barrault a deeper self through the fantasy of the other:

> not something erudite, not the famous Greek harmony of our grammar schools, not the Greece of bleached statues, but an archaic, juicy, human, anguished Greece in constant contact with the mystery of life: a magical Greece.[83]

Barrault was not alone in viewing the Candomblé as an allegory for a magical Greece. In Camus's *Orfeu Negro*, released the same year as Barrault's *Nouvelles réflexions*, the Candomblé becomes a moment in Orpheus's journey to the underworld to find the soul of Eurydice. Set in the mid-twentieth-century slums of Bahia and featuring Orpheus (played by Breno Mello) as a Black guitarist ready to play at the carnival, *Orfeu Negro* depicts the Candomblé as an authentic expression of contact between the living and the dead. The gold-clothed Orpheus attends a liturgy led by a cigar-smoking main priest and includes both an altar to Christ and a circle dance in which a female practitioner becomes possessed, writhing and screaming. The Macumba scene culminates as

Eurydice's spirit takes possession of an elderly woman standing behind Orpheus: Eurydice's acousmatic voice begs him not to turn around, and when he inevitably does and sees only an elderly woman, the voice bids Orpheus farewell forever.

Boulez never credited the Candomblé as an explicit influence on *Le Marteau*, and never would have stooped to the "simple ethnographic reconstruction" that we can read in Barrault's *Réflexions*. To take the Boulez of 1954 at his word would mean believing that the Candomblé had hardly made an impression on him. The natives exhibited "some impressive hysterical states," the composer wrote to Pierre Souvtchinsky, "but the rites and cults . . . addressed to God, to the devil, to the phallus or to the virgin, are always ineffectual rites and cults for their own ends." It is conspicuous that Boulez, at this stage of his development, distanced himself from Artaud—"I am more and more convinced that Artaud was on completely the wrong track." He dismissed the rituals for much the same reason that he dismissed Catholicism (which he must have seen reflected in the Candomblé): worshipping God or the devil, the virgin or the phallus is "ineffectual," in his words, since "hysteria [is] one of the most passive states."[84] To "reconstruct" hysteria in the manner of Artaud's *Pour en finir*, from this perspective, would be to aspire to a "passive state," while Boulez sought something more active and also more abstract, musically removed from Bahia. To "organize delirium" means to consciously create it, to *write* presence.

The accents of Boulez's frame drum, unlike a Candomblé bell pattern, are irregular, hardly an ostinato; the voice of Boulez's flute is neither repetitive nor diatonic in the manner of a Candomblé vocal melody. Yet this is Boulez's composerly conjuring trick. The rhythmic character of the "Commentaire" mirrors that of the *xirê*: starting with a regular pulse interspersed with accents, Boulez follows the poetic arc through which a practitioner, guided by rhythmic and timbral intensification, enters another state of being. He wrote this being into music. Barrault's all-too-obvious allegorization of Candomblé as "a magical Greece" is, I suggest, an apt analogy for Boulez's own (more covert) appropriation: sound itself became a kind of redemptive western allegory through which Boulez affirmed the mysterious power, the elemental force, of sound.[85] Even in Béhague's ethnographic account, the power that music can seem to wield over Candomblé practitioners becomes an oblique allegory for musical autonomy. "The immediate call to possession," he stated, "comes from the music itself."[86] Music wields its own mysterious powers: the effects of the Candomblé drums become an allegory for the immediate spiritual power of *the music itself,* a tacit acknowledgment of the autonomy of musical aesthetics. And "the music itself" was the site of Boulez's own allegorizing.

Musicology has encountered this situation before. Boulez appropriated an originally spiritual form without its original spirituality, a bid for musical purity along the lines of Igor Stravinsky's disavowal of his own ethnographic sources. The mythic power of a springtime rite becomes relocated, through a composer's disavowal of extra-musical influences, into the autonomous space of music. Debunking this modernist myth of "the music itself," Richard Taruskin cited the many folk songs that Stravinsky wrote into *Le Sacre du printemps* and demonstrated that Stravinsky invoked the poetics of the rite—whether a virgin sacrifice or the wedding depicted in *Les Noces*—to convey a primitive immediacy of consciousness. For Taruskin, Stravinsky's autonomous music was an endeavor to embody in musical form a Eurasianist dream of a united Russian spirit and Russian land between Asia and Europe. It was a land floating somewhere in the music itself.[87]

For Boulez, too, the primitive state evoked by a rite beckoned toward a sonic utopia, but this utopia was even less worldly. He did not call for a new national consciousness, nor did he imagine that the sounds of the ethnographic other could uncover a more original or more ideal political reality. Instead, his effort to forge the essence of the other's hysteria without representing a specific other reflected perhaps the oldest, purest, and quintessentially western philosophical dream: ontology.

CONCLUSION: TO HAVE DONE WITH
THE JUDGMENT OF ONTOLOGY

> . . . it is fatal *that, in its closure, representation continues.*[88]
>
> —JACQUES DERRIDA

There is perhaps no better term for Greek essence than "ontology." "A Greek invention first of all," to quote Derrida, the term refers to a discourse (*logos*) about being (*on*), premised on an ontological difference between particular things of the world and their metaphysical ground.[89] Drawing from Heidegger, Derrida held that ontology presupposes a difference between "*Seiend* (being in English, *étant* in French, *ens* in Latin)," and "*Sein* which means in French *Être*, in Latin *Esse*. In English, there is no way to translate the difference between *Seiend* and *Sein*," which is why translators sometimes render "*seiend* as 'being' with a lowercase 'b' and *Sein* as 'Being' with a capital 'B' which is rather problematic."[90] Lowercase "being" refers to an entity existing in its temporal and spatial specificity—we can think of the specific sounds of Boulez's "Commentaire," or the writhing body of Barrault's imagined "wounded man," as "beings" in this sense—whereas *Sein* (or Being) refers to a more abstract sense of presence.[91]

Being/*Sein* is presupposed before the act of writing; it refers to presence, here and now. It is also reconstructed after the moment of writing: my meaning or intention only becomes present—in hindsight—once a reader travels through the detour of my words and arrives at the end of my sentence. Being may therefore be understood as something that "takes place" both before and after my act of speech. It is before or after, never contemporaneous with, the moment of meaning. This is why Derrida used the phrase "written being": Being is always dependent on the temporal delay between *Seiend* and *Sein*, which becomes, in Derrida's philosophy, an ontological *différance* that makes possible the whole metaphysical game of presence and absence, ideal and sensible, inside and outside, signified and signifier—the old grid of western metaphysical dualisms.

To simplify somewhat the ontological difference that Derrida described from Heidegger, uppercase "Being" may be understood as something static; lowercase "being," as something kinetic: the two terms are somewhat like noun and verb.[92] The French *la présence*, which, as I described in the Prelude, connotes a general static sense of "being there" or there-ness, is only thinkable on account of the various kinetic "beings" that one can see and experience in a particular place and time. This is the rub, so to speak, of an ontology—*any* ontology— since static Being endures on a different temporal order than particular kinetic "beings." "The sign," wrote Derrida, "is conceivable only *on the basis of* the presence that it defers and *in view of* the deferred presence one intends to reappropriate."[93]

This is to recall a familiar temporal antinomy. Music is *here*, alive in its moment, yet it vanishes right away, beckoning a musician or a philosopher toward ideas and truths that are by nature of an ideal and permanent kind. A basic premise of ontology may be stated thus: that a discourse may close the gap between kinetic beings—the fleeting sounds, the transient scene, the performed presence—and the static sense of presence (in the sense of *praesentia*) from which these fleeting appearances derive, and toward which they point.

By observing that the signifier and signified, like "being" and "Being," imply distinct and incommensurate temporal orders, Derrida argued that the whole of western metaphysics, which "has been constituted in a system (of thought or language) determined on the basis of and in view of presence," had been operating under the spell of a fiction.[94] Presence, or Being, does not endure unchanged. Ontology, the bedrock of European philosophy, appears often in Derrida to be little more than a game of writing—though far from inane. It is a discourse that grapples with the nature of being through the *logos*; that is, through "reason, discourse, calculation, speech—*logos* means all that—and also 'gathering': *legein*, that which gathers."[95] If a *logos* is a "gathering," ontology gathers many disparate beings under the general sense of Being. This is why, for Lévinas, "ontology as first philosophy is a philosophy of power."

In Lévinas's view, philosophical discourses about Being had always been constituted through a process of appropriation-by-assimilation, since an ontology takes form as the other—whatever is outside of Being—becomes "gathered" within a western *logos*. However the term might be understood, ontology presupposes a specific relation between the knower and the known—a relation that was, for Lévinas, more than a mere analogy for actual political situations of inequality and injustice. As Europe asserted its "Being" through colonialism, through vast systems of military domination and economic exploitation, European philosophers laid down an intellectual machinery that would legitimize western dominance, an ontological thinking machine that is more abstract, purportedly pure, but no less imperialistic in orientation. Ontology is a "philosophy of power" because it assumes the priority of Being over beings, hence of European thought over the rest of the world. Lévinas described this "primacy of the same" by invoking Plato's dialogue

Meno, in which Socrates discovers that a slave with no prior education is able, through dialogue, to understand geometrical principles.
European philosophy had always hinged on the conviction that "I,"
the ego—the slave's eternal soul—already hold the seeds of knowledge
within the self. "Philosophy is an egology" because ontology assumes
that difference is but a mirage concealing sameness.[96]

Artaud and Barrault were after a kind of essence: the sensory barrage of the Balinese theater or the spasms of a Candomblé practitioner
became allegories for the Being of theater. Even for Artaud, this essence
was (sometimes) Greek: a Tarahumara rite that he witnessed in 1936
became, in his writings, "the rite of the kings of Atlantis as Plato describes it in the pages of *Critias.*" He continued:

> Plato talks about a strange rite which, because of circumstances
> that threatened the future of their race, was performed by the
> kings of Atlantis.
>
> However mythical the existence of Atlantis, Plato describes
> the Atlanteans as a race of magical origin. The Tarahumara, who
> are, for me, the direct descendants of the Atlanteans, continue to
> devote themselves to the observance of the magical rite.[97]

All this allegorizing amounted to a navel-gazing fantasy that a deeper
self might emerge from the other, somewhat like a Catholic cross
emerging from the Mexican soil.

By disavowing the "simple ethnographic reconstructions" that we
can hear in Artaud or read in Barrault, Boulez displaced these explicit
western allegories onto sound. Sound became "radically other," and
écriture became Boulez's "neutral medium." This is ontological appropriation: musical writing becomes the pure light through which a
composer writes the other into the ideal space of western music. "Real"
sounds, what Boulez called pure or neutral sounds, emerged for the
composer only when the specific sonic world that he heard in South
America, or that he encountered through recordings of Laotian or
Cambodian song, were effaced, neutralized, and made part of his abstract musical imaginings.

Is this not how an ontology—any ontology—is made? A process of
extraction and inscription makes reality thinkable beyond faulty appearances, a process of writing that makes the very distinction of reality

from appearance possible. However, studying Boulez might remind us, to play a bit with his own concepts, that sound does not "become ontological" until it passes through *écriture*. Ontology is neither a given nor is it a neutral medium—it only seems so, as if to name an ontology is to name what really is, which is the trick of the term. Ontology also cloaks the real with a shroud of mystery: a veil conceals many actual voices, individualized sounds that fall mute whenever an ontology comes into being. And this same veil often functions as a bolster for scholarly authority. Ontology is a writerly conjuring trick, though a peculiar one because it seems so innocuous, connoting the "in itself" of things—a real sound beyond language; a presence beyond what one can represent.

In recent decades, however, many have sought to rescue ontology from its historical baggage as a philosophy of power. For proponents of the ontological turn in anthropology, there are many possible ontologies. The anthropologist's job, according to Eduardo Viveiros de Castro, is not to "[explain] the world of the other," but instead to "[multiply] our world"—that is, to expand the discursive "worlds" of anthropology by letting the other remain other. "The Other [is] the expression of a *possible* world."[98] To make sense of this ontological turn in anthropology, David Graeber patiently distinguished what he termed Ontology$_1$, the philosophical discourse on being that stretches from Heidegger backward toward the Greeks, from Ontology$_2$, a newer and relativistic use of the term. Ontology$_2$ is not a *discourse about* being, but rather a substitute term for "mode of being" or "way of being"—as if the term directly connotes what really is, "beyond words." Otherwise said, any person or people might have or belong to an ontology; hence there are many ontologies out there. From this standpoint, Ontology$_2$ is no longer "a discourse (*logos*) *about* the nature of being," but, as Graeber writes, has become "a word for 'being,' 'way of being,' or 'mode of existence.' "[99]

The state of *santo bruto* cannot be judged as real or phony if the practitioner belongs to a completely different order of being. Yet, if it is an "illegal move," as Viveiros de Castro claims, for the anthropologist to call what appear to be magical moments like *santo bruto* either true or false, holding instead we are witnessing a radically other ontology, then the ethical field becomes flattened.[100] The idea that many other worlds exist, protected from the anthropologist's Eurocentric gaze by a shield called "ontology," seems to fall into an ethical dilemma familiar from the days of Franz Boas and his students. If we place the other in another "possible world"—which is, after all, of our making—then there is no basis for truth and no reason to take the other seriously. Hence no matter how "radical" or progressive, to quote Paul Rabinow, attempts to construct relativistic theories of cultural difference risk "[leading]—despite their intent—to a form of nihilism, a reduction of the Other to the Same."[101]

This is not the right place (and nor am I the right author) to recount the full scope of this anthropological debate.[102] I wonder, though, how different Ontology₁ and Ontology₂ really are. Whether one tries to make sense of Being or whether one wonders how forests think,[103] one still reaches beyond the human toward fundamental conditions that we cannot experience, but may comprehend—once again: is this not how an ontology, any ontology, works? Ontology has not changed much since Derrida or Lévinas wrote about "the West." It has only become a kind of trump card for scholarly authority, since, as Graeber suggests, "the problem with cultural relativism is that it places people in boxes not of their own devising": ontology "just substitutes a deeper box."[104]

In the musicological box, meanwhile, ontology seems to have "imperialized" how some scholars think about sound. Applying Eduardo Kohn's rather simple definition of ontology—"the study of 'reality'"—to the study of sound, we can see that sound often stands for just that: reality.[105] As we saw in Chapter One, Cox conceives of the "sonic flux" as an "immemorial material flow" that humans can actualize by making music, but that always goes beyond the human. Noise is Being itself: the form of presence through which any particular sound or piece of music can be understood. All human utterance and all musical expression are made possible by a supra-audible field of vibration, and it is to this invisible realm of sonic flux that all human music is bound, finally, to return.[106] This claim on behalf of the ontology of sound echoes that of other writers in the field of sound studies, including Steve Goodman, whose *Sonic Warfare: Sound, Affect, and the Ecology of Fear* claimed that an "ontology of vibrational force" lingers below everything we can consciously perceive about music—hence sound can act violently on us, creating fear at a gut level before we have a chance to think.[107] In *Sensing Sound: Singing and Listening as Vibrational Practice*, Nina Sun Eidsheim put forward a less frightening but similarly premised argument that musical performance is, first and foremost, an engagement with a primordial reality of vibrating matter.[108] While sonic flux resounds beyond human perception, vibration—which is Eidsheim's update to "noise"—becomes the elusive pure presence underlying what one can represent. Ontology, in this sense, is a means to reconfigure subjectivity: "if we reduce and limit the world we inhabit" by holding to preconceived notions about sound, she argues, "we reduce and limit ourselves."[109] A distinction abides between music-as-appearance (something created) and sound-as-reality; "sensing sound" allows one to break free of self-versus-other binaries that continually "reduce and limit" our self.

These studies of sound conceive ontology differently from anthropologists like Viverios de Castro in so far as Cox, Goodman, and Eidsheim examine what the aesthetics of specific Euro-western art practices (sound art, DJ-ing, underwater singing, etc.) can teach us about sound in general. Brian Kane has dubbed this kind of inquiry *onto-aesthetics*: avant-garde art practices become revealers of a timeless ontological condition.[110] In this respect, Cox, Goodman, and Eidsheim have something in common with Boulez and the modernists studied in the present book. First, they believe that sound reveals something like Hoffmann's "realm of infinite yearning," but without the yearning, without the lingering presence of God, and even without human beings at all. Second, each author claims that this vibratory realm is detectable only through new technology and is revealed only by the most cutting-edge avant-garde musical practices.[111] However, these authors differ fundamentally from their modernist forebears because musicians and scholars operate with different ethical imperatives. Artists are usually aware of making fictions. When scholars explore sound, however, the line between reality and fiction is often blurred. It is conspicuous, for instance, that when Cox, Goodman, or Eidsheim write about sound, they rely (sometimes covertly but usually quite explicitly) on their own experiences with *music*—the art produced, after all, by humans who sing underwater or install loudspeakers in art galleries. It is musical practice that is ultimately made to uncover—and to provide evidence for—a "revealed" ontology.

The problem I see is not with the ethical thrust of the "ontological turn" in anthropology or sound studies—in fact, I share a basic conviction held by each of the scholars of sound previously mentioned that one's attitude toward sound always implies an ethical orientation. The problem I sense has to do with the big term, "Ontology," the central philosophical idea that leads scholars down the windy discursive path toward sonic purity. No matter which historical understanding of ontology one takes up, it is worth reiterating that ontology is a Greek science first of all, a specifically *western* way of understanding presence, that which is real, solid, here and now. Ontology assumes that philosophy might close the gap between appearance and reality or might use words to make transience permanent.[112]

How could many ontologies be possible without the old uppercase Ontology? We can write over it but cannot really get outside of it. A repertoire of discursive sleights of hand is available to support this relativistic flattening, however, including Viveiros de Castro's affirmation that the other represents a *possible* world; "*Autrui* is the *possibility*, the *threat* or *promise* of another world contained in the 'face/gaze of the other', i.e., in its perspective," he writes, drawing (like Cox) from Deleuze. "Anthropology can make good use of this advice," he sums up:

> maintaining an Other's values implicit does not mean celebrating some numinous mystery that they might hide, but rather amounts to refusing to actualize the possibilities expressed by indigenous thought—choosing to sustain them as possible *indefinitely*, neither dismissing them as fantasies of others, nor by fantasizing ourselves that they may gain their reality for us.[113]

Even if the other is not a celebrated "numinous mystery," they would have to remain a mystery, no? Once again, the dilemma of cultural relativism must inevitably haunt any endeavor to ontologically relativize (or, to play with the Boulezian term, ontologically neutralize) the other. To take Viveiros de Castro seriously would be to forever bracket the truth and seriousness of the "face/gaze of the other": if the other is only ever an expression of a possible world, one whose actualization should be refused *a priori,* then ontology threatens a "deeper box" of nihilism.

But even if there is a great big virtual world out there for the anthropologist to discover, the philosophical terrain does not change much. In this flattened field in which many ontologies become equally possible—never actual, always boxed off—then "ontology" regains its original meaning. If any entity might have or belong to an ontology, then everyone and everything is equally "ontological" (and, then, why not have ontology on the beach? or ontology in bed?).[114] Though it may seem radical to think of many possible ontologies, as soon as the term is in play, there is only ever *one* ontology. It is still a discourse, a light through which to illuminate "beings," making other worlds part of our own.

It is striking to note, on this point, that at certain moments during *The Black Register*, Tendayi Sithole—whom, as I described in the Prelude, called Blackness an "ontological scandal," something extra-ontological, occluded and dehumanized under the light of being—becomes ambivalent. Ontology, defined by the "zones of being and non-being," has captured (or, to recall Derrida's "White Mythology," has metabolized or obliterated) Blackness by relegating it to the zone of non-being. "The black subject equated with ontology," Sithole states, "assumes the state of collapsibility and the result is the nothingness of blackness," which implies that any ameliorative position for thinkers who are dehumanized would have to be outside the domain of the ontological, since this domain is the very problem from the start. Colonial processes brought the human into being and colonial domination imposed being on the human. But at other moments during his narrative, Sithole begins to think of blackness as another kind of ontology, almost using the term in its anthropologically relativistic sense: "there is a subject, and there is blackness, as distinct ontological categories. The two ontologies are opposed to the point of irreconcilability."[115] "What does the black want?" He continues: "The black wants *to be*," making "the existential-ontological demand to be human."[116] In one moment, ontology is a form of ethnocentrism scandalized by blackness; in another, the black desires ontology. This apparent inconsistency does not imply any imprecision or lack of rigor on Sithole's part, but rather points up a telling indeterminacy. How does one reconfigure a term and concept that is always already Euro-western-centered outside Euro-western-centeredness?

Despite recent endeavors to ethically remediate the idea of ontology, the resonances between our present-day sonic ontologies and the sonic allegories of Boulez and Artaud's day should make us cautious about using ontology as a stand-in for reality. Of course, there is a great distance between Artaud's pure theater and Mexico, as between Bahia and Barrault's magical Greece. Simply describing Artaud and Barrault's writings is sufficient to uncover the ethnocentric mindset that we know (by now) to have been a part of artistic modernism. But somehow when the ontology of sound is in question, it becomes harder to answer: where is reality and where is appearance? For Clifford, all ethnography is (in some sense) surrealist because ethnography always involves aestheticizing its findings.[117] The other appears to me through the writing that I know, becoming comprehensible as my representation; the art forms and expressions of the other resonate with my perception of my own culture, and thus the other's culture, viewed against mine, becomes a form of art. In sum, *all* culture can be something of an ethnographic artifact *and* a work of art, real because farce.

If all ethnography employs surrealist procedures, at least tacitly, I would venture that sonic ontology-making is surrealistic too. Which amounts to a rather simple conclusion: ontology-making is, after all, just that—a *making*. But it is a peculiar kind of *poiesis*, since ontology claims to present things as they really are. Thinking through Derrida's conclusions about Artaud, however, I wonder if ontology really gets us closer to the real.

> To think the closure of representation is to think the tragic: not as the representation of fate, but as the fate of representation. Its gratuitous and baseless necessity.
>
> And it is to think why it is *fatal* that, in its closure, representation continues.[118]

Precisely as he sought to disavow an older metaphysical regime—in Derrida's words, to "kill the Father," both the religious Father who judges the world from afar and the Author-God who makes theater into a mere double of a metaphysical script—Artaud stayed within metaphysics. As soon as one acknowledges presence, it is already a representation. Presence is a mirage of the real, an illusory sur-reality vanishing like sound. We can see the limits of representation, its closure, but we cannot move beyond it. Instead, sound studies often "reconstructs" an old modernist conjuring trick. Ontology-making conceals the maker, becoming another discursive guise for Western Writerly Authority. Perhaps it is time to find a new tool. Or rather, perhaps it is time to have done with the conceit that sends us on endless discursive quests for sound beyond the human, or sound "post"-human. Let us dispense with *reality* once and for all.

Four

THE WRITTEN BEING OF SOUND

Cage and Derrida

EXCURSUS: THE BREATH OF GOD

Let us return to the Maverick Concert Hall during that one summer day in 1952. As David Tudor sat quietly with a stopwatch during the premiere of *4'33"*, John Cage's audience perhaps heard the composer's "all-sound music of the future" for the first time. This was the music for which Cage listened as he wrote his 1937 manifesto, "Future of Music: Credo," in which he dubbed the composer an "organizer of sound," one who, with the aid of emerging technologies of sound reproduction and an ever-growing body of recordings, "will be faced with the entire field of sound."[1]

4'33" was perhaps an expression of Cage's realization that we always face this entire field of sound; all one needs to do is listen. By 1948, Cage had already expressed his wish—in a parodic, Satiean manner—"to compose a piece of uninterrupted silence and sell it to Muzak Co. It will be 3 or 4½ minutes long—those being the standard lengths of 'canned' music—and its title will be Silent Prayer."[2] *4'33"* is this "silent prayer" and seems to well embody the composer's desire to rid his music of his own tastes and preferences, of the will to choose. Cage seems to have taken seriously Duchamp's instructions for *Erratum Musical* (1920, which I described in Chapter Two) for a composer to pull notes out of a hat: he is well known as a composer of chance, flipping coins to determine the combinations of pitches, durations, and dynamic markings in each measure of the third movement of his *Concerto for Prepared Piano and Chamber Orchestra* (1950–51) and the entirety of *Music of Changes* (1951). Any reader of Cage's writings may discover that the composer advocated letting go of authorial intention, surrendering the will to design or control sounds; instead, in his chance compositions as in the Maverick Concert Hall during the premiere of *4'33"*, Cage preferred to oust composerly intention in order to "let sounds exist." To quote Cage from a later conversation with Daniel Charles:

> Sounds don't worry about whether they make sense or whether they're heading in the right direction. They don't need that direction or misdirection to be themselves. They *are*, and that's enough for them. And for me, too. . . . A sound doesn't *have* its being, it can't be sure of existing in the following second. What's strange is that it came to be there, this very second.[3]

Cage's avowal that an entire field had been revealed, and his imperative to "let sounds just be sounds" also implied an attendant mode of listening. The Maverick Concert Hall became Cage's frame for *panaurality*, a mode of apprehension in which one attends to any and all sound, whatever comes to be here "this very second." Yet, to recall Cage's reproach, his listeners "didn't know how to listen": it would have taken awareness of Cage's words to know that one was experiencing sound in Cage's (natural, raw, spontaneous) sense.[4] It would have taken the right prompting, the proper orientation, to hear *4'33"* as an embodiment (and perhaps the most stripped-bare version) of the "all-sound music of the future." It would have taken the right prompting to listen in an unbiased, embracing, panaural way. One had to know Cage's speech.

The composer may not have been aware that when he expatiated about sound, present this very second, he was beholden to another, metaphysical kind of sound: the sound of speech captured in phonetic-alphabetic writing. Because phonetic writing inscribes the sounds of speech, which in turn signify things and ideas, it "is already, in itself, a form of duplication," as Michel Foucault once stated, since it represents not the signified but the phonetic elements by which it is signified; the ideogram, on the other hand, directly represents the signified, independently from a phonetic system, which is another mode of representation.[5]

In his 1963 essay, "Language to Infinity," Foucault used the figure of non-phonetic writing to cast the already-doubled nature of phonetic writing into relief: it is

[t]his presence of repeated speech in [phonetic] writing [that] undeniably gives to what we call a work of language an ontological status unknown in cultures where the act of writing designates the thing itself, in its proper and visible body, stubbornly inaccessible to time.

Whereas non-phonetic written forms convey meaning primarily through lines and shapes, "independently from a phonetic system"—which suggests that speech would be secondary to written characters—Foucault observes that in the case of phonetic writing speech must be primary. It is the presence of speech, repeated during the act of reading, that grants phonetic writing a distinct ontological status, creating a doubled, virtual space: "Writing, in Western culture, automatically dictates that we place ourselves in the virtual space self-representation and reduplication."[6]

Cage's "all-sound" became a figure in this virtual space of writing. The status of sound in Cage's wake is fundamentally tied with the status of the language one uses to name, to describe, or to theorize sound, to speak it into being. Sound is inseparable from "the ontological question of the modern phonetic language," to quote a phrase from Fuoco Fann, who draws from Foucault's thesis (in *The Order of Things*) that an "archaeological mutation" occurred during the late eighteenth century, altering the structuring conditions of European knowledge (the *episteme*). This epistemic shift, signaled by the emergence of the modern human sciences, gave form to a new order of language and to the figure of Modern Man (Foucault's *l'homme*), one who is both an object of knowledge and also a knowing subject—one who seeks to overcome one's own finitude by acquiring more and ever more knowledge. An attendant change commenced in the study of language, which indicated a profound alteration in the status of phonetic language for all Euro-western modernity.[7]

Prior to this epistemic shift, according to Hubert L. Dreyfus and Paul Rabinow, "as long as discourse provided a transparent medium of representation whose linguistic elements corresponded to primitive elements in the world," then, in Foucault's view, "representation was not problematic." It is around the turn of the nineteenth century that "man, as we know him today, makes his appearance and becomes the measure of all things"; at the same time, "representation suddenly [be-comes] opaque."[8] In Foucault's own words: "from the nineteenth cen-tury, language began to fold in upon itself, to acquire its own particular density, to deploy a history, an objectivity, and laws of its own."[9] It is as if phonetic writing in its modern form, with its density and objectivity, its ontological status, burrowed deeper and deeper into the virtual space of self-representation. In "Language to Infinity," Foucault used the figure of a mirror to illustrate this ontological status:

> since writing refers not to a thing but to speech, a work of lan-guage only advances more deeply into the intangible density of the mirror, calls forth the double of this already-doubled writing, discovers in this way a possible and impossible infinity, cease-lessly strives after speech, maintains it beyond the death which condemns it, and frees a murmuring stream.[10]

In Foucault's view, this murmuring stream of speech inscribed in phonetic writing overflowed the bounds of representation during Eu-ropean modernity, as if the voices murmured louder than the world they spoke about. Foucault's ideas in this relatively obscure essay of 1963 anticipate the critique of logocentrism and phonocentrism that Derrida would make well known by 1967.[11] It is worth recalling Derrida's words from the first page of *Grammatology* on which he termed logocentrism "the metaphysics of phonetic writing (for example, of the alphabet)," which, through the history of Euro-western thought, had been "noth-ing but the most original and powerful ethnocentrism."[12] Phonocen-trism connotes a metaphysical view according to which speech is the most ideal medium for thought: because speech unites the voice to the *logos* via the breath—a union that occurs spontaneously during the moment of utterance, *in this very second*—western metaphysics had aligned speech with the soul, with spirit, with interiority, and with Man, whereas writing had been considered the merely material double of speech, aligned with body, exteriority, death, with woman and the other.

In Derrida's view, phonetic writing is a kind of structuring model for the western metaphysical dualisms of speech/writing, spirit/body, and presence/absence, since phonetic writing, "the medium of the great metaphysical, scientific, technical, and economic adventure of the West," grants a metaphysical privilege to speech.[13] To quote John Lagerwey's Derridean account of the privilege given to speech in the west: "it is through using a phonetic writing that we have been led to see in writing a simple duplication of the 'living voice': speech—whether of man or of God—has the power to create things, or to realize them," and therefore it is "the use of human breath—to talk—which becomes the ontological model for the whole universe."[14] "The Chinese case," Lagerwey continues, "allows us to understand that this view is a reflection of our anthropocentrism."[15] Westerners may not be able to imagine a writing that came before speech; Lagerwey suggests that this writing always existed in China. Whereas phonetic writing copies the time it takes to say a word—one reads syllable by syllable, "[beginning] from the Alpha of intention to attain the Omega of [meaning]"—each Chinese character occupies the same amount of space and is distinguished by its number of brush strokes.[16] Essentially visual and spatial, Chinese ideograms originally resembled shamanic talismans or "imbricated talismanic graphs," in Fann's words, "the script, the image, and the representation of 'heaven and earth'" (*tian di* 天地); by contrast, western writing, which is essentially temporal and teleological, "from the beginning [represents] an ontological status of *being*: that is, the history and life of the spirit as 'self-presence.'"[17] Thus, for Hegel, a non-phonetic system like Chinese would "[menace] at once the breath, the spirit, and history as the spirit's relation with itself."[18]

It was precisely this anthropocentric and ethnocentric view of writing that Derrida meant to undermine. There is always a writing before the letter: the play of *différance*, the archi-writing, destabilizes the privilege of phonetic writing, undermining the *privileged presence*, the inaugurated moment. Though assessing "the Chinese case" is beyond my purview, in this chapter I will suggest that the privilege granted to the living voice, the breath of Man or of God, which is a bias that seems to stem from the very structure of phonetic writing, undergirds a particular modern orientation toward performance. If, according to the great metaphysical tradition Derrida described, the physical text is always outside speech as the body external to spirit, then the act of performance in its moment would spring from the same font of creativity as a vocal utterance, and once documented, represented or inscribed into materiality, would lose its force and privilege.

Taking recourse to Lagerwey's summation that speech had been the "ontological model of the universe" in the west, Fann synthesizes Foucault's notion that phonetic writing carries an ontological status unknown in cultures that use non-phonetic written systems with Derrida's view that "phonetic writing copies the sounds of words and is not only coextensive with but also equiprimordial with metaphysical thought." Fann sums up this bias toward speech, an ontological model of the universe that is itself modeled off the inaugural power of God:

> We have to breathe. We make phonetics while we breathe. With the phonetics our thoughts spring out of our mind. When this process occurs, it instantaneously creates things in the moment. The act of speech by itself has more power than anything else. As soon as we open our mouth, we say something, and something is created. This creative power stems from the root idea that God possesses an infinite creative subjectivity.
>
> In the Western view, breath represents God; breath also represents phonetics, and phonetics represent ideas. When phonetic sound is made, the breath, the phonetic, and God are forged as One. This is the power of God, or a power from God.[19]

That speech became the ontological model for the whole universe is evidenced by the opening pages of the Book of Genesis, in which it is the Creator's speech that allows the first light to shine, for the earth to be formed, and for man to walk upon it—suddenly, in a breath. And God passed this breath to man.

As God spoke existence into being, Cage spoke sound into being. This sound creates something spontaneously this very second—just like a voice. As I will suggest, the creative (theological) act of speech *is* the "ontological model" for Cage (and Cageians') ideas about sound and performance, since in the Maverick Concert Hall sound was to be spontaneous and natural, a raw moment of creation that cannot be mediated, duplicated, relived. Speech is the model of *suddenness*. Further, if panaurality connotes a mode of listening in which all sounds are equally attended to—and in Cage's most utopian moments, we become equal to sound and sound becomes equal to us—then speech must be the ontological model for this mode of listening. Nicholas Mathew has named this encompassing mode of listening *omniaudience*, a term that captures the "fantasy of totally inclusive listening" as well as the related (neo)liberal fantasy of total political inclusion: "the liberal ethic of listening is the other side of the liberal ethic of voice."[20] Omniaudience implies that we may—really: we *should*—apprehend all-sound *as if* each sound is a living voice. Our thought of sound is never far from the metaphysics of phonetic writing, and it is perhaps too easy to forget that phonetic writing, the only writing we (westerners) use, is first of all a medium for sonic presence. Sound studies seems to have missed the sound in S-O-U-N-D.

. . .

INTRODUCTION: SOUND AS *DIFFÉRANCE*

> Literature is not only illegitimate, it is also null, and as long as this nullity is isolated in a state of purity, it may constitute an extraordinary force, a marvelous force. To make literature become the exposure of this emptiness inside, to make it open up completely to its nothingness, realize its own unreality—this is one of the tasks undertaken by surrealism.[21]
>
> —MAURICE BLANCHOT

This chapter begins from the premise that musicians and philosophers face the same questions and approach the same problems, though, of course, they do so through different means. By narrating a series of events from Cage's (and Tudor's) career(s), I will demonstrate that even

before Derrida wrote of the "overwhelming" or "comprehension" of
écriture, Cage had expanded the notion of composition far beyond the
physical gestures of literal inscription. He had already flattened the actions of multiple performers onstage, the concordances produced (by
chance, as it were) between multiple loudspeakers, spoken words, the
piano, and even the vibrations of banal everyday objects, into his "all-
sound" music, claiming to have discovered the essence of composition
itself.

During the 1950s, as Derrida developed the basic convictions of
deconstruction through his readings of Husserl and as Cage gained
musical fame, there is no evidence (of which I am aware, anyway) that
the philosopher or composer knew of each other. Derrida was not yet
well known (in France or elsewhere) when Cage began using chance
operations—which, as we shall see, was one innovation among others
that enabled him to expand the notion of "composition." Even after
Derrida had published his famous trio of books in 1967, it is doubtful
that Cage, who is sometimes depicted from this period as a smiling,
shaggy-bearded vagabond who lived in an all-glass house in upstate
New York and who spent his days picking mushrooms and flipping
coins, would have cared too much about French poststructuralist philosophy.[22] Conversely, while I would wager that Derrida developed his
ideas about *écriture* and *différance* well before he published his book
trio, he probably did not pay much attention to contemporary notions
of composition or of writing in the domain of music.[23]

But the philosopher and composer moved in the same direction
around the theme of writing, as if the expansion of writing was already
taking place, waiting only to be codified and theorized. In this chapter,
I will suggest that *Cage's sound is Derrida's writing*, for the composer
had already made music become the exposure of the emptiness inside,
to paraphrase Maurice Blanchot's words about surrealist writing. Derrida and Cage, like the other philosopher–musician dyads I have described, seem to have begun from the same point, which may be termed
the nothingness or the nullity: the bare traces of pen scratches or of
ephemeral sounds that make the movements of music or the play of
signification begin, and which, in some sense, gives these forms of expression their "marvelous force." Otherwise stated, the composer and

philosopher began from the philosophical question of the "now," or of the present. Sound was, for Cage, an always-present condition of any and all music. Cage's sound is close to the Derridean notion of the *trace*, an empty non-presence that runs below and makes possible any positive notion of what music is. Tracing means temporalizing: a movement that makes presence (both *le présent* and *la présence*) possible while always already undermining its (or their) stability.

The main difference that I see between Cage and Derrida seems to lie in the former's belief in the eternal presence of sound, what Kahn dubbed Cage's "always sound," while Derrida would contend that the radicalized notion of *écriture* in fact destabilizes the very possibility of "always sound," or any stable, essential notion of sound having a total field that one might purely, naively perceive omniaudially. Whereas the overwhelming of *écriture* undermined, in Derrida's view, the founding concepts of ontology, Cage took the play of *différance*—the archi-writing, tracing, the emptiness or nullity—as the basis for an aesthetic position. And Cage's aesthetic position by and large privileges presence—and, I will demonstrate below, speech—cohering with the metaphysical epoch that, Derrida contended, "will never end," but whose "historical *closure* is, however, outlined."[24] French theory, I suggest, allows us to *see how* Cage sought the Being of sound, holding an ontological view about the nature of sound itself, and therefore allows us to see how Cage's aesthetic position deconstructs itself. Conversely, attending to Cage might allow us to sense that the medium of music, seemingly by its very nature but especially in Cage's world, is already bound with the questions of presence, being, and subjectivity that would so preoccupy Derrida.

The two sections to follow will demonstrate that Cage approached sound through two related, though seemingly distinct, paths. Section one attends to two Cage works that seem to best embody his ideal, as he put it in the 1957 essay "Experimental Music," for musicians to "let sounds be themselves rather than vehicles for man-made theories or expressions of human sentiments": his collaborative performance events, specifically the *Black Mountain Piece* of 1952 and a 1963 televised performance with Tudor in Berlin.[25] Cage's disavowal of the convention of musical writing (in the literal sense of notation or the Boulezian sense of "neutralization") was part of his effort to "let sounds be," though, as I will describe, Cage frequently took a double position, appearing at times to be both for and against intention, freedom, or intellection.

I will position the composer's collaborative performance works and his discursive positioning as part of the prehistory of a debate around the theme of presence that can be seen as formative for more recent studies of theater and performance. Since he started from sudden sound, "purely" of its moment, and then took this suddenness as the basis for an absolute conception of what sound is, Cage anticipated what Peggy Phelan would later term the "ontology of performance." "Performance's being . . . becomes itself through disappearance," she wrote. The "only life" of performance, on this view, is in the present, in what Erika Fischer-Lichte would term the "bodily co-presence" of actors and spectators, or, in the case of Cage, maybe the bodily co-presence of sound and us. As soon as performance becomes mediated, it is no longer performance.[26] Others (like Rebecca Schneider, Philip Auslander, or Amelia Jones) would contend, by contrast, that the performed moment is already "written," already produced by cultural practices, by tricks of media, and by the lingering traces of images and words that collect dust somewhere in an archive. Presence is unthinkable without the dust.[27]

Cage in fact *performed* both sides of this debate. On one hand, he was a sonic ontologist, believing in the pure presence of sound in its moment—a moment that, once philosophized (that is, ontologized) becomes eternal, the basis of "always sound"—while on the other Cage was something of a materialist. As section two will describe, he frequently used the language of systems, and like Derrida, took cues from Norbert Wiener's *Cybernetics*, another predecessor to the overwhelming of writing in Derrida's sense and to the expansion of composition in Cage. This is the second path: Cage and Tudor styled their works and their personae with an air of scientificity, of technical exactitude and technocratic advancement. By describing the event-performance *HPSCHD* of 1969 as well as *Rainforest*, a work of live electronic music that Tudor realized for the Merce Cunningham Dance Company in collaboration with Gordon Mumma, I will suggest that Cage's use of the language of systems (and Tudor's construction of a technological "rainforest") was the obverse side of his (or their) ontological understanding of sound. Cage's techno-utopianism wound up serving the same purpose as his invocation to "let sounds be," with the added implication that all modern society was soon to arrive at an ultimate state of being.

In the third section, I will briefly describe Cage's (mis)appropriations of ideas drawn from Eastern spiritual thought to demonstrate that his injunction to "let sounds be" was an affirmation of the privileged status of speech. By the concluding fourth section, French theory will enter the scene yet again. My final aim, drawing from Foucault's "Language to Infinity" and from Fann's inquiry into the ontological question of the modern phonetic language, will be to suggest that Cage's position on sound—his idea of letting sound be sound, of pointing his listeners toward whatever sounds happen to be *here*—was in fact beholden to, and functioned to bolster, the metaphysics of this language. The dichotomy between voice and writing, or between the inaugural breath of the Creator and the dead medium of inscription, or, by extension, between the momentary actions of a performer and the means of reproduction, of documentation, or of anything else that would mar the present by taking it out of itself: this dichotomy, which characterizes two sides of Cage's aesthetic position as well as dual scholarly positions on presence, is as old as Genesis.

BEING IN THE PRESENT: CAGE AND ONTOLOGICAL SOUND

Another oft-recounted event. During the summer of 1952—maybe 16 August, maybe not—Cage wrote a sketch of a performance piece that was to be enacted that afternoon at a small and politically progressive arts college in the mountains of North Carolina that he had visited periodically since 1948, giving lectures and teaching classes. When a few dozen students showed up to the Black Mountain College cafeteria that afternoon, wearing sandals and flannel and fresh from classes (for which they received neither grades nor degree credit), they sat in a quadrangular arrangement in the center of the cafeteria space and watched several of their teachers, who were positioned at various points around the audience, perform. Their recollections vary. Cage either sat or stood, on a ladder or behind a podium, reading the Bill of Rights, the

Declaration of Independence, or a text by Meister Eckhart; his partner and collaborator Merce Cunningham danced around the audience, maybe accompanied by a dog; Charles Olson and M. C. Richards read poetry from another ladder, or from the audience; Robert Rauschenberg's *White Paintings* may have hung from the ceiling, while on the ground Rauschenberg himself played radios and/or scratchy old vinyl records on a blaring wind-up record player; Tudor played a piano and/or a radio; Franz Kline's paintings may or may not have also been on display (and perhaps the artist was present somewhere, too); a group of other students or one of the artists was in charge of slide and/or film projections on the walls, showing clips of the college chef, a sunset, and/or abstract visual art; another student may or may not have been in a corner playing Asian instruments; at the end of the performance, a group of young children allegedly came through the performance space and poured coffee into white cups that had been placed among the crowd from the start.

It is not certain what happened during that one open-toed summer afternoon (or maybe evening). But we know that whatever happened . . . happened, and that is the charm of Cage's *Black Mountain Piece* (also known as the *Black Mountain College Untitled Event*), performed a couple weeks before the premiere of *4'33"*. *It happened.* People were there. The fact that different audience members later recalled the event differently—not remembering who was standing on a ladder and who was seated, who played a radio and who played a record, and so on—was, of course, part of the point.[28]

The *Black Mountain Piece* may be seen to embody (at least in memory, in the awareness that the "work" is not present, but once was) a resistance to what Phelan would term "the smooth machinery of reproductive representation necessary to the circulation of capital."[29] Tudor, who had discovered the writings of Artaud through Boulez, introduced the theater theorist to Cage (and to Richards, who would soon translate Artaud's *Le théâtre et son double*), and in the Black Mountain College cafeteria, Cage seems to have followed Artaud's rallying cry to liberate theater from its reliance on texts and on the figure of the author.[30] At stake for Artaud, as I described in the previous chapter, was the conviction that traditional western theater, with its "economy of representations," using Phelan's words, imposes "a vertical hierarchy of value," "erasing dissimilarity and negating difference," whereas performance, when it is lived in its moment, is a metonymic movement of "contiguity and displacement."[31]

The terms "contiguity" and "displacement" seem to well characterize what (one can imagine) unfolded in the BMC cafeteria, yet from our perspective, the only contiguity and displacement left is in the domain of the document. In a 1965 interview, Cage recalled that a movie had played on one side of the cafeteria while at the other end there were slide projections; he stood on one ladder and the poets on another; Rauschenberg played "an old-fashioned phonograph with a horn," and, in Cage's account, the dog stayed quietly to watch him. The audience, meanwhile, "could see itself": Cage conceived the configuration of seats as a "theater in the round"; four triangular arrays of seats faced the center of the room, with aisleways left between each array for the artists and spectators to move about the space as they pleased.[32]

Cage's hand-drawn sketch of the performance space—simply four triangles pointing towards the center—is one of the only documents that might give us a sense of what the cafeteria looked like. Richards later produced a sketch of a sort, and there are some curious dissimilarities between her recollection and Cage's.[33] Richard's sketch shows the configuration of performers in the space but includes neither the audience nor a configuration of seats; she indicates that Cunningham's dance path stretched, not between the aisles, but across the middle of the room; she was also convinced that Kline's paintings were on display whereas Cage recalled Rauschenberg's *White Paintings*: these are only three points of divergence between her and Cage's recollections—to say nothing of the varied recollections of auditors, who, as David Patterson has recorded, were sometimes wildly inconsistent.[34] The only certainty may be that Cage predetermined the time intervals during which each of his performers would act throughout the *Black Mountain Piece*'s 45-minute duration. "During periods that I called time brackets," Cage recalled, "the performers were free within limitations—I think you would call them compartments—compartments which they didn't have to fill, like a green light in traffic."[35] Patterson accounts, for instance, that Cage's handwritten note to the film projector operator (a BMC student) instructed them to begin at 16 minutes, to play freely until 23 minutes, to begin again at 24:30, and then to play freely until 35:45, and so on.[36] Each actor was programmed—so to speak—by a precisely timed on-or-off switch, and were free (within certain limits, anyway) to move about in the space or to conduct whatever actions they saw fit during the given time intervals.

Composing by intervals of time, which was Cage's first major innovation and is perhaps the defining method of his entire career, laid the foundation for him to conceive and enact indeterminate and performance-based works like the *Black Mountain Piece*. It was a technique that Cage likened to Rauschenberg's *White Paintings*; the composer later called his friend's blank canvases "airports for the lights, shadows, and particles," as if the paintings themselves were spatio-temporal containers in which various actions and movements could take place.[37] The composer also looked back in time toward one of his French predecessors, stating in a lecture delivered at BMC during his first summer there, "Defense of Satie" (1948), that "Beethoven was in error."[38] Satie, Cage's anti-Teutonic protagonist, may have agreed with Cage's view that the harmonic thrust of the nineteenth-century symphony was too heavy-handed, and that if there is any Truth to music, it lies in the subtle experience of the simplified, stripped-bare textures and the hypnotic rhythms of the *Trois Gymnopédies*; or, conversely, perhaps the Truth may reveal itself once music is banalized into the seemingly endless, meaningless loops of a work like *Entr'acte*. It was Satie's use of short, repeated phrases that seems to have inspired Cage to "defend" the old Arcachan cynic (which amounted, of course, to Cage's defense of Cage), and from this standpoint, the *Black Mountain Piece* may be seen as the ultimate (ontological?) *Furniture Music*. Not only would music vibrate meaninglessly, but even the performers themselves, the sounds of radios and records, and even the visual art on display, would come to occupy the space like light or heat, as comfort in any form.

If we could relive that unique one-time-only event—and this is the event's allure: *if only we could have been there*—then perhaps we would experience the resistance to documentation about which Phelan wrote when she declared "[p]erformance approaches the Real through resisting the metaphorical reduction of the two to the one." A performance like the *Black Mountain Piece* would put one in touch with the very dichotomy of presence, the temporal difference opened up between an ephemeral spectacle and whatever one might represent, document, and store away in the dusty archive corner. It would be impossible to reduce two to one in the case of the *Black Mountain Piece* simply because the work only "exists" as a series of recollections, no two alike. The *Piece* is rather like an artwork from the early 1990s that Phelan described in *Unmarked: The Politics of Performance* in which artist Sophie Calle collected viewers' recollections of a group of paintings that had been stolen from a museum in Boston. Calle's artwork consisted of these very recollections: "Calle places these commentaries within the representation of the museum. The descriptions fill in, and thus supplement (add to, defer, and displace) the stolen paintings."[39] In the case of the *Black Mountain Piece*, the recollections recreate the original, making the one-time-only event thinkable while also displacing it, adding representations on top of representations, and thus hinting at the strange excess that Phelan would term the "unmarked."

The unmarked is presence; more specifically, it connotes something like "the original," or the original presence: that which is *here* in its preciousness for a moment, and which may be envisaged in hindsight, but never *re*-presented, by attending to the gaps in a text, the inconsistencies of recollection, the *un*-representable within a representation. Phelan affirms that "the other arts, especially painting and photography, are drawn increasingly toward performance." This shift among various artforms toward the ambiguity and suddenness of performance may be seen as a side effect of a general turn away from the specific medium, what Rosalind Krauss called a "washing away" of the medium in favor of conceptual and performance-based art over the course of the twentieth century.[40] Calle's collection of recollections, and even the *Black Mountain Piece* as it is remembered in various overlapping recollections, escape capture by specific media and instead seem to revel in conceptual ambiguity. Phelan is something of a Postmodern Pater: all art aspires toward the condition of music, since music is a transient performance that always washes itself away. This washing ritual opens performance to the Real, foregrounding the curious ambiguity, or the nothingness, that is art's own condition of possibility.

It is conspicuous that Phelan began from this point of emptiness, the fleeting moment, and took the very un-graspability of the present as the basis for an ontology (somewhat like making an ontology out of the ineffable). If "[p]erformance cannot be saved, recorded, documented, or otherwise participate in the circulation of representations *of* representations," in her own words, then the *Black Mountain Piece* would maintain its integrity (its ontology). It was (and in some sense still is) an inaccessible "now" moment composed of various actors in a space for a time. The obverse position would hold that presence is only comprehensible through a retrospective game—much like the game I described in Chapter Two when noting that reading Varèse's words and understanding his concepts (of sound masses or zones of intensity) allows one to re-think and re-imagine, in hindsight, the structures and principles of his compositions, and thus to re-hear these compositions anew. Perhaps the most intriguing part of any "time-based art," to quote Rebecca Schneider, is to be found in "the fold: the double, the second, the clone, the uncanny, the *againness* of (re)enactment."[41] Schneider seems also to begin from the absence opened up between a performed moment and its recollection, or between presence and representation, and uses this very ambiguity to resist Phelan's ontology.[42] It is the supplement (the double or the re-creation) that makes the original thinkable; it is only in face of the reproduction that one may sense the aura of the original.

The *Black Mountain Piece* is (was?) all about this dichotomy of presence, and Cage would surely have held Phelan's position, an ontological understanding of the performed moment. Yet his manner of approaching the ontology of performance was always duplicitous, full of discursive sleights of hand that, when unpacked, seem to undermine the possibility of holding a stable position regarding sound, composition, or performance. The scene in the BMC cafeteria, for instance, would appear to affirm a listener's or performer's ability to improvise. The feedback between the performers in the BMC cafeteria and the chance concordances that might arise from Cage reading a lecture, Tudor playing a radio, and Cunningham dancing, among the other actions performed in the cafeteria, would cohere differently for each individual viewer, whose reactions would seem to have been as indeterminate as the performers' actions. But while Cage created a situation in which "freedom [was] granted," he also cautioned, "but not to do whatever you want."[43] Cage held a dual stance toward the notion of freedom throughout his career, a dual stance that necessarily complicates any claim to the true life of performance. It was as if his performers were free to dance, to play recordings or instruments, to project slides, and so forth, however they wished, but there were already unspoken limits.

Since Cage disdained the idea of improvisation—he would claim more than once that jazz was inadequate, stating that the idea of communication was inappropriate for new music—his participants were not to respond directly to each other.[44] The performance was to be freewheeling yet atomistic, as if each performer would simply go their own way, yet always with a certain flavor and feeling. "It wasn't simply that 'something' would happen," writes Benjamin Piekut, describing Cage's attitude toward trusted performers like Tudor,

> it was that the "right" thing happened, without exception. . . .
> With Tudor at the keyboard, Cage accepts whatever will come,
> . . . but this is not a real acceptance—he already knows he will
> approve of what is to come.[45]

One may presume that Cage knew he would approve of whatever was to happen in the cafeteria, too. The *Black Mountain Piece* did not simply "happen," but happened according to taken-for-granted prescriptions, a complicity among the performers, their audience, and Cage.

While there was no pure freedom for Cage's performers, there was (and is) no "pure" presence either, since an ephemeral work can only become a Work when it is read (and hence written). By the same token, without the various word piles, perhaps scholars of Cage or of performance art in general would have missed the first "Happening." This is how the *Black Mountain Piece* is often remembered. Even though Cage's endeavor, according to certain witnesses, was not at all unique since collaborative events always spontaneously "happened" at BMC—in a way, such events were the whole point of BMC—the *Black Mountain Piece* in particular has been taken to anticipate later performance movements. "Happenings are events that, put simply, happen," wrote Cage's student, Allan Kaprow, in 1961, channeling something from his mentor. "Though the best of them have a decided impact—that is, we feel 'here is something important'—they appear to go nowhere and do not make any particular literary point."[46] But the literary point practically screams: leave thought aside, jump into the bizarre, the banal, whatever is happening now, and thus find Being. Away with words, with concepts, with parameters, all the academic and intellectual shibboleths, and just . . . experience.

Kaprow is an odd mirror for Cage. The composer was not fond of Happenings, claiming that Kaprow imposed almost authoritarian mechanisms of control over the events that would unfold. "When I go to a Happening that seems to me to have intention in it I go away, saying that I'm not interested," wrote Cage. "Though I don't actively engage in politics, I do as an artist have some awareness of art's political content, and it doesn't include policemen."[47] This is a Cageian double position. By his own yardstick, the composer was also a "policeman," sometimes much more thorough than Kaprow. Why would all the performers in the BMC cafeteria need prescribed time brackets? This is to say nothing of certain works for piano, like the virtuosic *Music of Changes*, in which Cage demanded a kind of athleticism and rigor from Tudor that was far beyond anything Kaprow ever expected from the participants in Happenings. Cage loved Tudor (and I do not use the word lightly[48]) partly because the pianist abided so well by the composer's instructions and seemed to intuitively understand his intentions. Distancing himself from Kaprow was a discursive means for Cage to disavow intention in order to throw the veil of naturalness and spontaneity over his own no-less-controlled works.

It was precisely Cage's manner of occupying incompatible positions—affirming and denying the pure freedom of his performers, disavowing yet upholding the authority of the author, and elevating the presence of performance while also allowing for its "deconstruction" into the materials that produce it—that allowed the composer to forge an ontology of sound. If we recall that an ontology is, first of all, a *logos* of being, a discourse on existence, then one may sense a connection between Cage's endeavor to direct his listeners' attention, and to redirect his interpreters, toward the pure "now" moment of performance and the idea of ontology in general. Cage's discursive self-contradictions were his means to short-circuit the act of interpretation, hence to affirm that sound *is*—that it is unbeholden to reason, to memory, to representation. Any listener may suddenly perceive whatever is happening in the moment, taking any sound in the performance space as music; each listener will necessarily hear these sounds differently, each from a different perspective.

"Here we are concerned with the coexistence of dissimilars," Cage wrote, "and the central points where fusion occurs are many: the ears of the listeners wherever they are."[49] The composer foregrounded a basic condition of any and all music, since music is un-graspable, always self-effacing in its ephemerality and its perpetual dissimilarity. From this perspective, one may sense that sound, for Cage, was something of a trace; yet whereas Derrida was to take this underlying structure of difference as the starting point for his deconstruction of western metaphysics, Cage premised his position and authority on this peculiar absence. Sound became the site of the composer's own power. As in Ralph Waldo Emerson's affirmation of depersonalized perception—"I become a transparent eye-ball; I am nothing; I see all"—Cage's strategy of double positioning allowed the composer, by making himself "nothing," to make himself all.[50] It is in this sense that Cage's double positions may be taken as the very basis of his ontological understanding of sound: since he negated both freedom and its negation, both intellection and its negation, since he negated both composition and improvisation, he swept the table clean, so to speak. Sound, perceived suddenly, is the only remainder once one unravels Cage's intellectual Gordian knots—knots that were made to unravel themselves.[51]

To borrow Derrida's words, "the movement of supplementary representation," and specifically the movement of supplementary speech, "approaches the origin as it distances itself from it."[52] The audience's various recollections, as well as whatever one can read about Cage and his aesthetic position, make the *Black Mountain Piece* feel closer and closer. The origin comes into light, however, only on the condition that its reappropriation is impossible. The gap between *here*—the "here" described in a recollection and collected in an archive—and *there*—the "there" of the moment described, the event that unfolded in 1952—is widest when it seems to be nearly closed. In Cage, the composer's sense of presence, of "being there," is an ideal forged, carried, and relivable only if one is willing to follow Cage's words and the words of others. *Then* we know how to listen now.

• • •

One may ask: what about a different medium? The *Black Mountain Piece* has indeed vanished, after all, and is only available in traces that are written in the most literal sense—documents in an archive. It is worth attending to another event, differently documented, to test Phelan's claim about the ontology of performance as well as Cage's own claims about the nature of sound and composition. In contrast with the BMC event, this event is documented on video: we can see and hear exactly what happened.

On 21 January 1963, the touring duet of Cage and Tudor appeared onstage at the Berlin Kongresshalle in front of a packed house of suit-and-tie-wearing spectators who scratched their chins while Tudor (who was also suited-and-tied) walked about two pianos that were amplified via microphones and pickups.[53] Tudor stoically scraped debris against the strings and twiddled knobs on an amplifier to create sporadic blares, rings, and long tones. Cage, seated a few meters behind Tudor and next to composer Hans Heinz Stuckenschmidt and an interpreter, answered various questions from Stuckenschmidt and the Berlin audience. Tudor played works that Cage had composed for piano—or rather, Tudor realized them. During the performance, he returned periodically to a small table on which he had scattered bits of paper and variously shaped transparent cutouts. The piece(s) performed by Tudor on this program were among what James Pritchett termed Cage's "tool" scores: "works which do not describe events in either a determinate or an indeterminate way, but which instead present a procedure by which to *create* any number of such descriptions or scores."[54] Using the tools Cage provided, Tudor would "compose" the work on the spot.

While Cage and Tudor reveled in unpredictability, with the audience never knowing what was to come next, they also projected an aura of rigor and control. Though Tudor's actions seemed to be as free as the audience members' reactions, the appearance of freedom was negated at the same time that it was proffered, since behind Tudor's blares and scrapes, upon the table, lay the outlines of paper and transparencies.

Always with an affect of dry, cool detachment, Tudor put together his "score" and then went about the stage seemingly without regard for the interview that was taking place only a few feet away from him. Yet while the scrapes of metal on piano strings and the blares of loudspeaker feedback tended to interrupt or obscure certain things said by Stuckenschmidt or the audience (via the interpreter), when Cage spoke, the blaring and scraping tended to cease. It was clear who was in charge and who was to be in focus.

One question from the audience touched obliquely upon this apparent inconsistency. "Why, John Cage, are you against the word 'improvisation'?" With his characteristically deliberate drollery, Cage responded: "uh, I don't know now whether I am against it or for it." The audience laughed; perhaps they were familiar with Cage's (and Tudor's) tactic of sidestepping certain pointed critical questions, always with an attitude of quiet recalcitrance, especially in front of the German intellectual crowd.[55] Cage went on to explain that although he disdained improvisation, his works had nevertheless become more and more indeterminate. As if to demonstrate, he moved to a desk closer to Tudor, and with Stuckenschmidt and the interpreter quietly watching, he donned glasses, lit a cigarette, and began typing on a typewriter. As one familiar with Cage and Tudor's style during this period might expect, Cage's glasses, ashtray, and typewriter were grotesquely amplified via contact microphones. The rustle of the frame on his face, the twisting of the typewriter's platen knob, and the pounding of its keys must have been as deafening as the continued scraping of Tudor's piano.

Here and there, audience members continued to laugh. Cage surely knew what he was doing and what kinds of responses he and Tudor would provoke. His recalcitrance was both restively avant-garde, as if behind the audience's laughter it was Cage who had the last laugh, dodging pointed questions and disavowing profundity, and also betrayed his reliance on the very intellectual mechanisms against which he seemed to pose himself. This dependence is confirmed by the presence of writing. Cage premised his aesthetic position on estrangement, spontaneity, and anti-rationalism, yet the act and idea of writing—an idea quite literally *enacted* in the Berlin Kongresshalle—lent Cage a veil of literary austerity.

And so Cage wrote. After the pounding ceased, he stood again, putting a microphoned collar around his throat to read the text that he had newly composed:

> For many years now, we have been thinking of composition in terms of sounds, which are made up of their parameters: frequency, duration, amplitude, overtone structures, and whatever else one can think of. Now we have nothing to do with the parameters. We produce sounds without giving the parameters a thought. That means, let me suggest, that we are giving up thinking of composition, and in return we are getting composition itself.

We are getting composition itself. Cage made perhaps the ultimate ontological claim. By doing away with the parameters that composers had, over preceding decades, created to weigh and measure sounds according to their amplitude, frequency, or duration, and also by doing away with any conventional sense of organization or hierarchization among pitches, whether according to the rules of tonal harmony or the methods of serialism, Cage peered through western musical syntax toward the being of sound. The essence of "composition" in Cage's sense might be stated thus: sound "is" and "is" always; it only takes the right framing, the right mindset, the right medium, to hear the sounds of the room, the scratching of piano strings, the ring of amplifiers, or the cacophonous barrage of multiple performers, *as* an art of sound.

• • •

These two events, one a lost performance recalled by its participants and the other documented on video, allow us, despite differences in how these events have been mediated, and despite differences in both venue and content, to get a sense of what Cageian sound, "happening" only in its moment, would have sounded like. They also allow one to piece together what sound meant for Cage and for those close to him. Organized sound, liberated sound, or sound-by-chance: Cage's approach to sound changed throughout his career.[56] Yet he always remained a thinker of the being of sound.

Perhaps the image of Cage at the typewriter is the very symbol of the dichotomy of presence. The Black Mountain College and Kongresshalle performances both involve writing, whether Cage's scribbled instructions for the BMC cafeteria space, the recorded recollections of auditors, or the very act of writing on a typewriter. Beyond the literal sense of writing, though, I would wager that there was (and is) a broader sense of writing at play in each moment. "Differance is what makes the movement of signification possible only if each element that is said to be 'present,'" recalling Derrida's words, "appearing on the stage of presence, is related to something other than itself but retains the mark of a past element and already lets itself be hollowed out by the mark of its relation to a future element."[57] These Cage events are surely "written" in this broader sense since the "real" event is gone; even a video, playing presently, is already an invisible inscription on tape (or encoded in digits reorganized by YouTube), therefore the face-to-face is deferred even as it is portrayed.

However, there is a more specific Cageian sense of writing that I wish to foreground in order to focus the broader Derridean sense of *écriture* toward the present inquiry. If one takes Cage's words seriously about expanding composition beyond the limits of the written page, of any rational system of control, and so on, then *the whole event*—in 1952, in 1963, or any other time—*becomes composed*. The very idea of composition enlarges beyond then-established limits, encompassing any and every sound in a space for a time. These events, which were allegedly meant to oust intellection, prescription, parameterization, what have you—the bugbears of the western literate musical tradition—affirm through this very disavowal an even higher, absolute principle of organization. The essence of music is flattened into sound; sound is elevated back into essence. Every sound, every actor, every movement, belongs to a system.

CYBERSONIC MACHINES: CAGE
(AND TUDOR) AS MATERIALIST(S)

Cage's imperative to "let sounds exist" and his affirmation that he and Tudor had discovered "composition itself" indicate that the composer elevated sound into a transcendent status, akin perhaps to the realm of infinite yearning that Hoffmann once heard in Beethoven. But Cage seems—in a manner reminiscent of the scholars of sound that I cited toward the end of Chapter Three—to have emptied sound of the divine, of infinite yearning, and even (by his own words, anyway) of himself, his whims and tastes. "What if a B flat, as they say, just comes to me? How can I get it to come to me of itself, not just pop up out of my memory, taste, and psychology?"[58] Composing by chance and instigating large-scale collaborative performances were two means by which Cage sought to answer his own rhetorical question: sound may come to us of itself if it is created by chance, organized through an impersonal process rather than through an act of memory or of conscious choice. Regardless of the means through which one arrives at sound, however, in Cage sound is always ontological: a being in itself, something with its own life, sounding for a moment and then dying away, beckoning only for us to listen beyond ourselves.

In this section, I will examine another related means through which Cage sought this being of sound. During the 1950s and through the rest of his career, while he made philosophical claims about sound in general, Cage also thought of his works as systems, and frequently used the language of systems to describe what he was doing, casting himself as something of a technocrat. This was a common move, as Taruskin accounts, among post-war composers during the "zero hour" in which the American academy placed supreme privilege on technological innovation, and as artists on both sides of the Atlantic began taking the medium (and, specifically, the electronic medium) as a central part of music's message.[59] My endeavor in this section will be to demonstrate that the emphasis Cage placed on technology and his use of the language of systems nonetheless served a familiar purpose: to give form to the "now" moment and to foreground the sudden experience of sound. In Cage's most techno-crazed moments, "all-sound" and "always sound" appear as metaphors for an all-encompassing techno-utopia. Cage the materialist, in other words, was just as "ontological" as Cage the idealist.

It is well known that Cage had begun composing by chance after 1946, the year he began employing the gamut technique to fill in various intervals of time. In the manner of a "total serialist" (à la Boulez), Cage would select various pitches and pitch combinations, rhythms and rest durations, dynamic levels (i.e., volume), as well as extended techniques (atypical ways of playing an instrument, like slamming the piano lid), and arrange all these musical materials into a vast gamut; then, he would compose works by restricting himself to combinations of sounds derived from the gamut. It was only a matter of time, seemingly, before Cage took his hand off the wheel, flipping coins to make selections from his gamut in works of 1950–51 such as the *Concert for Prepared Piano and Chamber Orchestra* or *Music of Changes*.[60] Through the rest of his career, Cage relied on chance operations in one form or another to create more concertos, works for magnetic tape, for voice, or for the Black Mountain College cafeteria, among other collaborative performance events.

As his techniques of chance became more sophisticated, Cage began to search—in a Varèsean manner—for new technologies that would be obedient, not to his thought per se, but to the demands of sound itself. In a short text from 1966, Cage stated:

> what we need is a computer that isn't labour-saving but which increases the work for us to do, that puns (McLuhan's idea) as well as Joyce revealing bridges (this is [Earle] Brown's idea) where we thought there weren't any, turns us (my idea) not "on" but into artists.[61]

By imagining a computer that would widen the possibilities for composition, Cage anticipated the computerized chance machine he would use throughout the latter part of his career. To "pun as well as Joyce" requires finding many possible ways of relating unrelated ideas, building bridges by way of chance concordances; in surrealist fashion, the work of chance opens language to its own emptiness.

Before one such event, a large multimedia performance piece of 1969 titled *HPSCHD*, Cage found his Joycean computer. In *HPSCHD*, first staged at the University of Illinois at Urbana-Champaign, Cage invited seven pianists to come play harpsichords amid a swirling multimedia show, a precisely executed performance controlled by the ILLIAC II supercomputer. The harpsichordists were instructed to play specific works: Tudor, a collection of chance-determined compositions by Cage; another harpsichordist, a collection of works by Cage, Webern, Schumann, Beethoven, and others; another player was instructed simply to play anything by Mozart.[62] By following the random series of numbers generated by composer and programmer Lejaren Hiller's computerized chance program, Cage created parts for fifty-two tape players that would electronically produce wave frequencies at predetermined time intervals. These tapes were Cage's effort to expand the notion of musical scale beyond its traditional meaning: "each of the fifty-one tapes was composed using a different division of the octave," Pritchett explained,

> ranging from five to fifty-six tones. . . . These tones could, in turn, be microtonally inflected by any of 128 degrees (sixty-four sharp and sixty-four flat), so that there was an enormous number of available pitches.[63]

In the same space, Cage combined seven harpsichords, an instrument that is characteristically tinny and percussive, reminiscent of Europe's classical age, with electronically produced sound samples of microtonal scales. The event was therefore baroque in a figurative sense: the harpsichords must have sounded as alien and mechanical as the tapes, the cacophony of different keyboard repertoires blending with the cacophony of mechanized sounds. Further, as if the aural barrage was not enough, Cage and Hiller also used the chance computer program to predetermine at what times and in what sequences various slides and motion pictures (documentaries, clips from NASA, abstract visual plays of color, etc.) would be projected onto the large circular screen surrounding the auditorium throughout the duration of *HPSCHD*.

If we could reverse time and attend the premiere of *HPSCHD*, perhaps we would experience the techno-utopia about which Cage would begin to write during the late 1960s. In his essay "McLuhan's Influence" (1967), for instance, Cage avowed: "I believe . . . we do not live in the day of the invention of the wheel (which extended one's ability to get from one place to another)"; this mode is outdated. Rather, "we live as the effect of electronic inventions by means of which our central nervous systems have been exteriorized."[64] Cage rearticulated an idea that he had already put into practice in the Black Mountain College cafeteria: Artaud's cruelty, which he took in the early 1950s to connote a kind of sensory barrage that would affront an audience seated in the round.

An event-performance does not proceed linearly like a rolling wheel; it permeates each of the senses and, as it moves in all directions at once, expands our sensorium. Cage's inclusion of machines among his collaborators during the 1960s allowed him to extend this Artaudian principle beyond the human.

The vast network of human and non-human actors featured in *HPSCHD* may be termed a "cybernetic system."[65] Wiener's *Cybernetics* was on Cage's bookshelf, and while it is obvious that the composer took a cue from McLuhan's well-known affirmation "the medium is the message," he also followed the mathematician and philosopher Wiener's view that any system, mechanical or human, may be thought as a structure of communication, control, and feedback, a program organized by codes and administered by messages. This is precisely how Wiener conceived cybernetics, a neologism derived from the Greek word for "steersman" that he defined as "the entire field of control and communication theory, whether in the machine or in the animal."[66] Cybernetics involved conceiving of all living beings with their biological processes as well as machines with their many interrelated parts as so many proto-computers: "the ultra-rapid computing machine, depending as it does on consecutive switching devices, must represent almost an ideal model of the problems arising in the nervous system." Each level of *HPSCHD*, from the film and slide projections to the micro-tonal passages recorded on tape, was reducible, in some sense, to digits. The mathematical procedures by which Cage, in his own words, "[divided] the five octaves into all divisions: from five tones per octave to 56 tones per octave," employing "the binary function which is so implicit in the computer—zero or one" to conceive of the whole event as an elaborate system of on-and-off switches, rendered the whole scene "digital," in a literal and a figurative sense.[67] The electronic sounds are organized according to a code; the sounds produced by harpsichord may also, from this perspective, be seen as digital, on-and-off switches manned by the performers' own digits.[68]

In Cage's work and in his writings, the expansion of composition to encompass vast systems like the space inside the auditorium at the University of Illinois was an aspect of the composer's endeavor to draw an analogy between the scene enacted within a performance space and the general scene of modern techno-crazed American society. The whole of society, like *HPSCHD*, or like the webs of wires and chance concordances of electronic and acoustic sounds onstage at the Berlin Kongresshalle, was composed of circuits that communicate, feedback, and pulsate with signals just like the synapses of a nervous system or the media infrastructure of a modern city. Along this path, Cage may be termed a "positivist" of a sort as he trained his gaze toward systems, technology, and data. His words from a later interview affirm that the composer thought of the tape players, the visual effects, and the human performers in *HPSCHD* as so many machines:

> One thing I think that we do, that we don't know that we do as we think, is we move from one idea to another; but we don't go, as it were straight from one idea to the next idea; but rather we go back to something which is no idea at all, but from which ideas can be generated. We go through some point of instant erasure, or zero, or something like that. . . . This is the process that we make without knowing that we make it and which, in many cases, the machine absolutely requires us to make, or it won't work.[69]

It is the blank moment, the nothing or zero between movements of mind, that allows our circuits to reset and for our thought to function. In this passage, Cage gives another meaning to the "unmarked," that which escapes the movement of representation and only exists during a moment of performance. Inside the temporal flow that one might imagine as a progression from one idea to the next, one movement to the next, there is an absence, perhaps a negative time, that grants this flow its coherency. This need to return to zero accounts for the movement of consciousness as well as the movements of the machine; hence there is a deep structural similarity between our nervous system, as a vast internal system of on-and-off switches, and the external workings of the sounds, lights, and projections inside *HPSCHD*. Once thinkable as a mode of computing, our nervous systems may then be seen to enter into, and cohere with, the vast mediatized environment of the modern city—a rainforest of digital processes.

The zero moment to which (as Cage imagined) consciousness must return, however briefly, is like the zero in binary code; as Wiener continued, "the all-or-none character of the discharge of the neurons is precisely analogous to the single choice made in determining a digit on the binary scale."[70] If our conscious life proceeds by switching rapidly on and off, and therefore may be understood as a form of coding, then even the movements of mind must be a form of writing. When Derrida wrote of Wiener, this is the aspect of cybernetics that the philosopher most emphasized: "whether it has essential limits or not, the whole field covered by the cybernetic *program* would be the field of writing." If every human organization is structured like a machine, then the inherent privilege of the human being over animal or non-human actors would be undermined. Wiener, in this sense, may be seen to have anticipated Derrida's own effort to destabilize the anthropocentrism inherent in western notions about writing, "to oust all metaphysical concepts—including the concepts of soul, of life, of value, of choice, of memory—which until recently served to separate the machine from man."[71]

In a commentary about Derrida's words about Wiener, Christopher Johnson states that Derrida "situates the emergence of grammatology in the wider context of cybernetics, a movement or discipline which exercised its own, peculiar field of influence." During the 1950s and 60s, Johnson continues,

> the self-correcting, self-regulating "thinking machines" described by cybernetics were raising questions about the uniqueness of human consciousness and the life processes that supported it, and redrawing the traditional boundaries between human and machine, life and non-life.

If, as Johnson suggests, cybernetics "performed a kind of revealing function for grammatology," then Cage and Derrida can be seen to have responded to the same revelation.[72] Cage would have agreed with Derrida that the most crucial and furthest-reaching implication of Wiener's cybernetics had to do with the notion of life. Wiener rendered any system, organic or man-made, into a self-enclosed process of communication, hence the mechanical system becomes a model for social systems—Wiener accounted, for instance, that Margaret Mead was among those who encouraged him, "in view of the intensely pressing nature of the sociological and economic problems of the present age of confusion," to apply his notion of the cybernetic to social organization in general (a task he admitted to failing).[73]

No matter how big or small the system, in cybernetics life is quite literally "deconstructed." In the early pages of *Cybernetics*, Wiener describes an experiment in which he and a group of clinicians first anesthetized and decerebrated a cat and then stimulated the cat's nervous system by attaching electrodes to it. When they channeled regular rhythmic pulsations of electricity into the cat's nerves, they found that the rhythm and intensity of the electricity used to stimulate the cat's nervous system only sometimes corresponded to the rhythm and intensity of its muscular responses. The frequency of muscle pulsations (i.e., clonic vibrations) would sometimes have no apparent relation to the electrical signal. This was because the muscles responded to themselves.[74]

In Wiener's view, the nervous system is a machine, and conversely, the machine may be taken as something organic, self-enclosed and self-regulating in the manner of an organ or ecosystem. Wiener's theory still owed something to the very metaphysic that cybernetics seemed to go beyond—this was Derrida's critique, ultimately, of the cybernetic program. Even if cybernetics flattens out the distinction between man and non-man, a distinction that Wiener decried as crude and simplistic, cybernetics "must conserve the notion of writing, trace, grammè [written mark], or grapheme," in Derrida's words, "until its own historico-metaphysical character is also exposed."[75] It will have to conserve a notion of the external, material trace as opposed to the inner workings of the machine, which Wiener sometimes described using organic metaphors: the metaphysics of inside-outside became, in *Cybernetics*, an opposition of animate life to inanimate matter, and Derrida noted that Wiener,

> while abandoning "semantics," and the opposition, judged by him as too crude and too general, between animate and inanimate etc., nevertheless continues to use expressions like "organs of sense," "motor organs," etc. to qualify the part of the machine.[76]

Cybernetics was, in a sense, all about this tension between human and non-human, never questioning its own "historico-metaphysical" foundation.

For Cage and Tudor, meanwhile, the expansion of "writing," or the flattening of life into so many systems visible and invisible in Wiener's cybernetics, bolstered their endeavor to flatten every mode of expression in a space for a time into so many modalities of composition, hence to uncover composition's essence. They played off the same tension between life and its other that compelled Wiener; this tension allowed Cage and Tudor to imbue certain works with an air of machinic precision and also, at the same time, of organic unity. A work like *HPSCHD* would be an inhuman mechanism and a self-regulating natural organism at once.

Tudor extended this principle of organic unity in the machine by including the voices of everyday objects into machinic compositions. During the same year that Cage would premiere *HPSCHD* (1969, a year during which he temporarily left his position as music director for the Merce Cunningham Dance Company), Tudor "composed" a system of homemade oscillators, everyday objects, and loudspeakers to accompany a new production by the company, *Rainforest*. The music produced, a complex variety of constant droning tones that Tudor and Mumma captured and modified through a system of preamps, was the result of their experiments with transduction to "release the voices" of various everyday objects. To realize *Rainforest*, Tudor and Mumma first generated electronic frequencies—drones—from oscillators, applying these frequencies "by special transducers" to everyday objects. In other words, electronic sounds would be directed into objects; bits of wood, metal, glass, or plastic would be made to vibrate with the frequency of an electronic pitch (somewhat like affixing electrodes to a cat's nervous system), and then Tudor and Mumma would attach contact microphones to these objects to allow their voices to be heard. The final stage of communication would occur as the amplified voices of these objects, played through loudspeakers, would return to the objects themselves, creating a self-enclosed loop as the objects begin to resonate more, to sing louder, once they "hear" their own voices projected through the loudspeaker system.

In lieu of a score, Tudor sketched a diagram showing the system that produced *Rainforest*: on the left side, eight inputs refer to various signal generators—commercially available oscillators and other frequency producers designed by him and Mumma—and on the right, Tudor drew a loudspeaker. In between the oscillators and loudspeakers, his drawing indicates a complex web of wires leading from the oscillators to various objects at center, and from the objects to the preamps at right. The electronic drones produced were to be directed, through transducers, into up to eight acoustic objects (though with the Cunningham Company Tudor used only three or four), which Tudor termed "instrumental loudspeakers,"[77] and once the objects began to resonate, the pick-ups amplified their sounds by way of the preamps and mixers, pumping the sounds into the main speakers. *Rainforest* is a closed system of feedback; once the everyday objects begin to resonate, the system perpetuates the resonance without any need for human intervention or guidance.

As was typical, Cunningham's choreography was also a self-enclosed system irrespective of the music Tudor and Mumma would produce—and which the dancers in the company likely had not heard before the premiere of *Rainforest* on 9 March 1969 at the State University of New York at Buffalo.[78] Cunningham's dancers wore faded, ripped, and vaguely flesh-toned skin-tight leotards designed by Jasper Johns and moved about a black stage filled with dozens of floating *Silver Clouds* (pillows made of Mylar) that the Bell Labs engineer and technological experimentalist Billy Klüver had fashioned for Andy Warhol. While Cunningham's choreography was characteristically non-representational, the story behind his conception of *Rainforest* has been a starting point for writers who have related the piece to a kind of ecological system. According to dance scholar David Vaughan, for instance, Cunningham conceived of *Rainforest* while reading *The Forest People*, an ethnographic study of Mbutu Pygmies in what was then the Belgian Congo by the British American anthropologist Colin Turnbull. Vaughan quotes Cunningham's own account of an episode from Turnbull's book: attempting to follow his interlocutors into the forest, the anthropologist—much taller than they—found himself "constantly hung up by a branch in some way," much to the amusement of his guides.[79]

Cunningham's account of this source adds basically nothing to the dance other than a (vaguely bigoted) tinge of exoticism—elsewhere he would add a tinge of autobiography, stating that the piece recalls a rainforest near Centralia, Washington, that he remembered from childhood.[80] These accounts bolster the nature metaphor in *Rainforest*'s title, which is itself a marker of the tension between organic and non-organic, life and machine, that formed the basis of Cunningham's (or Cage's, or Tudor's) poetics during this time. The choreography of *Rainforest*, for six dancers, can be described as an alternation between long, protracted poses and sudden bursts of exaggerated, swift movement. The dance was a series of trios and duets in which a new character came onstage to replace another (who did not return), and which culminated in a long solo by Cunningham in which he moved quickly about the stage, scattering the silver pillows with a rapid-fire series of spins.[81]

This denouement was not characteristic of the rest of the piece, however. In the opening sequence, for instance, dancer Barbara Lloyd Dilley sat in front of Cunningham, and they stretched their arms outward and slowly rotated about each other. Suddenly seated, Cunningham maintained a yogic pose—back upright with one knee raised over the other—as Dilley crawled around and about him, facedown. When Albert Reid entered stage left, poised in a broken akimbo with one arm stretched backward, the trio leapt into a rapid succession of quick gestures: Cunningham lifting Dilley from the ground and walking about the stage in something of a strut, Reid twirling around and running about the stage, and Dilley spinning widely with her arms outstretched. And suddenly static again: Dilley poised on one leg, bent over facing away from the audience with one hand on Cunningham's shoulder as he slowly circled her on all fours.

The same tension between life and the machine that formed the basis for Wiener's cybernetics became a theme of Cunningham's dance and has been a theme in its reception. The poetics of Cunningham's choreography took shape through these contrasts between seemingly "non-human," almost freeze-frame postures, and quick-paced, fluid, and evidently expressive ("human") movement. Some interpreters of *Rainforest*, taking a cue from the title, have drawn analogies between the movements of the dance and the movements of other human ecosystems. Dance and theater scholar Roger Copeland, for instance, proposed a structural homology between the actions onstage and the movements of a cityscape. "Cunningham never gives us 'stories' about the city," he wrote, but offers us . . . the dense spatial and rhythmic texture of urban life embodied in simultaneous occurrences, the dissociation of what we hear from what we see, sudden reversals of direction, and unpredictable entrances and exits. . . . What we witness is the deep structure of urban life, not the photographic surface.[82]

A rainforest is a system; the city is a system; Cunningham's *Rainforest* is a system, too: organic and mechanical, fleshy and metallic, alternating between slow robotic movement and rapid human flailing.

Had audiences looked downward into the orchestra pit during *Rainforest*'s premier, they would have seen another system: a miscellany of black boxes, a plethora of wires, and two men quietly huddled over the mess, bringing *Rainforest* to life.[83] The occasional growls, rumbles, and squeaks that resulted from Tudor and Mumma's repositioning of transducers and contact microphones could very well be read as "noise" imitations of a forest ecology. When later questioned about *Rainforest*, though, Tudor seems to have avoided linking the sounds produced by his and Mumma's electro-acoustic system too explicitly with the sounds of a natural ecosystem. Rather, as in Copeland's use of structural homology, Tudor claimed that his process of creating live electronic music sought, from the start, to bring forward the "natural" sounds that a loudspeaker could produce—the configuration of oscillators, transducers, and preamps did not imitate the sounds of a forest; rather, this configuration *was* the metaphorical forest. "I feel that I have something that I can call my work when I discover a natural process, or when I discover an instrument as a natural object," Tudor stated during a 1972 interview on French radio:

> That's how my piece *Rainforest* came about, because for many years I've felt that loudspeakers are an obscenity—or, at any rate, it's a false notion . . . they don't exist because the attempt was made to create something to reproduce sound. . . . To me a loudspeaker is a vibrating membrane and is capable also of creating sound by its vibration. And so I was dreaming one day and I thought how nice it would be to have a whole rainforest of loudspeakers.[84]

Like Wiener, therefore, Tudor applied an organic metaphor to his and Mumma's systems, endowing a mechanical contrivance—the

THE WRITTEN BEING OF SOUND   209

loudspeaker—with its own nature. If a loudspeaker may become a natural object, then there is no longer an inherent privilege of the human
over the non-human. This notion of a techno-natural (eco)system was
to become the crux of Mumma's *cybersonics*, his own Wiener-esque neologism to connote the kind of feedback created between acoustic and
electric instruments in works such as *Rainforest*. By extending "the concept of 'collaboration' . . . to technological levels," Mumma conceived
the "cybersonic" as "a situation in which the electronic processing of
sound activities is determined (or influenced) by the interactions of
sounds with themselves—that interaction itself being 'collaborative.' "[85]

As in *HPSCHD*, in which humans and machines may have appeared
to a spectator as so many collaborators in a spectacle forged by chance
concordances and discontinuities, in *Rainforest*, a part-electronic, part-
acoustic system would collaborate with itself. At the same time that
the traditional notion of life was being deconstructed, Cage and Tudor
played between themes of organic and non-organic—another double
position. Organic structures are broken down into their component
parts as systems of on-and-off switches, from the macro-social level
all the way down to the nervous system, and vice versa: we all belong
within a modern technological rainforest.

> Automation. Alternation of global
> society through electronics so that world
> will go round by means of united
> intelligence rather than by means of
> divisive intelligence (politics,
> economics). Say this idea has no basis
> in fact but arose through brushing of
> misinformation. No sweat. It arose
> (the idea exists, in fact).[86]

Cage's ideas about technology blend, in this excerpt from his poem,
"Diary: How to Improve the World (You Will Only Make Matters
Worse)" of 1965, with a utopian vision. All intelligence may be united
through electronics; Cage followed McLuhan's idea that new media
may expand our sensorium, imagining that this expansion may enable
us to become one with each other in a big self-regulating, self-sufficient
"thinking machine." All of society seems poised to arrive, in Cage's

view during this time, at an ultimate collective state of being. Automation creates alternation: our nervous systems expand outward into the rainforest of modernity.

It is conspicuous that Cage's techno-utopianism wound up affirming the same call to "just be" in the present that he would frequently voice elsewhere. As important as technology was for his compositional method and for the realization of certain collaborative works from his later period, Cage wielded technology in much the same way as he wielded Artaud's ideas about theater, or, as we shall see in the next section, as he wielded ideas drawn from Eastern sources. Cage's techno-craze was the obverse side of his belief in the "ontology of performance," since when we are confronted by a barrage of multimedia stimuli, when composition expands to encompass any and every sound, or when our nervous systems expand into an electronic rainforest, we can only perceive suddenly, awakening to the "now" moment. When sound is dispersed into systems, into its various materials and networks of human and non-human actors, the interior of the human being is exteriorized while the exterior world of signals becomes the model (in Wiener or in Mumma) for any communication, between people or within the self. All of society becomes a vast composition; composition becomes the hidden structure of society. The curtain of history and tradition is pulled aside. Cage hoped we may freshly arrive at the now, born anew to presence. "Contemporary music is not the music of the future nor the music of the past," Cage asserted in his lecture, "Composition as Process" (1958), "but simply music present with us: this moment, now, this now moment."[87]

But the cat is still dead. The main premise of Cage's bid to presence, and the obverse side of his utopian affirmation of sensorial expansion and perceptual immediacy, is the zero or the nothing. By returning to zero, tossing aside memory as well as the normative forms and techniques of western music, Cage traversed this emptiness inside (to recall Blanchot's words again). The art of Cage started from the trace, the empty non-presence out of which any sound, any music, any creativity may emerge. However, while there is a possibility that one may awaken to the now and that new music may pave way toward ever more progress, ever more creation, there must also be the possibility of entropy.[88] A work like Tudor and Mumma's *Rainforest* may eternally self-create, or it may disperse and decay in the manner of Jean Tinguely's *Homage to New York*, the twenty-three-foot-long sculpture composed of bicycle wheels, motors, a piano, a go-cart, and bathtub, among other various bits of metal, that self-destructed in the sculpture garden of the New York MOMA one spring day in 1960.[89] Perhaps a self-consuming and imploding machine would be a truer structural homology (and homage) to the city than a self-creating rainforest. In any case, the zero or the nothing was the void from which Cage seems to have begun, and the place toward which he pointed his listeners: disavow thinking and just be; cast off prejudice and expand the senses. The zero is certainly the place from which Cage began to speak. And it was his speech that filled the silence.

THE SPOKEN BEING

In a lecture delivered at Julliard on 27 March 1952, five months before the Black Mountain College event and the premiere of *4'33"*, Cage faced an audience of musicians and scholars who seem to have been primed to undermine his aesthetic position. In the early part of this Julliard lecture (which would later form part of *A Year from Monday*), Cage bashes Beethoven yet again: according to the normative prescriptions of western music, a listener must "confuse himself to the same final extent that [a] composer [does] and imagine that sounds are not sounds at all but are Beethoven. . . . Any child will tell us: this is simply not the case." Once the confusion is sorted out, Cage affirms, then we may perceive that sounds are simply sounds, not an emanation of any particular author's mind.

The Julliard sound archive includes a recording of Cage's lecture and shortly after this statement about what a child would say, Tudor enters with a deafening blam on the piano. He performs works by Cage, Morton Feldman, and Christian Wolff through the rest of Cage's lecture. Cage emphasizes sudden apprehension, pitching his anti-intellectualism intelligently, once again, facing an intellectual crowd.

> That is to say, one has to stop all the thinking that separates music from living. . . . The wisest thing to do is to open one's ears immediately and to hear a sound suddenly before one's thinking has a chance to turn it into something logical, abstract, or symbolical.[90]

Cage's Julliard lecture bespeaks his conviction that abandoning choice to chance, abandoning parameterization to thoughtlessness, allows one to grasp—suddenly, *voilà!*—the in-itself of composition. As he stated, "with contemporary music there is no time to do anything like classifying. All you can do is suddenly listen, in the same way that when you catch a cold all you can do is suddenly sneeze." Cage's words about suddenly listening well sum up the same essential message he would articulate throughout his career. "Contemporary music is not so much art as it is life."[91] Thought is not required; it is only necessary to be, suddenly, here and now.

It is well known—and has become something of a thought cliché—that the kind of sudden perception Cage advocated was Buddhistic. Cage's self-positioning has allowed the composer to be remembered as a kind of sonic sage, or, to quote Caroline A. Jones's dubious dubbing, a "Zen master" of the avant-garde.[92] The Julliard lecture is perhaps the first public event at which Cage mentioned his studies with D. T. Suzuki, the Japanese apologist for Zen Buddhism whose lectures at Columbia University Cage had attended—though, as Patterson accounts, Suzuki only started lecturing at Columbia during the spring or fall of 1952, thus when Cage gave his lecture in March, he could not have studied with Suzuki for more than a couple weeks or months. And "study" probably meant auditing a lecture, maybe two. Zen Buddhism was a fresh appropriation, and, to play on one of Cage's own phrases, was something of a cheap imitation.[93] (If Boulez had taken this tact, one can imagine he might have devotedly transcribed Buddhist chants or more thoroughly read about Chan before making his knowledge public.)

Perhaps because Cage was always quite vocal about his borrowings from Suzuki's Zen and other Eastern sources via Alan Watts or Ananda Coomaraswamy, many scholars have followed his footsteps in construing various spiritual practices as vehicles for the same sudden apprehension—the *voilà* moment. When Pritchett claimed in *The Music of John Cage*, for example, that Cage learned from Zen to "rid [himself] of conceptual thought in order to apprehend ultimate Reality," Pritchett anticipated a refrain that has echoed in more recent Cage biographies by David Revill, Rob Haskins, and especially Kay Larson, all of whom allege that the composer experienced something akin to sudden enlightenment.[94] They all take Cage's words against composerly intention seriously, and also take seriously Cage's grab-bag method of appropriation, his manner of cribbing ideas from Coomaraswamy or from Suzuki, always with an air of American transcendentalism à la Henry David Thoreau. By failing to distinguish these various sources, Cage biographers as well as Cage scholars tend to conflate all of these sources in the same way that Cage did.[95] The basic "facet of Cage's contact with Asian culture," according to Patterson, was "the way in which he studied, absorbed, and sifted through a variety of texts during the 1940s and 1950s, extracting with single-minded discrimination only those malleable ideas that could be used metaphorically to illuminate" his own "artistic themes" or to "reinforce the tenets of his own modernist agenda."[96]

Unpacking anew Cage's Eastern influences is a task beyond the present scope: it suffices to say here that Cage took themes and ideas from various sources—and his friendships with Joseph Campbell and Aldous Huxley should not be overlooked—to construct a "perennial philosophy" of sound.[97] Borrowing a phrase from Robert H. Sharf, Cage (and sometimes Cage scholars) used (and sometimes use) "Zen" as a marker for a "noncontingent, transcultural, nondual spiritual gnosis that underlies all authentic religious inspiration."[98] The same suddenness applied, in Cage's view of new music, to all authentic sonic inspiration. Sudden awakening, living life as it is, and apprehending things as they are: these are among the westernized Zen tropes that Cage took to indicate a transcendent, universal spirituality. Zen was therefore a kind of "romantic, ahistorical, and acultural idealization," to cite Fann's words about Suzuki, whose efforts to promulgate Zen during the mid-twentieth century tended to bolster a "view held by the Western world for the last few hundred years of a country like China as an anti-progressive 'immobile empire.'"[99] But even as Cage invoked Suzuki—that is, even as he invoked an already reconstructed version of Zen that Suzuki promulgated in the west—the composer also avowed, in characteristic fashion, that "what I do, I do not wish to be blamed on Zen."[100] Another double position: Cage appropriated the aura of "Zen," really the idealized and romanticized—in a word: Americanized—aura of Beat Zen, while also declaring his independence from Suzuki. With Cage there was always an out.

During the question-and-answer session after Cage's Julliard lecture, a couple of the audience members (two male voices I cannot recognize) tried to undermine Cage's discursive strategy of double positioning with regard to the theme of presence.[101] One audience member pointed out that Cage's compositions (like those by Feldman and Wolff) were not purely of "sound," but rather of certain deliberately conceived sounds—the composer used some method of choice and thus of exclusion, which undermines the whole premise of just "being there." Cage elided his auditor by claiming that while he did employ compositional methods, during the act of performance, "we weren't remembering: we were being in the present."

In listening to this exchange, I get the sense that Cage's invocation of Suzuki was a timely tactic, as if the composer knew that his avowals about sudden perception would not hold up under serious academic scrutiny. Suzuki's Zen was the perfect discursive shield. After Cage stated "we weren't remembering," another questioner leapt to the microphone to press Cage's presentism. Their dialogue was quick paced, with one man cutting off or talking over the other:

> RESPONDENT: In order to live our lives in the future, in order to be able to keep on living, we have to, uh, draw upon experience which we've had in the past.
>
> CAGE: Why?
>
> RESPONDENT: Well, how can . . . what?
>
> CAGE: Why?
>
> RESPONDENT: *Why?!* Because . . . uh . . . how do you learn . . . how do you walk? You walk because you've understood either in the mind or . . .
>
> CAGE: Yes, but I don't walk by asking myself how do I do it. I simply walk.
>
> RESPONDENT: Yes, but at one point . . .
>
> CAGE: And I'm not drawing on my previous experience.
>
> RESPONDENT: In one point in your life you had to have the experience of finding out how to walk . . .
>
> CAGE: Well, fine. Then let it go.
>
> RESPONDENT: Or you have to find out from your parents talking

THE WRITTEN BEING OF SOUND 215

how to talk. And I don't see how, uh, you can live your life completely . . .

CAGE [*PRESUMABLY WALKING ACROSS THE STAGE*]: Yes, but you see as I walk now it's no longer a problem. [*Laughter and applause from the audience shortly follow.*]

This exchange sums up Cage's double position and also demonstrates how he held his (doubled) ground. He excluded the past in favor of the "now"; but, if one follows his line of thinking, the "now," conversely, becomes the eternal condition of composition itself. We move beyond the simple "now" toward uppercase "Now," or uppercase "Being"—a kind of stasis. Therefore, while Cage could be taken (on the surface, anyway) to have worked against any kind of nominal logic that would pin down what music is—since he wanted to escape intellection and affirm "pure" now-ness, always dispersing, always refusing—this very slipperiness became a means for Cage to revive ontology as a discourse on what is, or what is "now," in this very moment.

Presence is a kind of ontological myth. Maybe learning to walk was an inopportune choice; Cage's questioner could have simply pointed out that Tudor had to remember a lot of notes in order to "not remember," to "be in the present." In fact, we *are* only able to walk because we have walked before. Many steps lead up to the present, and while one does not need to think about every step one has taken in order to walk now, nevertheless our past experience remains invisibly, unconsciously constitutive with regard to how, why, and where we walk. Cage put himself right in the middle of this apparent tension between experience "now" and the conditions of this experience, between the present moment and the absent past, disavowing memory even as he was already beholden to it. And out of this temporal antinomy, this double negation, came an endless flurry of speech. The Q and A went on intensively for twenty minutes or so, with various auditors trying to pin Cage down to one side of a coin. Cage responded every time by discursively flipping the coin.

CONCLUSION: THE SPACE OF WRITING

In poetically opaque prose, Foucault begins "Language to Infinity" by invoking writers as recent (to him) as Blanchot and as distant (to us and to him) as Homer. "Writing so as not to die, as Blanchot said, or perhaps even speaking so as not to die, is a task undoubtedly as old as the word." Death and the figure of the singing bard become central in Foucault's description of the role of breath and of speech to sustain life in the space of a text: "it is quite likely that the approach of death—its sovereign gesture, its prominence within human memory—hollows out in the present and in existence the void toward which and from which we speak."[102] Foucault's depiction of phonetic language in "Language to Infinity" might be summed up like this: phonetic writing is already, by its nature, a double of a double, since writing represents a spoken representation; there is a gap between the spoken signifier (for Saussure, the "acoustic image") and the ideas that words activate (their signifieds); by the time of Euro-western modernity, and particularly in modern literature, this gap widened, indicating a new situation for language and knowledge.

"Language to Infinity" appeared a few years before *The Order of Things* (1966), in which Foucault describes a gradual transformation of the western *episteme*, beginning with a description of the cosmic order of the Renaissance in which "signs and similitudes were wrapped around one another in an endless spiral," the things of the earth mirroring the heavens above and joining language and things in a "profound kinship."[103] This Renaissance *episteme*, in which words, like the things of the world, possess an *intrinsic meaning*, is as distant from us moderns as is Crollius's 1624 *Traité des signatures*, in which the author affirms that

> the stars are the matrix of all the plants and every star in the sky only the spiritual prefiguration of the plant, . . . and just as each herb or plant is a terrestrial star looking up at the sky, so also each star is a celestial plant in spiritual form.[104]

This Renaissance world is, in Foucault's words, "folded in upon itself," with microcosm mirroring macrocosm and all beings falling into place within a larger cosmic scheme. By the Classical Age (the seventeenth and eighteenth centuries), however, language is no longer "ontologically interwoven" with things, but becomes instead an artificial grid made to represent the order of the world. Human beings belong within this broader order, a grand table created by God, and language only has validity when words represent this already-existing order of things. "The role of man was to clarify the order of the world," Dreyfus and Rabinow explain to summarize Foucault's view: "[t]he key was that the medium of representation was reliable and transparent."[105] Once Modern Man emerged and became the measure of things, however, replacing God and throwing the whole notion of an already-ordered universe into doubt, the reliability and transparency of representation became compromised. This "archaeological mutation" created an unstable epistemological ground on which we still stand (according to the Foucault of 1966).[106]

The growing autonomy of language is perhaps the crux of Foucault's narrative of the break into Euro-western modernity. With Cervantes, for instance, "resemblances and signs [dissolve] their former alliance; similitudes . . . become deceptive and verge upon the visionary or madness": Don Quixote imagines his world as if he lives in an old tale; local inns become castles, and ladies become fair maidens; he "reads the world in order to prove his books."[107] In the works of Marquis de Sade, the scenes and characters are a screen for a kind of desperate "desire battering at the limits of representation"; violence, sexuality, and desire "extend, below the level of representation, an immense expanse of shade" that still hovers over us.[108] Writers like Cervantes and Sade, in other words, put language at a further and further remove from a reality that their words neither resembled nor represented—and the birth of modern literature, for Foucault, betrayed the fact that any domain of the human sciences might come to exist, finally, like literature, in the "infinite space" of language itself. This is the context for Foucault's observation, in "Language to Infinity," that phonetic language represents the sounds of speech. Phonetic writing is already a double, already one level removed from the representation of things.

In *The Order of Things*, this doubled nature of phonetic writing seems to take on its own life: Foucault observes that sound, conspicuously, became a primary focus of philological study. With Franz Bopp and the birth of modern philology, "language is treated for the first time . . . as a totality of phonetic elements"; "language exists when noises have been articulated and divided into a series of distinct *sounds*. The whole being of language is now sonorous [*Tout l'être du langage est mainte- nant sonore*]."[109] As the new fields of biology and economics made pos- sible the modern notions of life and labor, in other words, so philology gave birth to language, which was no longer a transparent medium for the representation of things but rather a discipline on its own, an auton- omous and instable intermediary.

I am struck by the role speech sounds seem to have played in Fou- cault's claim that,

> [f]rom the nineteenth-century, language began to fold in upon itself, to acquire its own particular density, to deploy a history, an objectivity, and laws of its own. It became one object of knowl- edge among others, on the same level as living beings, wealth and value, and the history of events and men.[110]

A deep connection between this new writing of the human sciences, premised on a "sonorous being" of language, and the writing of litera- ture, is a consistent undercurrent in *The Order of Things*.

> Throughout the nineteenth century, and right up to our own day—from Hölderlin to Mallarmé and on to Antonin Artaud— literature achieved autonomous existence, and separated itself from all other language with a deep scission, only by forming a sort of "counter-discourse," and by finding its way back from the representative or signifying function of language to this raw being that had been forgotten since the sixteenth century.[111]

In a striking turn, literature allowed language to be used once again in its raw being (*être brut*), returning to the order of resemblance that characterized the Renaissance *episteme*. Words would no longer be linked to things through a process of representation but would directly *produce presence*.

It is possible to read this moment of *The Order of Things*, and to un- derstand the murmuring streams and mirror games in "Language to In- finity," as affirmations of a positive power of literature: to create worlds and to resemble these worlds in a raw or original way. In my reading, however, Foucault was not optimistic. The return to (*ramonter*—literally a "re-mounting" or re-ascension of) the "raw being" of language had commenced, in the decades leading to Artaud, at an even further remove from reality than any person who lived prior to the modern *episteme* could have imagined. Not only would writers of fiction play the game of language to infinity, *but so would writers in the human sciences*, the sciences that claimed privileged access to the truth of Man— for Foucault, a recent invention. Foucault positions sound at the heart of this linguistic game of mirrors. When he writes that the "presence of repeated speech in writing undeniably gives to what we call a work of language an ontological status unknown in those cultures where the act of writing designates the thing itself, in its proper and visible body, stubbornly inaccessible to time,"[112] the non-phonetic writing of the other appears again, this time as a writing *without an ontological status*, or at least without the kind of ontological status that characterizes phonetic writing. A sonic presence, then, defines the ontology of phonetic writing as distinct from a character that depicts an object or thing directly— without the doubling of speech, without the game of mirrors.

It may seem counter-intuitive to attribute Cage's ideas about sound, and his means of producing sounds, to this doubled nature of phonetic language. After all, the composer avowed that sound is always around us: it is *not* written; in fact, by simply "being in the present" with sound, we may disavow any traditional notion of writing and expand the scope of "composition." Yet there was always a particular privilege granted to speech in Cage's works. That Cage articulated his aesthetic position through speech—spoken lectures, interviews, and manifestoes—is all too obvious. What is less obvious is that speech may be the "ontological model" for Cage's aesthetic position, and even for his works.

The *Black Mountain Piece* or *4'33"*, for instance, exist as collections of speech: each work "is" (quite literally) a phonetic double. Recollection is all that remains; the sounds in the room are long gone. Rather than foregrounding the magic of the performed moment as a resistance to documentary representation, Cage's performance events—at least as these events may be remembered now—are guaranteed by speech, and Cage seems to have foregrounded this specific aspect of musical reception as a feature of his works. In other words, the *Black Mountain Piece* or *4′33″* seem to point up their own constructed-ness in speech, in the writings and narratives captured in recollections and in texts.

At the same time that certain of his works seem to be *about* speech in so far as it is speech that maintains them, it is also conspicuous that many of Cage's works *featured* speech. At Julliard as in the Black Mountain College cafeteria, Cage (like Olson and Richards) was an orator. One can imagine that whether Cage read the Declaration of Independence, the Bill of Rights, or a text by Meister Eckhart during the *Black Mountain Piece*, he likely orated a democratic narrative, or fragments of many narratives in which the themes of individual rights and independence from parochial old-world authority would blend well with the mystical ideas Cage took from Eckhart. By glancing through his citations to Eckhart elsewhere, for instance, one may get the sense that medieval Christian mysticism fulfilled the same purposes for Cage as did his Asian sources. Cage sometimes wielded Eckhart's words to affirm his own endeavors to jumble disparate elements together into immersive spectacles: "the soul is the gatherer-together of the disparate elements," Eckhart wrote, "and its work fills one with peace and love."[113] Sometimes the listener's awakening to peace and love would be accomplished, Cage avowed, by a kind of divine awakening:

> one must achieve this unselfconsciousness by means of trans-
> formed knowledge. . . . Then we shall be informed by the divine
> unconsciousness and in that our ignorance will be ennobled and
> adorned with supernatural knowledge.[114]

Sometimes Cage's Eckhart sounds like Satie's Péladan, striving toward the mastery of feminine otherness as part of a grander spiritual quest: "Earth has no escape from heaven: flee she up or flee she down heaven still invades her, energizing her, fructifying her, whether for her weal or for her woe."[115] Ultimately, though, Cage used Eckhart to affirm the call to just be in the present: through sudden perception, one may, in Eckhart's words, be "innocent and free to receive anew with each Now-moment a heavenly gift"; "Dear God," he exclaimed, "I beg you rid me of God."[116]

But Cage was never quite rid of God. If, by using a phonetic writing, we "have been led to see in writing a simple duplication of the 'living voice,'" to recall Lagerwey's words, and if "speech—whether of man or of God—has the power to create things, or to realize them," then Cage's notion of sound, and his manner of discursively framing his sound, was often a realization of speech. Cage's American mystical speech filled the cacophony in the Black Mountain cafeteria, and in the Berlin Kongresshalle, his speech accompanied Tudor: he explained to his audience (always, of course, with the familiar elusiveness) about indeterminacy and, after pounding on a typewriter and attaching a microphone to his vocal cords, he orated the expansion of composition.

Since Cage spoke, and since certain of his words have persisted—in memory, in texts—as a kind of linguistic double, I would suggest that Cage's notion of sound always involved the doubled nature of phonetic writing. This is one sense of the "written being" that Derrida would soon describe: Being, like Cage's sound, had been produced in and through writings. Being was always a discursive creation made by philosophers—it was literally "written in" to many texts—and with the epistemic break into modernity described by Foucault, this being had become just as instable—just as impossible to affirm—as the representative function of modern language.

In his own poetic prose, Fann synthesizes Derrida and Foucault's views about phonetic language, contending that with the epistemic break that heralded European modernity, the doubled nature of this language intensified. This break had far-reaching, and ultimately devastating, consequences for knowledge, creating a chasm between language and reality into which the modern knowing subject had fallen, somewhat like Don Quixote, lost somewhere in a world of words. To make clear Foucault's notion of the growing autonomy of language, Fann writes a brief narrative in first person. His words seem to perform the inaugural power of the modern phonetic language, and, by linking this power to the speech produced in certain forms of popular music, he draws out the implications of Foucault's own sense that the modern phonetic language had become ever more autonomous yet ever more precarious.

> I hear myself when I speak; therefore, I make a representation of the world when I speak, live, and labor. I hear the inner narrative of self regardless of whether I speak or not; therefore, I experience the endless murmuring stream of consciousness. These narratives and murmurings are not "outside me, outside my breath,

at a visible distance"; they do not "cease to belong to me." This has been the fundamental nature of phonetic speech since Homer's time. Rock and roll music particularly revived this nature—you are not *enchanted* by the radical or intense melodies or rhythms. Rather, you *hear the voice*, a form of *speech* as lyrics. When you hear the singer *speak*, you hear yourself *speak*. Rock and roll music no longer *concerns* representation: rather, it *concerns* the production of presence. It is inside you, inside your breath, at a proximately visible distance; it does not cease to belong to you. In short, it is the most radical and intense *modern production of presence.*[117]

Cage was not a rock n' roller, yet this performative mini-narrative about the modern phonetic language seems to speak loudly and clearly about Cage's sound. Cage was never too far from God, for when God said there should be light, there was light; when Cage said sound was pure, there was pure sound. "Speech," to recall Fann's trenchant words, "the sound, the voice, the breath—is identified as creator, or spirit, which is supreme in the West. We believe in speech." This belief in speech did not only refer, in Cage, to spoken language. As I have suggested throughout this chapter, for Cage it was *suddenness* that mattered. With new music, all one can do is suddenly listen: it is the momentary presence of an action, a gesture, an utterance, that escapes materiality. This belief in performance, in the pure presence of the performed event that is inaugurated in a moment, reflects this deep belief in the power of speech, since speech is of the moment; it precedes and always transcends writing. The sudden act of speaking and creating was the true model of Cage's view of performance, perhaps the very model of the ontology of performance.

Aside from moments in which Cage spoke, therefore, I would like to suggest that there is another sense in which his works may be understood as "spoken," or, to invoke Derrida's phrase again, there is another way to understand Cage's sound as a "written being." Cage's whole aesthetic position was premised (sometimes implicitly and sometimes explicitly) on the oppositions between the organic and the mechanical, the living and the artificial, memory and suddenness, and, by extension, between mediation and liveness, inscription and performance: *each of these oppositions are an allegory and alibi for the doubled nature of phonetic writing.* The dualism of inside and outside, of body and soul, the breath of the Creator (whether of God or of Cage) and the fallen exteriority of the document all replicate the metaphysics of phonetic writing.

• • •

Derrida's "written being" has two related connotations when thought in relation to Cageian modernism, one in which a work contains speech or takes form through speech; the other in which speech becomes the ontological model, the metaphysical foundation, for a work—even if the work does not feature the literal act of speaking. If we hold, with Phelan, that a nonverbal action is beyond writing, then performance *is* the metaphysics of this inaugural phonetic speech; it reduplicates the metaphysical divide between the material and ideal, between writing and voice.

Cage's sound is écriture: there "is" no sound in Cage without the ontological double of sound in (and as) writing, in his texts and the texts written about him, in the archive of recollection, or in the writing of technological reproduction. There "is" no sound without the inaugural power of speech. Sound was a weapon with which the composer thwarted certain critics, emptying the author, disavowing intellection, and sometimes wielding technology, all as a guise or disguise of an unbridled egotism and fundamental duplicity. Cage's sound was a white musical mythology.

While Cage and Derrida seem to have traversed the same emptiness, the play of traces and the silence at the heart of cultural meaning, they moved in opposite directions, and so too have scholars of performance. When looking back on the performed moment, we tend either to uphold an ideal of performance, alive in its moment, or else to disperse the performed moment into various materials and actors, traces and documents. By positioning Cage as a forerunner of the recent scholarly debate(s) around presence, I have tried to move elsewhere: to look through Cage's ways of conceiving sound, and through divergent scholarly ways of approaching presence, and toward the "conditions of possibility" (so to speak) that have shaped how presence may be thought. For Foucault, with the growing opacity of language during the nineteenth century, critical thought in the west took two related paths. Transcendental philosophy and new empirical fields arose at the same time. On this view, either we become positivists like Wiener, interested only in the observable, in the myth of a universal calculus, in systems composed of on-and-off switches. The whole world, its machines, its animals, its people, is an elaborate set of cybernetic systems. Or we move in the opposite direction toward *a priori* investigation. Kantian philosophy questions what makes representations possible; it

> uncovers a transcendental field in which the subject, which is never given to experience (since it is not empirical), but which is finite (since there is no intellectual intuition), determines in its relation to an object . . . all the formal conditions of experience in general; it is the analysis of the transcendental subject that isolates the foundation of a possible synthesis between representations.[118]

These two divergent modes of thought, one positivist and the other geared toward *a priori* inquiry, are two sides, for Foucault, of the archaeology of modernity.

We still belong to this Kantian dynasty. Cage, and by extension, modern music to our day, can be seen as endless series of variations on this theme: the obsession with form, on one hand, and the obsession with pure sound on the other. Through various means of thinking, making, and theorizing musical forms, through techniques and technologies, through the lofty terminology of analysis, and through the technocratic craze of Cage's mid-century or of our own moment in which anyone with a computer can be a musician—all of this appears as the obverse side of a covert yet fundamental belief in the Being of sound. This historical *a priori*, to borrow a Foucauldian phrase, is the condition of possibility for the presence and liveness debate. The "mythical speech" or the "phonetic breath" may lead one to rejoice in the transient life of performance. Or we declare that truth is the product of actors, objects, techniques—in a word: writing. Our thought about presence divides, and may only ever divide, between materialism and idealism, those two great ontological machines.

Postlude

A SIMULACRUM OF A PRESENCE

• • • "It got right through to me." Cage was at first shy to demonstrate his vocal style to John Lennon. During a 1972 televised short film titled *John & Yoko in Syracuse, New York*, Cage appeared with Lennon and Yoko Ono around a table, smoking and conversing about voice.[1] Ono (Cage's longtime friend[2]) speculated that stress causes certain people to speak in the high register. She explained that women's voices remain higher than men's because women are suppressed in society, as if strangled, forced to speak from the nose and throat. The vocal screechiness of certain dictators, Hitler included, could also be explained by the tremendous stress of their situation. If one cannot relax, one's voice must go higher. A bearded Cage, laughing, asked if his own voice had become so low on account of his relaxed spirit. While Ono affirmed "yes, you're very relaxed," a smiling Lennon conjectured that Cage's bass voice was well suited to say "Om."

The conversation veered toward microphones and singing, and Cage said cheekily, "well, you've never heard me sing." After some light goading from Ono and Lennon, Cage demonstrated his vocal style: a kind of low ululation on a "wah" vowel. He modulated the pitch downward, gurgling and vibrating in his throat as if a choking engine, and then ascended to a final short "ah." "Beautiful," said Ono right away, and as Cage leaned forward with a wide puppy-dog grin, he asked Lennon "did you like it?" The former Beatle confirmed: "it got right through to me."

The current narrative has described the rise of various ontological attitudes toward sound from Cage's French predecessors up to his own mid-century moment. Having examined these predecessors and having listened for ontological sound in various configurations, I wager that the ground has been laid to question whether this ontological lineage ever really ended. This chance 1972 meeting between an avant-garde guru, a performance art celebrity, and a singer–songwriter icon may seem an odd place for us to end, but the work of Cage, Ono, and Lennon could be said to coalesce around at least two familiar themes. The first, of course, is presence: one only needs to recall the hordes of screaming Beatles fans, images of Ono's *Cut Piece* (1964), and Cage's amplified typewriter to see that each of these artists approached the theme of liveness in his or her own way—or at least that liveness, stage presence, shock value, and so forth remain central in their critical images. And Lennon's reference to "Om" also bespeaks a common hippie-dippieness behind each of these artist's aspirations to presence—Cage had already, in his own way, imagined that there is no heaven, no hell below us, no countries, no possessions: "Imagine all the people / Livin' for today." Or, in Cage's words: "we weren't remembering: we were being in the present."

Second, and keeping in view the weight each of these artists attached to "being there," the work of Cage, Lennon, and Ono can also be said to coalesce around the decay of various "literate" art traditions in the twentieth century. The fame (and auction value) of Lennon's lyric sheets attest to the fact that he basically never used notation, more or less eliding musical writing altogether, while Ono's performance art can be seen as part of a revived oral tradition afforded by the advent of video recording—another form of documentation without literal inscription.[3] Cage, as we have seen, had already expanded composition beyond the score, and by the time of this obscure television special, he had added his vocal gymnastics to his repertoire of sonic experiments.

These vocal gymnastics fell, like the scrape of Tudor's piano strings or the sounds of the Maverick Concert Hall, under the banner of "composition itself" in Cage's expanded sense. In 1970, he composed the text *Mureau* by "subjecting all the remarks of [Henry David] Thoreau about music, silence, and sounds . . . to a series of I Ching operations," thus composing, as he put it, "a mix of letters, syllables, words, phrases, and sentences."[4] In listening to a 1972 recording of Cage reading *Mureau*, one senses that his list should have gone in reverse: Cage begins with full sentences, but through the course of the performance, he begins to isolate syllables and to prolong the sounds of particular vowels, as if introducing new vocal elements gradually through the (hour-long) performance.[5]

Though these vocal sounds have a written text as their basis, Cage's vocal style veers away from notation, intensifying the music of phonetics—the clicks of consonants and the grinding of his throat's phonic metal. His modulations, his drones, his quick ascensions on certain repeated vowels, his growls and yelps, were not written. And while Lennon included his own nonsense syllables on famed Beatles tracks—"I am the Walrus / Goo goo g'joob!"—Cage affixed contact microphones to his throat, performing the broken syllables and gurglings that he demonstrated for Ono and Lennon while on the road with Tudor. A live recording of *Mesostics Re Merce Cunningham (Untitled)* made in Germany (presumably during the 70s), for instance, which was later released as part of the collection *The Art of David Tudor* (2013), features Tudor's live electronic music—in which the hum of oscillators or recordings of insects and other natural phenomena would be played through vast arrays of homemade distortion devices to produce various drones, chirps, and white noise—accompanying Cage's vocals. The electronic squeaks and blares (which surely were deafening) seem to pair well with Cage's own verbal swoops, vibrating yells, and low drones (as if Artaud's spirit from *Pour en finir avec le jugement de Dieu* was onstage with the Cage–Tudor duo).[6]

In thinking through Cage, Lennon, and Ono's respective oral traditions, that one hippie-dippie syllable sticks in my mind: "Om." More could be said about Lennon and Cage's meanderings into (westernized, hippie-fied, Orientalist) spiritualism, but not here.[7] It suffices only to speculate that the former Beatle was not bluffing when he said that Cage's voice "got right through to me." Cage and Lennon seem to represent dual sides—maybe avant-garde and kitsch—of a technologically revived oral tradition, or perhaps an electronically invigorated expansion of composition to include all kinds of musical utterance previously limited to oral transmission.

Which brings us back, in closing, to the Derridean question of the enlargement of writing. When Richard Taruskin observed that the advent of electronic media of musical reproduction signaled the waning of the western literate musical tradition, foreshadowing the possibility that we would enter a new postliterate musical phase, he stuck with a literal, commonsense idea of writing. "[T]he one musical medium," he wrote, "that originated in the twentieth century—namely, the electronic—is the one that depends least on writing" in the sense of musical notation. But, to invoke Cage's words once again, when we stop thinking of composition in this limited sense—via parameters, scores, and other writerly methods—we get "composition itself." Which suggests, perhaps, that when a whole era disavows composition in the limited sense (which is exactly what happened during the late twentieth century) composition enlarges to encompass previously oral expressions into a new form of technologically reproducible writing. To play with a Derridean phrase, the end of the "literary" musical tradition might mean the beginning of a new written sonic tradition, leading eventually to the inscription of sound in digits planted in mp3 files, democratized through widely available and user-friendly media of musical production like GarageBand, and broadcast instantly across the globe via corporate powerhouses like Amazon or seemingly transparent ontological machines like YouTube.

> And thus we say "writing" for all that gives rise to an inscription in general, whether it is literal or not and even if what it distributes in space is alien to the order of the voice: cinematography, choreography, of course, but also pictorial, musical, sculptural "writing." . . . All this to describe not only the system of notation secondarily connected with these activities but the essence and the content of these activities themselves.[8]

Of course, such questions can only be raised but not pursued here. The present study is meant to describe the decay of a certain era of modernism, focused on a group of composers whose works and aesthetic positions center on the problematics of presence and *écriture*. To keep playing with Derrid-isms, though, these composers might be seen as the last composers of writing, and the first composers of ontological sound.

We can still hear this sound. Through the late twentieth century and up to our present, the idea of liberated sound, as well as the related notion that composition arrives "in-itself" once it is freed from the score, are so frequently invoked—in music highbrow, lowbrow, and no-brow—that it is all too easy to forget that sound did not always exist in its present forms. Some would say we are in the great era of performance—of recorded performance, that is, where all repertoires are at our fingertips. Others may hold on to the idea of the face-to-face, of bodily co-presence as a basis of authenticity. In either case, the murmuring flow of speech continues—an endless speech captured in texts; the flowing language to infinity. One may question what sound is, what it means or has meant, what use can be made of it to understand culture, selfhood, or any other topic of scholarly exchange. Often the discourse matters more than "being there" (and especially if "being there," presence, *is* the basis of a discourse). Perhaps there "is" no music or sound without a written presence today, since music surely needs discursive media (especially if it is to generate capital). Perhaps the closure of an epoch of musical metaphysics signaled the dawning of an epoch of ontology. The production of musical presence ended when an epoch of simulated presence began.

> Since the trace is not a presence but the simulacrum of a presence that dislocates itself, displaces itself, refers to itself, it properly has no site—erasure belongs to its structure.[9]

The present is still too crowding, after all, too confusing, too present to imagine.

NOTES

Acknowledgments

1. Michel Foucault, *The Courage of Truth: The Government of Self and Others II; Lectures at the Collège de France 1983-1984*, trans. Graham Burchell (New York: Palgrave Macmillan, 2012), 5, 6.

2. Fuoco B. Fann, *This Self We Deserve: A Quest After Modernity* (Berkeley: Philosophy and Art Collaboratory, 2020), vii, 79; italics in original.

Prelude

1. John Cage, in Richard Kostelanetz, *Conversing with Cage*, 2nd ed. (New York: Routledge, 2003), 70; David Nicholls, *John Cage* (Urbana and Chicago: University of Chicago Press, 2007), 58-60.

2. John Cage, *A Year from Monday* (Middletown: Wesleyan University Press, 1969), 134.

3. "Here we are concerned about the coexistence of dissimilars, and the central points where fusion occurs are many: the ears of the listener wherever they are. This disharmony, to paraphrase Bergson's statement about disorder, is simply a harmony to which many are unaccustomed." John Cage, *Silence: Lectures and Writings by John Cage* (Middletown: Wesleyan University Press, 1973), 12.

4. See Cage's "Future of Music: Credo," in *Silence*, 5.

5. Cage, "Experimental Music," in *Silence*, 8.

6. In her discussion of 4'33", Lydia Goehr remarked that although "Cage's 'work' reflects an attempt to shed music of its institutionalized constraints imposed by composer, performer, and concert hall," Cage nevertheless "maintained

control (however minimal) over the music" by using the traditionally established framing of score, piano, and venue. Cage "aims to bring music back into the real or natural world of everyday sounds," but despite "whatever changes have come about in our material understanding of musical sound . . . the formal constraints of the work-concept have ironically been maintained." Lydia Goehr, *The Imaginary Museum of Musical Works: An Essay in the Philosophy of Music*, rev. ed. (New York: Oxford University Press, 2007), 264.

7. Roland Barthes, "The Death of the Author," in *Image-Music-Text*, trans. Stephen Heath (New York: Hill & Wang, 1977), 148; for the connection between Cage and Barthes's "Death of the Author," see G. Douglas Barrett, *After Sound: Toward a Critical Music* (New York and London: Bloomsbury, 2016), 22.

8. Kyle Gann, *No Such Thing as Silence: John Cage's 4'33"* (New Haven and London: Yale University Press, 2010); Dieter Daniels and Inke Arns, eds. *Sounds Like Silence; John Cage, 4'33", Silence Today: 1912, 1952, 2012* (Leipzig: Spector Books, 2012).

9. For the connection between Cage and Satie, see Alan M. Gillmor, *Erik Satie* (New York and London: W. W. Norton, 1988), 36, and Cage's own essay, "Defense of Satie," in *John Cage: An Anthology*, ed. Richard Kostelanetz (New York: Da Capo Press, 1970), 77–84; for Satie and the everyday, see Nancy Perloff, *Art and the Everyday: Popular Entertainment and the Circle of Erik Satie* (Oxford: Clarendon Press, 1991) and Steven Moore Whiting, *Satie the Bohemian: From Cabaret to Concert Hall* (Oxford and New York: Oxford University Press, 1999); for the collapse of aesthetics and banality vis-à-vis Duchamp and conceptual art, see Donald Kuspit, *The End of Art* (Cambridge, UK: Cambridge University Press, 2004).

10. Douglas Kahn, *Noise, Water, Meat: A History of Sound in the Arts* (Cambridge, MA, and London: MIT Press, 1999).

11. Kahn, *Noise, Water, Meat*, 9; italics in original.

12. Kahn, *Noise, Water, Meat*, 191; italics in original.

13. Richard Taruskin, "Ne Plus Ultra (Going as Far as You Can Go)," in *Music in the Late Twentieth Century: The Oxford History of Western Music*, vol. 5 (New York: Oxford University Press, 2010), 67–73.

14. Philip M. Gentry, *What Will I Be: American Music and Cold War Identity* (New York: Oxford University Press, 2017), 121.

15. Jonathan D. Katz, "John Cage's Queer Silence; or, How to Avoid Making Matters Worse," *GLQ* 5, no. 2 (1995): 231–252.

16. Caroline A. Jones, "Finishing School: John Cage and the Abstract Expressionist Ego," *Critical Inquiry* 19, no. 4 (1993): 628–665.

17. De Man described the "allegory of reading" in Proust, noting that while the narrator of *À la Recherche du temps perdu* invites the reader, through lush descriptions of various phenomena, to plunge right into Marcel's world, Proust nevertheless foregrounds the act of reading—since Marcel's love of novels is what compels his imagination—and therefore imposes a distance. An "allegory of read-

ing," in this sense, refers to the self-reflexive nature of À la Recherche, to the fact that the work is, in some sense, "about" reading. For de Man, Proust's novel thus "deconstructs" itself, since it is impossible, by nature, to experience Marcel's sensory world naively and simply *and* to take these phenomena, as Proust seems to imply, as a meta-reflection on the very act of reading, creating, and interpreting literature. For Hans Ulrich Gumbrecht, therefore, de Man's "allegory of reading" describes literary works that foreground the inadequacy of language's referential power. Literary "deconstruction" in de Man's sense occurs when a work demonstrates, through its own narrative logic, that "language cannot refer." Paul de Man, *Allegories of Reading: Figural Language in Rousseau, Nietzsche, Rilke, and Proust* (New Haven and London: Yale University Press, 1979), see esp. 57–78; Hans Ulrich Gumbrecht, "Presence Achieved in Language (With Special Attention Given to the Presence of the Past)," *History and Theory* 45, no. 3 (2006): 318.

18. Jacques Derrida, *Of Grammatology*, trans. Gayatri Chakravorty Spivak (Baltimore and London: Johns Hopkins University Press, 1997), 7; italics in original.

19. Derrida, *Of Grammatology*, 7.

20. See Suzanne Lüdemann, *Politics of Deconstruction: A New Introduction to Jacques Derrida* (Stanford: Stanford University Press, 2014).

21. John Lagerwey, "Dieu-Père/Dao-Mère: dualismes occidentaux et chinois," *Extrême-Orient Extrême-Occident*, Hors-série (2012). Translation is mine.

22. Derrida, *Of Grammatology*, 3.

23. Derrida, *Of Grammatology*, 9.

24. Derrida, *Of Grammatology*, 9.

25. Henri Bergson, *Matter and Memory*, trans. Nancy Margaret Paul and W. Scott Palmer (New York: Zone Books, 1991), 150; italics in original.

26. Hans Ulrich Gumbrecht, *Production of Presence: What Meaning Cannot Convey* (Stanford: Stanford University Press, 2004).

27. Carolyn Abbate, "Music—Drastic or Gnostic?," *Critical Inquiry* 30, no. 3 (2004): 505–536.

28. This sense of presence will be taken up in Chapter Four in relation to Cage. Peggy Phelan, *Unmarked: The Politics of Performance* (London and New York: Routledge, 1993), 146; see also Erika Fischer-Lichte, *The Transformative Power of Performance: A New Aesthetics*, trans. Saskya Iris Jain (London and New York: Routledge, 2008), see esp. 38–74.

29. Derrida; see the section "The Written Being/The Being Written," in *Grammatology*, 18–26.

30. Derrida, quoted in Ning Zhang, "Jacques Derrida's First Visit to China: A Summary of His Lectures and Seminars," *Dao: A Journal of Comparative Philosophy* 2, no. 1 (2002): 153.

31. Quoted in Zhang, "Jacques Derrida's First Visit to China," 154.

32. Peter Salmon, *An Event Perhaps: A Biography of Jacques Derrida* (London and New York: Verso, 2020), 5.

33. Salmon, *An Event Perhaps*, 154.

34. Arthur Schopenhauer, *The World as Will and Representation*, vol. 1, trans. E. F. J. Payne (New York: Dover Publications, 1969 [original German 1818]), 257; italics in original.

35. Michael Gallope, *Deep Refrains: Music, Philosophy, and the Ineffable* (Chicago and London: University of Chicago Press, 2017), 10. And again: "if music is a sensuous immediacy, it cannot be immediate to our experience without taking recourse to some form of mediation" (246).

36. "Worum es hier geht, wird deutlicher, wenn man Schopenhauers Verweis, die Musik sei 'unmittelbar Abbild des Willens selbst,' ersetzt durch die andere Formulierung, sie sei 'Verkörperung des Willens,' weniger ein 'Abbild' als eine alternative Modalität seiner Wirklichkeit." Hans Ulrich Gumbrecht, "Von Geschmack zu Intensität: Lässt sich der existentielle Stellenwert von Mozarts Musik historisch erschließen?" Conference presentation; cited with the author's permission.

37. Salmon, *An Event, Perhaps*, 78. "*Différance* will thus be the movement of play that 'produces' (and not by something that is simply an activity) these differences" by which a concept is named, since "the signified concept is never present in itself"; "every concept is necessarily and essentially inscribed in a chain or a system, within which it refers to another and to other concepts, by the systematic play of differences." Radicalizing this play of differences into *différance*, Derrida stated that *différance*, which is not itself a concept, is "the possibility of conceptuality." Jacques Derrida, "Differance," in *Speech and Phenomena and Other Essays on Husserl's Theory of Signs*, trans. David B. Allison (Evanston: Northwestern University Press, 1973), 140, 141.

38. To quote Bennington: "the fundamental thought" for Derrida

> is that everything, everything one might want to give an account of—everything we might be inclined to think of in ontological terms—has to be thought of in terms of the structure of the trace, where there are never anywhere any self-present elements at all. . . . [T]he trace is always trace of a trace. All that there "is" is trace structures where everything is what it is only in being fundamentally and originarily involved with what it is not.

Geoffrey Bennington and Alberto Moreiras, "On Scatter, the Trace Structure, and the Opening of Politics: An Interview with Geoffrey Bennington," *Diacritics* 45, no. 2 (2017): 40.

39. Fuoco B. Fann, *This Self We Deserve: A Quest After Modernity* (Berkeley: Philosophy and Art Collaboratory, 2020), 12, 34; italics in original.

40. Ernst Theodor Amadeus Hoffmann, "Beethoven's Instrumental Music," in *E. T. A. Hoffmann's Musical Writings: Kreisleriana, The Poet and the Composer, Music Criticism*, ed. David Charlton, trans. Martyn Clarke (Cambridge, UK: Cambridge University Press, 1989), 96. To quote Hoffmann's famous essay: "Music reveals to man an unknown realm, a world quite separate from the outer sensual

world surrounding him, a world in which he leaves behind all precise feelings in order to embrace an inexpressible longing" (237). And Schopenhauer:

> [Music] does not . . . express this or that particular and definite joy, this or that sorrow, or pain, or horror, or delight, or merriment, or peace of mind; but joy, sorrow, pain, horror, delight, merriment, peace of mind themselves, to a certain extent in the abstract, their essential nature, without accessories, and therefore without their motives. Yet we completely understand them in this extracted quintessence.

Arthur Schopenhauer, *The World as Will and Idea*, vol. I, trans. R. B. Haldane and J. Kemp (London: Kegan Paul, Trench, Trübner & Co., 1909), 338.

41. This is not to say that music was ever neatly separable from writing during Hoffmann or Schopenhauer's nineteenth century. Rather, the very idea of music's autonomy and its spiritual power was partly an affordance of written scores and print technology: Thomas Christensen has demonstrated, for instance, that four-hand piano transcriptions allowed musicians and critics, in the words of Austrian piano pedagogue Eugen Eisenstein, to "awake[n] the spirit and breath dormant in these forms"—that is, in transcriptions of Haydn or Beethoven playable by a pair of friends at a piano. "A meaningful, radiant performance" may bring this spirit to life, giving the listener a sense—maybe a fantasy—of the event that was to occur in the concert hall. Eugen Eisenstein, *Die Reinheit des Clavier Vortrages: Dem Idealismus in der Tonkunst* (1870), quoted in Thomas Christensen, "Four-Hand Piano Transcription and Geographies of Nineteenth-Century Musical Reception," *Journal of the American Musicological Society* 52, no. 2 (1999): 266. See also Adrian Daub, *Four-Handed Monsters: Four-Hand Piano Playing and Nineteenth-Century Culture* (New York: Oxford University Press, 2014). For Schopenhauer the Rossini-loving flautist, see Yael Braunschweig, "Schopenhauer and Rossinian Universality: On the Italianate in Schopenhauer's Metaphysics of Music," in *The Invention of Beethoven and Rossini: Historiography, Analysis, Criticism*, eds. Nicholas Mathew and Benjamin Walton (Cambridge, UK: Cambridge University Press, 2013), 283–304.

42. For Hoffmann and Schopenhauer's historiographical importance vis-à-vis the philosophy of romantic music, see Karol Berger, *A Theory of Art* (New York and Oxford: Oxford University Press, 2000), esp. 133–138.

43. I am indebted to Fuoco B. Fann's insights into the term and concept of ontology from comparative historical and philosophical perspectives. In personal correspondence as well as his writings, Fann has linked the ideas of many major thinkers—Michel Foucault, Derrida, and Lévinas among them—to contend that ontology, a central thread running through all western philosophy, has bolstered the privilege granted in western thought to phonetic language (as opposed to non-phonetic languages), and has also buttressed the modern knowing subject's anthropocentrism. See Fann, *This Self We Deserve*, esp. 12–17, 25–34, 49–50, 132–142, and below.

44. Emmanuel Lévinas, *Totality and Infinity: An Essay on Exteriority*, trans. Alphonso Lingis (The Hague, Boston, and London: Martinus Nijkoff, 1979 [original French 1961]), 43–44.

45. See Sylvia Wynter, "On How We Mistook the Map for the Territory, and Re-Imprisoned Ourselves in Our Unbearable Wrongness of Being, of *Désêtre*," in *Not Only the Master's Tools: African-American Studies in Theory and Practice*, eds. Lewis R. Gordon and Jane Anna Gordon (London and New York: Routledge, 2006), and "Unsettling the Coloniality of Being/Power/Truth/Freedom: Towards the Human, After Man, Its Overrepresentation—An Argument," *CR: The New Centennial Review* 3, no. 3 (Fall 2003); Tendayi Sithole, *The Black Register* (Cambridge, UK: Polity Press, 2020).

46. Lévinas, *Totality and Infinity*, 43–44.

47. Ning Zhang, "Interview with Jacques Derrida: The Western Question of 'Forgiveness' and the Intercultural Relation," *Comparative and Continental Philosophy* 12, no. 1 (2020): 14.

48. Things are, thankfully, changing: the ambiguous and ever-growing field of sound studies has finally begun to be "remapped," and the intellectual debt that Global North scholars of music and sound owe to the South is beginning to be recognized anew. See Gavin Steingo and Jim Sykes, *Remapping Sound Studies* (Durham: Duke University Press, 2019).

49. Zakiyyah Iman Jackson, "Outer Worlds: The Persistence of Race in Movement 'Beyond the Human,'" in José Esteban Muñoz, "Theorizing Queer Inhumanisms: The Sense of Brownness," *GLQ: A Journal of Lesbian and Gay Studies* 21, nos. 2–3 (June 2015): 215.

50. Geoffrey Bennington, *Interrupting Derrida* (London and New York: Routledge, 2000), 15; italics in original.

51. See Eitan Y. Wilf, *School for Cool: Academic Jazz and the Paradox of Institutionalized Creativity* (Chicago and London: University of Chicago Press, 2014).

52. According to Louis Menand, the Golden Age of American higher education (1945–1975) saw "the adoption of a self-consciously scientific model of research" as federal money poured into universities to fund scientific research during the Cold War era. "The idea that academics . . . could provide the state with neutral research results on which pragmatic public policies could be based was an animating idea in the 1950s university." The rise of the "research professor," who denied explicit political "ideology" so as not to offend his or her grantors, coincided with the inclusion of music composition in the university. Louis Menand, *The Marketplace of Ideas: Reform and Resistance in the American University* (New York and London: W. W. Norton, 2010), 73–75. In this context, Taruskin wrote, "it was successfully argued that technically advanced music composition could be regarded as a form of scientific research," which amounted to "giving up all pretense to the kind of subjectivity normally associated with the arts." Richard Taruskin, "*Et in Arcadia Ego*; Or, I Didn't Know I Was Such a Pessimist Until I Wrote This Thing," in *The*

Danger of Music and Other Anti-Utopian Essays (Berkeley: University of California Press, 2009), 8–9.

53. Cultural pluralism—an attitude of "Who Cares If You Listen?"—went hand in hand with a positivistic view of knowledge—hence "The Composer as Specialist" (the original title of Babbitt's infamous essay). Martin Brody, "'Music for the Masses': Milton Babbitt's Cold War Music Theory," *The Musical Quarterly* 77, no. 2 (Summer 1993): 162–164.

54. Jennifer Iverson, *Electronic Inspirations: Technologies of the Cold War Musical Avant-Garde* (New York: Oxford University Press, 2019), 23–48; Brian Kane, *Sound Unseen: Acousmatic Sound in Theory and Practice* (New York: Oxford University Press, 2014).

55. "Modernity is not a phenomenon of sensitivity to the fleeting present; it is the will to 'heroize' the present." Michel Foucault, "What Is Enlightenment?," in *The Foucault Reader*, ed. Paul Rabinow (New York: Vintage Books, 2010), 40. As in Benjamin Piekut's usage, I will use "avant-garde" in a conceptual register in this book, not to refer to specific movements (like Dadaism, surrealism, or the like) but rather to the "revolutionary ethos" that, in Matei Calinescu's words, characterizes the "sharp sense of militancy" and "heroic . . . struggle for futurity" that many twentieth-century artists shared. Benjamin Piekut, *Henry Cow: The World Is a Problem* (Durham and London: Duke University Press, 2019), 2; Matei Calinescu, *Five Faces of Modernity: Modernism, Avant-Garde, Decadence, Kitsch, Postmodernism* (Durham: Duke University Press, 1987), 95–97.

56. Fann, *This Self We Deserve*: for Derrida, see esp. 12–15, 77, and 132–142; for Foucault, see esp. 4–30, 68–70, 79–94, and 166–177; for Lyotard, see 64–70; for Lévinas, see 49–51; for Deleuze, see 97, 143–146, and 176–179; for Baudrillard, see esp. 99–102, 146–156, and 186–210. See also Michel Foucault, *The Order of Things: An Archaeology of the Human Sciences* (London and New York: Routledge, 2002 [original French 1966]); Jean-François Lyotard, *The Postmodern Condition: A Report on Knowledge*, trans. Geoff Bennington and Brian Massumi (Minneapolis: University of Minnesota Press, 1984 [original French, 1979]); Gilles Deleuze, *The Logic of Sense*, trans. Mark Lester (New York: Columbia University Press, 1990 [original French 1969]); Jean Baudrillard, *The Conspiracy of Art: Manifestos, Interviews, Essays*, trans. Ames Hodges (New York and Los Angeles: Semiotext(e), 2005).

57. Fann explicates Baudrillard's contention that "the modern nourishment we take in, the modern clothes that we wear, the modern car that we drive, and the modern images and messages that we receive do not define or justify our notion of consumption"; rather, in Baudrillard's words, "consumption is not a material practice, nor is it a phenomenology of 'affluence.'" "[C]onsumption is *the virtual totality of all objects and messages ready-constituted as a more or less coherent discourse. If it has any meaning at all, consumption means an activity consisting in the systematic manipulation of signs*" (italics in original). Consumption has

reversed into "post-consumption," the systematic manipulation of the signs of things to support the fictive, precarious sense of individual choice and freedom. Jean Baudrillard, *The System of Objects*, trans. James Benedict (London and New York: Verso, 2020 [original French, *Le système des objets*, 1968]) 218; see *This Self We Deserve*, 191.

58. Fann, *This Self We Deserve*, 27. And see from 86:

> This notoriously tricky inversion from "I" to "We" is one of the ramifications of modern knowledge. Modern thinking, Foucault argues, reduces "the whole being of things to thought" by "ramifying the being of thought right down to the inert network of what does not think." The fundamental ramification of thought is: we think, therefore we are. I no longer think but we think. Our thinking is based on modern knowledge. Knowledge is Power, Power is Truth, and Truth is Knowledge. It sounds like a riddle, nonetheless, an ontological riddle. Knowledge is linked with Power. Power is linked with Rationalization.

59. Fann, *This Self We Deserve*, 203; italics in original. "We are cool and no longer able to scream anymore," Fann writes, citing Jameson's well-known comparison between Van Gogh's colorful and meaning-laden *Pair of Boots*—which practically scream with the alienation of the world of the peasant worker who wears them—and Andy Warhol's *Diamond Dust Shoes*, "a random collection of dead objects" (205), superficial, shimmering yet meaningless. In the context of Fann's French-inflected inquiry, Warhol's shoes appear as simulacra in Baudrillard's sense: they are not quite "copies" of an original collection of shoes, but rather a one-dimensional X-ray-colored reproduction that ducks the question of "the original." In Jameson's reading, it is useless to try and find in Warhol's shoes a depthful expression of the world of the consumer who wears them; the shoes offer nothing of the poetic amelioration that Van Gogh sought through vibrant brushwork. But it is precisely in their shallowness that Warhol's shoes speak volumes about the contemporary. Whereas for Deleuze our rebirth into simulation offers a positive alternative to the history of western aesthetics, for Baudrillard simulacra and simulation indicate an ever-more profound stuck-ness, namely a far-reaching *banalization*. With Duchamp's readymades as with pop art à la Warhol or Jeff Koons, in Baudrillard's words, "all the banality of the world passes into aesthetics, and inversely, all aesthetics becomes banal: a commutation takes place between the two fields of banality and aesthetics, one that truly brings aesthetics in the traditional sense to an end." Baudrillard, *The Conspiracy of Art*, 92. Fann writes:

> We are stuck in the current knowledge, and we are stuck with fetish objects and dead objects. We are affectless after all. Modernism is waning like a daydream. The modern and the postmodern remain utterly distinct in their meaning with respect to the social function, the economic system, and the

sphere of culture in the contemporary world. While the modern is a nostalgic dream haunting us like a specter, the postmodern with its "plagues" is before our own eyes.

Fann, *This Self We Deserve*, 205.

60. Perry Anderson, *The Origins of Postmodernity* (London and New York: Verso, 1998); Fredric Jameson, *Postmodernism; or, The Cultural Logic of Late Capitalism* (Durham: Duke University Press, 1991).

61. Lyotard, *The Postmodern Condition*, 79.

62. Foucault, "What Is Enlightenment?"

63. A "contemporary" artist, according to Paul Rabinow, is fully conscious of the afterlives of modernism, taking up modernist forms and attitudes at a second order level of engagement; Paul Rabinow, *Marking Time: On the Anthropology of the Contemporary* (Princeton and Oxford: Princeton University Press, 2008). For Amir Eschel, this historical distance grants both contemporary artists and their audiences the ability to reflect upon, to better understand, and to productively work through certain traumas and forms of estrangement particular to the era after the Holocaust. "Poetic thinking," in the contemporary, is a means of personal autonomy; Amir Eschel, *Poetic Thinking Today: An Essay* (Stanford: Stanford University Press, 2020). Sianne Ngai, meanwhile, has argued that "our" contemporary time, far from the avant-garde battle cries of the past, has committed itself to a range of banal "aesthetic categories"—the cute, zany, and interesting—hence "our" aesthetic experience today is primarily shaped by the low-level amusements generated by "cute" advertising and commodity culture, "zany" slapstick comedy and the bustling bodies of corporate life, or the "interesting" information put forward on the internet, in news, in contemporary art criticism, in academic books, etc. Personal autonomy is, at best, a dull thrill; Sianne Ngai, *Our Aesthetic Categories: Zany, Cute, Interesting* (Cambridge, MA, and London: Harvard University Press, 2012).

64 Gumbrecht, "Presence Achieved in Language," 318.

65. Gumbrecht, *Production of Presence*, 54.

66. Derrida, *Of Grammatology*, 14.

67. Derrida stated during the China seminar:

Deconstruction or *déconstruction* existed already in the French dictionary, although it was not in common use before I used it. In the French dictionary, it means the way of analyzing and decomposing machinery or structural grammar. It has a technical or grammatical sense. It means de-constituting, decomposing complex linguistic or technical machinery. Now, when I used this word, I was trying to translate or transform in my own way a German word, *Destruktion*, used by Heidegger to refer to precisely the way of analyzing and de-constituting the history of ontology, of classical (and what we call vulgar) ontology, which is the main stream of

Western philosophy. Neither *Destruktion* nor deconstruction means destruction. There is no connotation of destruction within this word. It is a way to undo the structure through memory or genealogical procedures; there is nothing negative in this.

Quoted in Zhang, "Jacques Derrida's First Visit to China," 153.

68. Bennington, *Interrupting Derrida*, 9, 11.

69. Adriana Cavarero, *For More Than One Voice* (Stanford: Stanford University Press, 2005).

70. In *Jazz as Critique: Adorno and Black Expression Revisited*, Okiji focuses on collective sound-making to ethically remediate Adorno's ideas about popular music, positioning jazz as a "gathering in difference," meanwhile Pettman's *Sonic Intimacy: Voice, Species, Technics* began with the vibrations inside the mother's womb and ended with a plea for us to listen to "the voice of the earth," an imagined post-human voice that warns of ecological crisis. Fumi Okiji, *Jazz as Critique: Adorno and Black Expression Revisited* (Stanford: Stanford University Press, 2018); Dominic Pettman, *Sonic Intimacy: Voice, Species, Technics (or, How to Listen to the World)* (Stanford: Stanford University Press, 2017).

71. James Clifford, "On Ethnographic Surrealism," *Comparative Studies in Society and History* 23, no. 4 (1981): 550.

72. Clifford, "On Ethnographic Surrealism," 546.

73. Lydia H. Liu, "iSpace: Printed English After Joyce, Shannon, and Derrida," *Critical Inquiry* 32, no. 3 (2006): 520.

74. Mary Ann Smart, "Michel Leiris and the Secret Language of Song," *Representations* 154, no. 1 (2021): 95.

75 Lawrence Kramer, *Music as Cultural Practice: 1800–1900* (Berkeley: University of California Press, 1990), 212–213, and see especially 178–215; for a (lengthy) synopsis of Derridean terms culminating in a deconstructive reading of Chopin's Prelude in A minor, see Rose Rosengard Subotnik, *Deconstructive Variations: Music and Reason in Western Society* (London and Minneapolis: University of Minnesota Press, 1996), 39–147; for deconstruction and Mahler, see Martin Scherzinger, "The Finale of Mahler's Seventh Symphony: A Deconstructive Reading," *Music Analysis* 14, no. 1 (1995): 69–88; and for general reflections on music and deconstruction during the 1990s, compare Martin Scherzinger, "Music in the Thought of Deconstruction / Deconstruction in the Thought of Music," *Musicological Annual* 41, no. 2 (2005): 81–104, and Christopher Norris, "Music Theory, Analysis and Deconstruction: How They Might (Just) Get Along Together," *IRASM* 36, no. 1 (2005): 37–82.

76 See Abbate, "Music—Drastic or Gnostic?," 531, 532.

77. Rings defines this deictic power as the "attention-directing (or 'pointing') character" of language about music, noting that Vladimir Jankélévitch's descriptions of the music of Ravel or of Fauré, for instance, may sway a reader's apprehension of

this music. Philosophical writing is not simply descriptive; it is also transformative. Steven Rings, "Talking and Listening with Jankélévitch," in Michael Gallope and Brian Kane, "Colloquy: Vladimir Jankélévitch's Philosophy of Music," *Journal of the American Musicological Society* 65, no. 1 (Spring 2012): 218–223.

78. Fann demonstrates that Foucault's 1963 essay "Language to Infinity" anticipated Derrida's own critique of the metaphysical privilege granted in western thought to phonetic writing in *Grammatology*. Since, as Foucault wrote, "writing, in Western culture, automatically dictates that we place ourselves in the virtual space of self-representation and reduplication" "since writing refers not to a thing but to speech," phonetic writing had been thought to carry "an ontological status" unknown in cultures that use non-phonetic written systems (like China). In a similar way, the fact that a phonetic text is a "double" of speech, representing things through the medium of speech, meant, in Derrida's view, that "alphabetic writing is 'representing a representer, supplement of a supplement,' which indeed 'increases the *power* of representation.'" Observing this similarity in Foucault and Derrida's thought regarding phonetic language, Fann writes: "while Derrida and Foucault argued over [other] issues, they had one thing in common: the question of phonetic language, specifically, the privilege granted [in western thought] to phonetic language." Fann, *This Self We Deserve*, 37, 133, and 140; italics in original.

79. Jacques Derrida, "White Mythology: Metaphor in the Text of Philosophy," in *Margins of Philosophy*, trans. Alan Bass (Chicago and London: University of Chicago Press, 1982 [originally 1971]). Citations will be in parentheses throughout the next section.

80. Salmon, *An Event, Perhaps*, 4.

81. Michael Naas writes: "Derrida argues in 'White Mythology' that the text of philosophy, of metaphysics, is full of metaphors and that philosophy can never escape figurative language. Metaphor itself can thus never be understood completely from within philosophy since metaphors will always have been used to explain metaphor." Michael Naas, *Taking on the Tradition: Jacques Derrida and the Legacies of Deconstruction* (Stanford: Stanford University Press, 2003), 41

82. Naas has suggested that Derrida's analysis of metaphor centers on the dual figures of sun and earth, the two principal metaphors at work in western philosophy.

> Metaphysics, . . . according to Derrida, has conceived of metaphor in terms of either the sun, presence and light, or the ground, in terms of *either* "dialectical idealism . . . the *relève (Aufhebung)*" . . . *or* foundationalism, "the desire for a firm and ultimate ground, a terrain to build on, the earth as the support of an artificial structure."

Naas, *Taking on the Tradition*, 43; italics in original.

83. "An Interview with Jacques Derrida on the Limits of Digestion," *e-flux Journal* 2 (January 2009).

84. See also Elizabeth Rottenberg, "Devouring Figures: The Last Seminars of Jacques Derrida," *Philosophy Today* 55 (2011): 177–182. Rottenberg describes Derrida's use of *Little Red Riding Hood* as an allegory for the tendency of phonetic language to swallow or "maw" the other. "But what goes via interiorizing devourment, i.e. via orality, via the mouth, the maw, teeth, throat, glottis, and tongue—which are also the sites of cry and speech, of language—that very things can also inhabit that other site of the visage or the face, i.e., the ears, . . . the visible and therefore audiovisual forms of what allows one not only to speak but also to hear and listen" (Derrida, quoted on 179). Here Derrida links the act of consumption, of swallowing and incorporating the other into the same, to the mouth, hence to the voice. Thus the act of incorporation is not just the figurative devouring of Riding Hood by the animal's "maw"—the wolf devours the grandmother and thus becomes the Grand-maw—but is also sonic, since while it is the voice that ultimately speaks, the ear hears.

85. G. W. F. Hegel, *The Philosophy of History*, 148, 149, 153, and 157; quoted in Fann, *This Self We Deserve*, 53–54.

86. Fann, *This Self We Deserve*, 54.

87. Hegel, *The Philosophy of History*, 299; quoted in Fann, *This Self We Deserve*, 57.

88. Fann, *This Self We Deserve*, 57.

89. Sithole, *The Black Register*, 30.

90. Sithole, *The Black Register*, 234.

91. Wynter, "On How We Mistook the Map for the Territory," 119.

92. Wynter, "Unsettling the Coloniality of Being/Power/Truth/Freedom," 264.

93. "The hand of blackness has no magic wand, but the pen whose ink is the liquid (sweat, blood, and tears) that drips from the injured and suffering body." Sithole, *The Black Register*, 2, 4, 5, and 12.

94. Wynter, "On How We Mistook the Map for the Territory," 118.

95. Zakiyyah Iman Jackson, *Becoming Human: Matter and Meaning in an Antiblack World* (New York: New York University Press, 2020).

96. Wynter, "On How We Mistook the Map for the Territory," 119.

97 The imperative to "unlearn and relearn what we know" is the guiding light for Fann's own *Quest After Modernity,* including his insightfully lucid assembly of Derrida, Lévinas, Michel de Certeau, Baudrillard, and Robert Young around the notion of ontology as a fundamentally western ethnocentric *logos* of being. See *This Self We Deserve*, sections on Hegel, history, and "ontological imperialism": 48–59; for unlearning and relearning, see "A Note to the Reader" (vii–viii) and the lecture titled "Know Thyself" (157–211).

98. To recall some of Derrida's words, "My death is structurally necessary for the pronouncing of the *I*." Peggy Kamuf explicates this citation from Derrida's *La Voix et le phénomène*: "if the 'I' must be able to function with the same meaning in my absence, then that absence—my death—is structurally inscribed in the

possibility of its repetition, the ideality of its meaning." Derrida uncovers "the essential relation to 'my own death' inscribed in the very possibility of discourse. 'I,' like any other sign [i.e., *now*; *presence*], can have meaning only if it 'remains *the same* for an I-here-now in general.'" Peggy Kamuf, *Book of Addresses* (Stanford: Stanford University Press, 2005), 54.

99. The phrase "fieldwork in philosophy," and the idea of bridging empirical observation with "concept work," or the creation of philosophical concepts apropos to what is observed, is owed to Paul Rabinow. See Paul Rabinow, *The Privilege of Neglect: Science as a Vocation Revisited* (Berkeley: Anthropology of the Contemporary Research Collaboratory, 2020), 41–44.

100. These included Abbate's recollection of watching Ben Heppner as he cracked his high G's during a performance of *Der Meistersinger*, or suddenly seeing Wagner's chorus as if they had emerged from a Holocaust documentary.

101 This perspective is informed by Paul Rabinow and Anthony Stavrianakis's discussion of what Foucault termed *foyers d'experience*, or crucibles of experience and experimentation. See Paul Rabinow and Anthony Stavrianakis, *Inquiry After Modernism* (Berkeley: Anthropology of the Contemporary Research Collaboratory, 2019), 5–21; and Rabinow, *The Privilege of Neglect*, 2–22.

Chapter One

1. Caroline Potter explains: "The title is an invented word which has connotations of naked Greek boys doing exercise." Caroline Potter, *Erik Satie: A Parisian Composer and His World* (Woodbridge: Boydell Press, 2016), 6.

2. Henri Bergson, *Time and Free Will: An Essay on the Immediate Data of Consciousness*, trans. F. L. Pogson (Mineola: Dover Publications, 2001 [republication of original 1913 English translation, London: George Allen]), 105.

3. Bergson, *Time and Free Will*, 14–15; bracketed French terms are from Henri Bergson, *Œuvres* (Paris: Presses Universitaires de France, 1963), see 13–14 for this passage.

4. Jessie Fillerup, *Magician of Sound: Ravel and the Aesthetics of Illusion* (Berkeley: University of California Press, 2021), 9–10 and 50–92. Fillerup describes various Ravelian strategies for creating musical illusion, including perpetual ascent: "the impression that the music follows a steady upward curve that seems to culminate in a sonic apex" (76); transformative ascent—moments of character transformation often accompanied by a harp to "mark inward or outward metamorphosis" (225); the illusion of mechanization or of mechanical motion (111–116); and, finally, of motion or stasis.

5. For Pythagoras and the monochord, see Flora R. Levin, *Greek Reflections on the Nature of Music* (New York: Cambridge University Press, 2009), 6–16; for Schopenhauer, see the Prelude; for Derrida, see "Differance," in *Speech and Phenomena and Other Essays on Husserl's Theory of Signs*, trans. David B. Allison (Evanston: Northwestern University Press, 1973), 138–142. Derrida described *dif-*

férance as "the movement that makes signification possible," referring to the Saussurian premise that a language is constituted by differences and that linguistic signifiers—which are in themselves arbitrary—are only intelligible according to their relations within a system of differences. Seeking the conditions of possibility for this linguistic sense of difference, Derrida stated that *différance* is "the movement of play that 'produces' . . . these differences." Attending to this movement allowed him to observe that signifiers and signifieds are never contemporary and their interplay delays and defers the "full presence" of any particular referent. This sense of *différance* as the perpetual deferral of presence, a game of "temporalizing," is reminiscent, I suggest, of musical temporality, since "each element that is said to be 'present' . . . is related to something other than itself but retains the mark of a past element and already lets itself be hollowed out by the mark of its relation to a future element."

6. By the same token, as Gumbrecht suggested, Schopenhauer's affirmation that music presents a copy (*Abbild*) of the will itself is best understood if we understand *Abbild* to connote not a "copy" in the literal sense, but an alternate modality of the will's reality (see the Prelude).

7. Oscar Wilde, *Intentions* (London: Unicorn Press, 1945 [original 1891]), 47; Friedrich Nietzsche, *The Birth of Tragedy and The Case of Wagner*, trans. Robert Kaufmann (New York: Vintage Books, 1967); Jean Baudrillard, *The Conspiracy of Art*, ed. Sylvère Lotringer, trans. Ames Hodges (New York and Los Angeles: Semiotex(e), 2005), 112–113; and *The Perfect Crime*, trans. Chris Turner (London and New York: Verso, 2008), 9, 17; see also Fuoco B. Fann, *This Self We Deserve: A Quest After Modernity* (Berkeley: Philosophy and Art Collaboratory, 2020), 152–156, and Fillerup, *Magician of Sound*, 20.

8. Fann, *This Self We Deserve*, 153. In this passage, Fann quotes Baudrillard's *Passwords*, trans. Chris Turner (London and New York: Verso, 2003), 66.

9. Alexis Roland-Manuel, *Erik Satie: Causerie faite à la Société Lyre et Palette* (Paris: Roberge, 1916); Ann-Marie Hanlon, "Erik Satie and the Meaning of the Comic," in *Erik Satie: Music, Art and Literature*, ed. Caroline Potter (Farnham: Ashgate, 2013), 19–48; see also Potter, *Erik Satie: A Parisian Composer and His World*, 43.

10. Erik Satie, "A Musician's Day," in *A Mammal's Notebook: The Writings of Erik Satie*, ed. Ornella Volta, trans. Anthony Melville (London: Atlas Press, 2017), 112.

11. Caroline Potter, personal correspondence.

12. Matei Calinescu, *Five Faces of Modernity: Modernism, Avant-Garde, Decadence, Kitsch, Postmodernism* (Durham: Duke University Press, 1987), 5; quoted and explicated in Fann, *This Self We Deserve*, 116–117.

13. Christoph Cox, *Sonic Flux: Sound, Art, and Metaphysics* (Chicago and London: University of Chicago Press, 2018).

14. For Satie the minimalist, see Edward Strickland, *Minimalism: Origins*

(Bloomington and Indianapolis: Indiana University Press, 1993), 124–134; for Satie the proto-surrealist, see Daniel Albright, *Untwisting the Serpent: Modernism in Music, Literature, and Other Arts* (Chicago and London: University of Chicago Press, 2000), esp. 185–197; for Cage's Satie, see John Cage, "Defense of Satie," in *John Cage: An Anthology*, ed. Richard Kostelanetz (New York: Da Capo Press, 1970), 77–84, and Alan M. Gillmor, *Erik Satie* (New York and London: W. W. Norton, 1988), 36; for Satie and the everyday, see Nancy Perloff, *Art and the Everyday: Popular Entertainment and the Circle of Erik Satie* (Oxford: Clarendon Press, 1991) and Steven Moore Whiting, *Satie the Bohemian: From Cabaret to Concert Hall* (New York: Oxford University Press, 1999).

15. Satie, quoted in Potter, *Erik Satie: A Parisian Composer*, 145.

16. Examples of this phenomenon, for Fillerup, include the relentless left-hand ostinato in the first movement of Poulenc's *Trois mouvements perpétuels* (1918) or the music-box-like repetitive motives that Stravinsky used to depict the hustle and bustle of the Strovetide Fair in *Petroushka* (1911). There is a curious interplay between repetitive motives or ostinati that basically stay the same through many repetitions and the feeling of change. Fillerup, *Magician of Sound*, 44–48.

17. Bergson, *Time and Free Will*, 100.

18. Bergson, *Time and Free Will*, 100; italics in original.

19. Henri Bergson, *Matter and Memory*, trans. Nancy Margaret Paul and W. Scott Palmer (New York: Zone Books, 1991), 94.

20. Henri Bergson, *Duration and Simultaneity with Reference to Einstein's Theory*, trans. Leon Jacobson (Indianapolis, New York, and Kansas City: Bobbs-Merrill Company, 1965), 52; emphasis added.

21. Keith Salley, "On Duration and Developing Variation: The Intersecting Ideologies of Henri Bergson and Arnold Schoenberg," *MTO: A Journal of the Society for Music Theory*, 21, no. 4 (2015). For Kent Cleland, meanwhile, Bergson's emphasis on the indeterminateness of time and the interpenetration of past moments paved the way for Cage and his circle to compose indeterminate works. Kent Cleland, "The Temporalist Harp: Henri Bergson and Twentieth-Century Musical Innovation," *The European Legacy*, 16, no. 7 (2011): 953–967.

22. Arved Mark Ashby, *Absolute Music, Mechanical Reproduction* (Berkeley: University of California Press, 2010), 74.

23. Steven Rings, "Talking and Listening with Jankélévitch," in Michael Gallope and Brian Kane, "Colloquy: Vladimir Jankélévitch's Philosophy of Music," *Journal of the American Musicological Society* 65, no. 1 (Spring 2012): 218–223.

24. Patrick Gowers dates Satie's "Rosicrucian phase" to a roughly four-year span from 1891–95, but, as we will see, the seeds were planted several years earlier. Patrick Gowers, "Satie's Rose Croix Music (1891–1895)," *Proceedings of the Royal Musical Association*, 92nd session (1965–1966): 1–25.

25. Erik Satie, from *The Chat Noir Journal*, 9 February 1889, quoted in Whiting, *Satie the Bohemian*, 77.

26. Fillerup describes the illusion of transformation in *Les Entretiens de la Belle et de la Bête*, a movement of Ravel's ballet *Ma mère l'Oye* (1912) in which the Beast's transformation into a Prince occurs as two themes—the high-register Beauty theme and the growling contrabassoon Beast theme—play around each other until a harp glissando marks an abrupt transition. A cello reiterates the Beast theme in a higher register and with a more refined manner, signaling that the Beast has changed form. Fillerup, *Magician of Sound*, 51–53.

27. Whiting, *Satie the Bohemian*, 132–133.

28. Joséphin Péladan, *Le Vice suprême* (Paris: Librairie des Auteurs Modernes, 1884), 1–2:

Elle est seule.

Plein d'ombre alanguie et de silence berceur, clos à la lumière, clos au bruit, le boudoir circulaire a le recueillement rêveur, la somnolence douce, d'une chapelle italienne, aux heures de sieste; *buen retiro*, semblable à l'étage d'une tour ronde, sans baie ses murs elliptiques, ou cloutée d'argent aux plis, la pourpre héraldique étale, en un satin violet plein de rouge, son deuil royal et sa magnificence triste. . . .

Sur ses formes Parmesanes, le peignoir de soie violette a des froissements pareils à des moues de lèvres, à des caresses timides et effleureuses. Un bras que la retombée de la manche dénude, encouronne sa tête aux cheveux roux et lourds, l'autre pend avec des flexibilités de lianes, des souplesses de lierre et le dos des doigts pointus touche le peluche rase du tapis.

Par un bayement de l'étoffe la gorge apparaît, filigranée de l'azur des veines qui transparaissent. Les seins très séparés et placés haut sont aigus, les mules tombées, les pieds nus ont cet écartement de l'orteil que le bandelette du cothurne fait aux statues: et le sortir du bain amollit de matité douillette tout cet éphébisme à la Primatice. On dirait l'Anadyomène de ces primitifs qui, d'un pinceau encore mystique, s'essayent au paganisme renaissant, un Botticelli où la sainte déshabillée en nymphe, garde de la gaucherie dans la perversité d'une plastique de stupre : une vierge folle de Dürer, née sous le ciel italien, et élégantisée par un mélange de cette maigreur florentine où il n'y a pas d'os, et de cette lombarde où il n'y a pas de graisse.

La paupière mi-close sur une vision entrevue, le regard perdu dans les horizons du rêve, la narine caressée par des senteurs subtiles, la bouche entr'ouverte comme pour un baiser,—elle songe. . . .

Elle ne songe à rien, ni à personne, ni à elle-même.

Cette absence de toute pensée énamoure ses yeux, et entr'ouverte ses lèvres minces d'un sourire heureux.

Elle est toute à la volupté de cette heure d'instinctivité pure, où la pensée, ce balancier inquiet et toujours en mouvement de la vie, s'arrête ; où la per-

ception du temps qui s'écoule, cesse, tandis que le corps seul vivant s'épa-
nouit dans un indicible bien-être des membres. Ses nerfs au repose, elle ne
perçoit que la sensation de sa chair fraîche, souple, dispose ; elle jouit de
la félicité des bêtes, de ces vaches de Potter, accroupies dans l'herbe haute,
repues et qui reflètent une paix paradisiaque dans leurs gros yeux clignés.

29. Joséphin Péladan, *How to Become a Mage: A Fin-de-Siècle French Occult
Manifesto*, trans. K. K. Albert (Woodbury: Llewellyn Publications, 2019 [original
1892]), 18.

30. Péladan, *Le Vice suprême*, 327.

31. Péladan, *Le Vice suprême*, 327: "L'auto da-fé, même criminel, prouve la
foi des bourreaux, et la foi des victimes; et la foi est le levier qui fait l'œuvre de
Dieu. . . . La passion est une roue qui tourne, à senestre dans le mal; imbécilité de
l'arrêter. Il faut la faire tourner à dans le bien. C'est la roue du Tarot, c'est le cœur
de l'homme."

32. Robert Pincus-Witten, *Occult Symbolism in France: Joséphin Peladan and
the Salons de la Rose-Croix* (New York and London: Garland Publishing, 1976),
see esp. 217–223.

33. "Péladan idolized Wagner," wrote Gillmor, "as a philosopher of the new art.
He is known to have attended performances of *Parsifal* in Bayreuth . . . and, like so
many of his generation, he responded deeply to the lofty idealism of the German
master's 'sacred festival drama,' with its . . . overriding 'Christian' message." Gillmor, *Erik Satie*, 74.

34. Whiting, *Satie the Bohemian*, 150–151; Pierre-Daniel Templier, *Erik Satie*,
trans. Elena L. French and David S. French (Cambridge, MA: MIT Press, 1969),
13–14.

35. Erik Satie, "Epistle the First of Erik Satie to Catholic Artists and to All
Christians," in *A Mammal's Notebook: The Writings of Erik Satie*, ed. Ornella
Volta, trans. Antony Melville (London: Atlas Press, 2014), 103.

36. Erik Satie, "To the Editor of the Parisian Newspaper 'Gil Blas,'" in *The Writings of Erik Satie*, ed. Nigel Wilkins (London: Eulenburg Books, 1980), 150.

37. Satie, "To the Editor of the Parisian Newspaper 'Gil Blas.'"

38. Erik Satie, *Écrits* (Paris: Éditions champs libre, 1981), 114:

Il me revient que l'on ose murmurer contre Ceux qui ont le soin de la défense
de l'Art et de la Foi Catholiques. C'est une démence. Les insensés qui pous-
sent la révolte jusqu'à ce point d'aberration sont les impies, les hérétiques,
les apostats, les déicides, les affilés de l'odieuse secte maçonnique, les mer-
cenaires de l'Art, les écrivaines prévaricateurs. Qu'ils se taisent, ceux qui
vivent de l'humaine corruption; ils n'ont point le droit de parler à la face
de leurs juges. Parce que le monde se laisse volontiers guider par le Mal,
ils se sont faits les propugnateurs de l'abomination. Ils ont chassé Dieu du
foyer, jeté le trouble parmi les simples, souillé l'âme splendide de l'Enfance,

détruit les saintes institutions des siècles de grandeur. Ils ont fait de l'Art la source des plus coupables plaisirs.

Le temps de leur domination est fini. Il faut qu'ils connaissent la confusion et le châtiment suprêmes. Le monde chrétien abjure la faiblesse, les complaisances funestes et le respect humain. Dieu a voulu que Nous fussions éprouvés dans l'affliction, afin de fortifier Nos âmes pour le combat d'où doit sortir la Régénération de la société occidentale. Nous levons pour cette œuvre.

Some phrases taken from Nigel Wilkins's translation: see *The Writings of Erik Satie*, 46.

39. Whiting accounts that Satie, by this time, had created his own church, the Église Métropolitaine d'Art, an obvious spin-off from Péladan's Church of the Rose-Croix: "[a]t the very moment when Péladan, in his *Bulletin mensuelle*, publicly repented of his past extravagance and promised greater sobriety of expression in the future, Satie adopted [Péladan's] positions nearly wholesale and inflated them to the point of absurdity." Whiting, *Satie the Bohemian*, 163.

40. Roger Shattuck affirmed that the strange interplay of transcendence and banality, religiosity and boredom, forms the bedrock of Satie's avant-gardism:

Satie challenges us not to be impressed but to be bored. He says in effect: Here are the naked features of our world. If they provoke you or bore, you will have reacted constructively, for either way you will be forced to move. This is the meaning of a staggering sentence contained in one of his late notebooks, a sentence that describes his entire being: "Experience is one of the forms of paralysis." The child, like the true Bohemian, has not yet defined his life by excluding alternate ways of behaving. The "lessons" of experience can begin to cripple our freedom. There remains one form of paralysis which is even more devastating. In Satie's world the supreme heresy would have been the honeyed advertising slogan "They satisfy." If experience is a form of paralysis, satisfaction is a form of death. In his hands music never became an exercise in self-contentment. It was a means of upholding our freedom.

Roger Shattuck, *The Banquet Years: The Origins of the Avant-Garde in France; 1885 to World War I* (New York: Vintage Books, 1968 [originally 1955]), 185.

41. Gillmor, *Erik Satie*, 90–91:

There is extant a strange document in the composer's ornate calligraphy which outlines the "program" of the new church. . . . He had in mind a figure of 1,600,000,000 [people] for his black-robed and gray-hooded "Peneants noirs convers," while the "Peneants noirs profès," robed in black and white, would number 8,000,000, the "Peneants gris," a mere 40,000, the "Peneants blancs," 200, the "Cloistriers," 50, and the "Définiteurs," 10 . . . with Satie himself in the triple role of founder, high priest, and sole adherent of the sect.

See Roger Shattuck, *The Banquet Years: The Origins of the Avant-Garde in France; 1885 to World War I* (New York: Vintage Books, 1968 [original 1955]), 113–144.

42. R. C. Grogin, *The Bergsonian Controversy in France 1900–1914* (Calgary: University of Calgary Press, 1988), 123–124; Mark Antliff, *Inventing Bergson: Cultural Politics and the Parisian Avant-Garde* (Princeton: Princeton University Press, 1993), 4–5; for Russell's critique of Bergson, see Antliff, *Inventing Bergson*, and Suzanne Guerlac, *Thinking in Time: An Introduction to Henri Bergson* (Ithaca and London: Cornell University Press, 2006), 13.

43. Paul Gauguin, letter to Vincent van Gogh. Paris, on or about Friday, 13 June 1890. "Vincent van Gogh: The Letters," *Van Gogh Museum*, accessed 25 February 2021: http://vangoghletters.org/vg/letters/let884/letter.html

44. Bergson, *Matter and Memory*, 134.

45. Bergson, *Matter and Memory*, 134.

46. Gilles Deleuze, *Bergsonism*, trans. Hugh Tomlinson and Barbara Habberjam (New York: Zone Books, 1991), 51–72. For a helpful musicological take on Bergson's memory cone, see Daniel M. Grimley's description of Frederick Delius's 1911 *Song of the High Hills*. A rhapsody, idyll, and hill song follow one after another, and in each subsequent repetition of each section, Delius introduces variations and rhythmic elaborations on prior motives. Each section of Delius's piece, Grimley asserts, functions like a new layer of the cone: every variation coexists (virtually) with its theme. Daniel M. Grimley, "Music, Landscape, and the Sound of Place: On Hearing Delius's *Song of the High Hills*," *Journal of Musicology* 33, no. 1 (2016): 40.

47. Deleuze, *Bergsonism*, 55, 56–57.

48. Fae Brauer, "Capturing Unconsciousness: The New Psychology, Hypnosis, and the Culture of Hysteria," in *A Companion to Nineteenth-Century Art,* ed. Michelle Farcos (New Jersey: John Wiley, 2019); Hubert L. Dreyfus and Paul Rabinow, *Michel Foucault: Beyond Structuralism and Hermeneutics*, 2nd. ed. (Chicago: University of Chicago Press, 1983), 121–122; Georges Didi-Huberman, *Invention of Hysteria: Charcot and the Photographic Iconography of the Salpêtrière* (Cambridge, MA: MIT Press, 2003).

49. In her study of various images of Charcot's lethargic and hysterical patients—all women—pictured next to tuning forks, Carmel Raz suggests that the experiments at the Salpêtrière indicated "that specific kinds of sounds had privileged access to the nerves, a motif that haunts the long nineteenth century and continues to resonate into the present day." The vibrations of tuning forks could, in frighteningly "drastic" fashion, ban the mediation of words and affect the body immediately. Carmel Raz, "Of Sound Minds and Tuning Forks: Charcot's Acoustic Experiments at the Salpêtrière," *AMS Musicology Now*, 23 October 2015: https://musicologynow.org/of-sound-minds-and-tuning-forks-charcots-acoustic-experiments-at-the-salpetriere/

50. Albert de Rochas, *Les Sentiments: La Musique et le geste* (Grenoble: Librairie Dauphinoise, 1900), 158.

51. Rochas, *Les Sentiments*, 158:

Nous en avions pour garants non seulement le témoignage de Lina qui, à l'état de veille, déclarait ne les avoir jamais exécutées ni vu exécuter, mais ce fait qu'il était matériellement impossible qu'elle les connût; telle une danse polonaise provincial ancienne qu'elle a retrouvée sans hésitation, avec tout ses gestes caractéristiques . . . ; telle aussi la danse javanaise dont la musique venait d'être écrite pour le première fois par M. Saraz et où les mouvements si particuliers des mains ont été reproduits avec une netteté extraordinaire.

52. "In one experiment with Lina," composer Joscelyne Godwin writes in his study of French *Music and the Occult*,

Rochas used one of [Charles] Henry's inventions, the *polyphone*. This was a music-box that translated rhythms into mild electric shocks. Lina, connected to it, thought that she was hearing the music itself, and reacted to the pieces exactly as if they had been played out loud. Rochas' conclusion was that music can be perceived without ears, which seemed to him to put the existence of the astral body beyond a shadow of a doubt.

Joscelyn Godwin, *Music and the Occult: French Musical Philosophies, 1750–1950* (Rochester: University of Rochester Press, 1995), 159; italics in original.

53. Connecting Rochas's photos of Lina's dances, Charcot's iconography, and late-nineteenth-century theatrical realism, Mary Ann Smart clarifies:

it is precisely this voyeuristic intrusion into the intimate space of the female subjects that makes the representations so titillating. Not only is the female form displayed for observers, but we are given the impression of having full access to her interior self: the splayed poses of the visible body, whether of an actress or hysterical patient, are taken as convincing representations of the character within.

The female medium, rid of conscious mechanisms of control and rendered into what historian Renée Altergott trenchantly called a soluble medium, seemed suddenly to bare all before the observer's gaze. Mary Ann Smart, *Mimomania: Music and Gesture in Nineteenth-Century Opera* (Berkeley: University of California Press, 2004), 20; Renée Altergott, "Towards Automatism: Ethnomusicology, Surrealism, and the Question of Technology," conference paper delivered at the Institute of Modern Languages Research, London, England (Surrealism and Music in France, 1924–1952), 8 June 2018.

54 Bergson, *Time and Free Will*, 13; emphasis added.

55. Henri Bergson, "De la simulation inconsciente dans l'état d'hypnotisme," *Revue Philosophique de la France et de l'Étranger*, 22 (1886): 525:

Dès la première séance, nous réussîmes à les hypnotiser en les regardant à l'improviste de très près, et en maintenant fixés ours eux, pendant sept à huit secondes, nos yeux grands ouverts; aujourd'hui, il nous suffit de poser brusquement une main sur leur tête et d'attirer ainsi leur regard sur le nôtre pour les plonger instantanément dans cet état de stupeur qui caractérise l'hypnotisme le mieux prononcé: les yeux restent démesurément ouverts et fixes, la physionomie perd toute expression intelligente; enfin, Ton observe tous les phénomènes cataleptiques habituels: insensibilité générale, obstination à conserver indéfiniment les attitudes suggérées par le magnétiseuse.

56. Todd Cronan, *Against Affective Formalism: Matisse, Bergson, Modernism* (Minneapolis: University of Minnesota Press, 2013), 93; italics in original.

57. Bergson, *Time and Free Will*, 44.

58. Bergson, *Matter and Memory*, 184; italics in original.

59. Guerlac, "Duration."

60. Bergson, *Matter and Memory*, 184; italics in original.

61. Deleuze, *Bergsonism*, 20; italics in original.

62. Jacques Barzun put it most concisely:

Hume's demonstration was the logical end of Empiricism—the mind shaped by things "out there." Kant posited a mind that acts like a waffle iron on batter. The difference explains the name Idealism: the philosopher, instead of going from thing to idea, goes from idea to thing.

Jacques Barzun, *From Dawn to Decadence: 1500 to the Present; 500 Years of Western Cultural Life* (New York: HarperCollins, 2000), 508.

63. Gilles Deleuze, *Kant's Critical Philosophy: The Doctrine of the Faculties*, trans. Hugh Tomlinson and Barbara Habberjam (Minneapolis: University of Minnesota Press, 1984), 24.

64. The phrase "simulacra of belief" comes from Deleuze's reading of David Hume, who elaborated a theory of human nature in which the very principles that allow humans to understand the world produce erroneous beliefs and delusions. As Deleuze writes: "Kant owes something essential to Hume: we are not threatened by error, rather and much worse, we bathe in delirium." Knowledge cannot derive from experience: I cannot know that the sun will rise tomorrow, instead, "*I infer and I believe*" that it will, based upon memories, which I join into a causal chain. "Hume posits the question of the subject and situates it in the following terms: *the subject is constituted inside the given*." The threat of delirium arises when the principle of causality "forges fictive causal chains, illegitimate rules," and "simulacra of belief." Gilles Deleuze, *Pure Immanence: Essays on a Life*, trans. Anne Boyman (New York: Zone Books, 2001), 40, 43; italics in original. He "[establishes] the concept of *belief* and [puts] it in the place of knowledge. He [laicizes]

belief, turning knowledge into a legitimate belief." Hume's subject, according to Deleuze, is therefore constantly haunted by error: it lies to itself, invests in fantasy, and lives according to fictive beliefs. Gilles Deleuze, *Empiricism and Subjectivity: An Essay on Hume's Theory of Human Nature*, trans. Constantin V. Boundas (New York: Columbia University Press, 1991), ix, 107; italics in original.

65. "The truth is," Bergson writes, "that an existence can only be given in an experience." When it is a question of a material object, this experience will be one of external perception; when it concerns the mind or spirit (*esprit*), "it will be called intuition." Guerlac, "Duration."

66. Nietzsche, *The Birth of Tragedy*, 34.

67. Nietzsche, *The Birth of Tragedy*, 38.

68. Bergson, *Time and Free Will*, 45.

69. Bergson, *Time and Free Will*, 43.

70 See Brian Kane, "*L'Objet Sonore Maintenant:* Pierre Schaeffer, Sound Objects and the Phenomenological Reduction," *Organized Sound* 13, no. 1 (2007): 15–24.

71. Edmund Husserl, *Ideas: General Introduction to Pure Phenomenology*, trans. W. R. Boyce Gibson (New York: Macmillan, 1931), 103.

72. Deleuze, *Bergsonism*, 43; italics in original.

73. "The possible has no reality," wrote Deleuze; "conversely, the virtual is not actual, but *as such possesses a reality*. Here again Proust's formula best defines the states of virtuality: 'real without being actual, ideal without being abstract.'" Deleuze, *Bergsonism*, 96; italics in original.

74. Fuoco B. Fann's insights into the status of illusion as well as the question of representation in modern art and aesthetics motivate the present study, specifically his discussion of the notion of simulation, which I take to be roughly equivalent to "the virtual" in Deleuze. For Deleuze "*simulacrum* [was] a crucial art-historical term" that the philosopher leveraged "to resolve the predicament of representation": that is, to resolve a "futile debate" between "mind/heart, . . . external/internal, image/reality, representation/presence," which Fann terms "the old grid" structuring European thought. He clarifies that Deleuze "advocates reversing Platonism by uplifting the simulacrum over the world of representation," which is to say that simulation—or the virtual—stands opposed to the "old grid," providing an alternative to the old dichotomies of appearance and reality, or illusion and the real. However, while Deleuze believes that simulation might "perhaps even . . . 'cure' the dichotomies prevalent in discourses of the human sciences"—dichotomies that have their basis in the old grid (or instance, the knowing subject versus the unthought, man versus his doubles in Foucault's sense)—Jean Baudrillard finds simulation endlessly problematic because "Reality is a Western implementation." Either way, however, "for better or for worse, simulation overthrows representation." I owe the following discussion of the opposition between illusion and virtuality, between Bergson and Deleuze's Bergson, to these insights.

See Fann, *This Self We Deserve*, 143–147; and for the opposition of illusion with "integral reality" via Baudrillard, see esp. 153–155.

75. Deleuze, *Bergsonism*, 56–57; italics in original.

76. Deleuze, *Bergsonism*, 55.

77. Deleuze, *Bergsonism*, 55; italics in original.

78. Fann, *This Self We Deserve*, 97.

79. Fann, *This Self We Deserve*, 41.

80. In Bergson's words:

a complex feeling will contain a fairly large number of simple elements; but, as long as these elements do not stand out with perfect clearness, we cannot say that they were completely realized, and, as soon as consciousness has a distinct perception of them, the psychic state which results from their synthesis will have changed for this very reason.

Bergson, *Time and Free Will*, 84; see Deleuze, *Bergsonism*, 42.

81. Deleuze, *Bergsonism*, 80.

82. The *élan vital* is "a virtuality in the process of being actualized, a simplicity in the process of differentiating, a totality in the process of dividing up: Proceeding 'by dissociation and division,' by 'dichotomy,' is the essence of life." Deleuze, *Bergsonism*, 94.

83. Deleuze, *Bergsonism*, 106.

84. Fernand Léger, quoted in *Satie Remembered*, ed. Robert Orledge, trans. Roger Nichols (Portland: Amadeus Press, 1995), 74–75.

85. Darius Milhaud, *Notes Without Music*, trans. Donald Evans (London: Calder and Boyars, 1952), 105.

86. As Caroline Potter suggests, *Furniture Music* had an earlier origin, even as early as 1916, according to an unsubstantiated account by an owner of a Parisian venue (named Emile Lejeune) who stated that Satie improvised on a piano during the *entr'acte* of a collaborative artistic event. Satie allegedly called his amblings "furniture music" and avowed: "I want the visitors to circulate." Whether or not this account is accurate, certainly by 1917, around the time Satie conceived *Socrate*, he had written his first movements of *Musique d'ameublement*. Potter speculates, in fact, that *Socrate* may have been originally imagined "as furniture music, as an inherently multimedia project which incorporated Grecian dancers against various antique-themed backdrops in imagined spaces." Potter, *Erik Satie: A Parisian Composer*, 146–155.

87. "Ballet instantanéiste en deux actes, un entr'acte cinematographique et la Queue du chien de Francis Picabia; Musique d'Erik Satie—Film réalisé par René Clair." Poster for the *Théâtre des Champs-Élysées*, December 1924, catalogued as an *affiche typographique*, BNF Gallic, accessed 26 September 2017: http://gallica .bnf.fr/ark:/12148/btv1b531185420/f1.item.r=Rêlache%20Satie

88. Wassily Kandinsky, "On the Question of Form," in *Kandinsky: Complete*

Writings on Art, eds. Kenneth C. Lindsay and Peter Vergo (Boston: Da Capo Press, 1994), 243.

89. "In the 'great realism' (as exemplified in the art of Henri Rousseau) the external-artificial element of painting is discarded, and the content, the inner feeling of the object, is brought forth primitively and 'purely' through the representation of the simple, rough object." Peter Selz, "The Aesthetic Theories of Wassily Kandinsky and Their Relationship to the Origin of Non-Objective Painting," *Art Bulletin* 39, no. 2 (1957): 131.

90. Kandinsky, "On the Question of Form," 243.

91. Kandinsky, "On the Question of Form," 245.

92. The "abstracted or abstract forms (lines, planes, patches, etc.) are not important in themselves," Kandinsky concludes of abstraction, "but rather for their inner sound." Kandinsky, "On the Question of Form," 244.

93. Satie coined several neologisms, *phonométrographe* and *phonométrographie* among them, to counter his critics and to belittle his contemporaries: others included *pyrotechniques*, techniques for dealing with the force of "explosive sounds" (by stuffing cotton into ones ears); *phonologie*, which is "superior to music," "more varied," and "gives a better return on investment"; something called a *motodynaphone*, which an amateur musician could use to show up a professional; and finally, *philophony*, which sums up the methods and intentions of the other terms, pointing to the future. "The future," indeed, "lies with philophony." Erik Satie, "*Ce que je suis*," translated as "What I Am," in *A Mammal's Notebook: The Writings of Erik Satie*, 108.

94. Rogers interprets Satie's words to Cocteau as evidence that the composer understood music as a vibrational medium, taking seriously contemporaneous scientific studies of resonance and vibration. Satie's words to Cocteau, however, are the only evidence cited to support this claim—and, I repeat, it is dangerous to take the composer at his word. See Jillian C. Rogers, *Resonant Recoveries: French Music and Trauma Between the World Wars* (New York: Oxford University Press, 2021), 115.

95. Hence Joseph Auner would later appropriate Satie's own term to describe the "phonometrographic attitude" that by and large characterized the *fin de siècle*. Joseph Auner, "Weighing, Measuring, and Embalming Tonality: How We Became Phonometrographers," in *Tonality 1900–1950: Concept and Practice*, eds. Felix Wörner, Ullrich Scheideler, and Philip Rupprecht (Stuttgart: Franz Steiner Verlag, 2012), 25–46.

96. "Cette expérience, qui est un complexe inné d'intuitions et de possibilités musicales, est basée avant tout sur une *expérience du temps* spécifiquement musicale—*du khronos*—, par rapport à laquelle la musique proprement dite ne joue que le rôle de réalisatrice fonctionnelle." Pierre Souvtchinsky, "La Notion du temps et la musique (réflexions sur la typologie de la création musicale)," *La Revue musicale* 20, no. 191 (May–June 1939): 72; italics in original.

97. "Or, toute cette variété de types et de modifications du *temps psychologique* serait insaisissable, si à la base de toute cette complexité d'expérience ne se trouvait la *sensation primaire*—souvent subconsciente—*du temps réel, du temps ontologique.*" Souvtchinsky, "La Notion du temps et la musique," 72; italics in original.

98 Souvtchinsky, "La Notion du temps et la musique," 72; italics in original.

99. Vladimir Jankélévitch, *Music and the Ineffable*, trans. Carolyn Abbate (Princeton and Oxford: Princeton University Press, 2003), 6.

100. Jankélévitch, *Music and the Ineffable*, 36–37.

101. Jankélévitch, *Music and the Ineffable*, 45.

102. Jankélévitch, *Music and the Ineffable*, 47, 48.

103. Deleuze, *Bergsonism*, 34.

104. Henri Bergson, *Creative Evolution*, trans. Arthur Mitchell (New York: Henry Holt, 1911), 11.

105. Cox, *Sonic Flux*, 37.

106. Cox, *Sonic Flux*, 38.

107. Cox, *Sonic Flux*, 119.

Chapter Two

1. Edgard Varèse, from a letter to André Jolivet of 19 July 1935, in Edgard Varèse and André Jolivet, *Correspondance 1931–1965*, ed. Christine Jolivet-Erlih (Geneva: Contrechamps, 2002), 113; this translation from Klaus Kropfinger, "'You Never Took the Simple Path': Varèse's Liberation of Sound and the Delimitation of the Arts," in *Edgard Varèse: Composer, Sound Sculptor, Visionary*, eds. Felix Meyer and Heidy Zimmermann (Woodbridge: Boydell Press, 2006), 158.

2. Richard Wagner, *Richard Wagner's Prose Works*, vol. 5, *Actors and Singers*, trans. William Ashton Ellis (New York: Broude Brothers, 1966 [reprint of 1896 London edition]), 92.

3. Many posthumous appellations abound, an "astronomer in sound" or a "sound sculptor visionary" among them. See Malcolm MacDonald, *Varèse: Astronomer in Sound* (London: Kahn & Averill, 2003), and *Varèse: Composer, Sound Sculptor, Visionary.*

4. By echoing Wagner's words about Beethoven, Varèse seems to have used the composer of the Ninth Symphony the same way: that is, to say something about himself. "[A]s much as Beethoven is the explicit subject of the *Beethoven* essay, Wagner himself is its implicit subject." K. M. Knittel, "Wagner, Deafness, and the Reception of Beethoven's Late Style," *Journal of the American Musicological Society* 51, no. 1 (1998): 51.

5. Edgard Varèse, "The Liberation of Sound," *Perspectives of New Music* 5, no. 1 (Autumn–Winter 1966): 12.

6. Hubert L. Dreyfus and Paul Rabinow, *Michel Foucault: Beyond Structuralism and Hermeneutics*, 2nd. ed. (Chicago: University of Chicago Press, 1983), 30.

7. Varèse, "The Liberation of Sound."

8. Georges Bataille, "Base Materialism and Gnosticism," in *Visions of Excess: Selected Writings, 1927–1939*, ed. and trans. Allan Stoekl (Minneapolis: University of Minnesota Press, 1985), 45–52.

9. Bataille, "Base Materialism and Gnosticism," 51.

10. This latter phrase derives from Fann's aperçu about the modern speaking subject in a rich discussion of Foucault's archeology of the human sciences alongside Habermas's reading of Foucault: the "Modern man [or Foucault's *l'homme*] rebuffs Metaphysics but declares his own Myth." I am indebted to Fann's insights into the precarious status of *l'homme* and modern knowledge, drawing from Foucault. See Fuoco B. Fann, *This Self We Deserve: A Quest After Modernity* (Berkeley: Philosophy and Art Collaboratory, 2020), 25–30.

11. According to Caroline Potter, there is little evidence that Satie and Varèse were more than acquaintances, though Varèse spoke highly of Satie's 1893–95 *Messe des Pauvres*. The two composers also had friends in common: according to biographer Fernand Ouellette, Satie wrote to Varèse after the latter moved to New York, conveying a sad message in August 1918: "Our poor Debussy is dead. He has been very ill, dear fellow that he was, for a long time." Louise Varèse wrote of her visit with Satie during a trip to Paris in 1921 (without Edgard, who was back in New York finishing *Amériques* and establishing the International Composer's Guild):

> Satie came to see me at the apartment a friend had loaned me on the noisy rue Notre-Dame de Lorette and, warned by Varèse, I had provided a bottle of cognac. He was the image of the person Varèse had described to me: pointed beard, derby hat, stick in one hand, gloves in the other, and the most mischievous eyes I have ever seen, behind crooked pince-nez. He stood his cane in a corner by the door, put his gloves in his hat, and sitting down, placed them on the floor beside his chair. Then he said "*Oui, oui. Et comment va ce brave garçon?*" He was full of his recent travels. He had gone to Brussels! Then he talked about *Alice in Wonderland*, which he adored. He wanted to make a ballet of it. Would I write it? He was the only Frenchman, he said, who understood English humor (his mother had been English—or Scottish?) and the only composer whose music "understood Alice." I sincerely agreed with him. Besides the *Gymnopédies*, I had heard some of his piano pieces which Carlos [Salzedo] played and had read the Satie nonsense that enlivened every page. He promised to have scores sent to Varèse and he did.

Caroline Potter, *Erik Satie: A Parisian Composer and His World* (Woodbridge: Boydell Press, 2016), 62–66; Erik Satie, quoted in Fernand Ouellette, *Edgard Varèse*, trans. Derek Coltman (New York: Orion Press, 1968), 44; Louise Varèse, *Varèse: A Looking-Glass Diary; Volume 1: 1883–1928* (New York: W. W. Norton, 1972), 161.

12. In his biography of Varèse, Ouellette consistently paints the composer as a rugged individualist, unbeholden to his teachers and predecessors in Europe. Ouellette quotes correspondence with Varèse about the latter's departure from the Schola: "The reason I left him [d'Indy] was because his idea of teaching was to form disciples. His vanity would not permit the least sign of originality, or even independent thinking, and I did not want to become a little d'Indy. One was enough." Varèse, quoted in Ouellette, *Edgard Varèse*, 14; see also Robert M. Crunden, *Body and Soul: The Making of American Modernism* (New York: Basic Books, 2000), 44.

13. Guido Magnaguagno, "'Little France': Varèse and the New York Dadaist Scene," in *Varèse: Composer, Sound Sculptor, Visionary*, 76–81. See also Olivia Mattis, "Varèse and Dada," in *Music and Modern Art*, ed. James Leggio (New York and London: Routledge, 2002), 129–162.

14. Edgard Varèse, "Jérôm s'en ca-t'en guerre," *The Sackbut* 4, no. 5 (December 1923): 146; emphasis added.

15. "Where Hausmann wrote *fmsbwtözäu*," Daniel Albright accounts, "Schwitters devised a pronunciation guide (*fümms bö wö tää zää Uu*)." Schwitters transformed the strings of consonants into lines of pronounceable sound poetry in a rondo form, culminating in the chanted recitation of the German alphabet. Daniel Albright, *Untwisting the Serpent: Modernism in Music, Literature, and Other Arts* (Chicago and London: University of Chicago Press, 2000), 288.

16. Sophie Stévance, "Les operations musicales mentales de Duchamp. De la 'musique en creux,'" *Images Re-vues* 7 (2009).

17. "The choice of the readymades is always based on visual indifference and, at the same time, on the total absence of good or bad taste." Duchamp, in Pierre Cabanne, *Dialogues with Marcel Duchamp*, trans. Ron Padgett (New York: Viking, 1971), 48.

18. As curator Ya-Ling Chen wrote of *Erratum Musical*, "the aesthetic experience of listening to a piece of music is transformed into an abstract experience of experiencing an abstract space." Such garbled turns of phrase characterize readings of Duchamp's readymades, in critic Donald Kuspit's words, "a Gordian knot that no intellectual sword can cut," since the readymade "collapses into banality the moment the spectator takes it seriously as art, and becomes serious art the moment the spectator dismisses it as a banal object." Ya-Ling Chen, "Erratum Musical, 1913," *Tout-Fait* 1, no. 1 (1999); Donald Kuspit, *The End of Art* (Cambridge, UK: Cambridge University Press, 2004), 23.

19. I reference the 1927 version of Varèse's *Amèriques* performed by the San Francisco Symphony on the album *American Mavericks* (2012).

20. Varèse, "The Liberation of Sound," 12. Jonathan Bernard outlines various ways of understanding Varèse's aural "spaces." He explains, for instance, how the composer arranged his pitch clusters and then transposed certain symmetrical chordal structures from one instrument group to another, one register to another.

Bernard clarifies that *"timbre, rhythm/duration, linear succession,* and *dynamics,* applied separately or in combination,"* constitute the various "criteria for segmentation" in Varèse's music—that is, the criteria by which the analyst might distinguish one sonic grouping from the rest. See Jonathan W. Bernard, *The Music of Edgard Varèse* (New Haven and London: Yale University Press, 1987), esp. 43–85; italics in original.

21. Varèse, quoted in Peter Garland, "Americas," *Soundings* (Spring 1974): 115.

22. Varèse, quoted in Garland, "Americas," 115.

23. For a virtuosic parsing of the various motifs Varèse uses in *Ameriques* (fifteen in total, apparently), see Keith Tedman, "Edgard Varèse: Concepts of Organized Sound," PhD dissertation (University of Sussex, 1983), 262–264.

24. Edgard Varèse, "New Instruments in Orchestra Are Needed, Says Mr. Varèse," *Christian Science Monitor* (1922); quoted in Carol J. Oja, *Making Music Modern: New York in the 1920s* (New York: Oxford University Press, 2003), 33.

25. Varèse, "New Instruments in Orchestra Are Needed."

26. Edgard Varèse and Alcopley, "Edgard Varèse on Music and Art: A Conversation Between Varèse and Alcopley," *Leonardo* 1, no. 2 (1968): 194.

27. Varèse, "New Instruments in Orchestra Are Needed."

28. Fernand Ouellette, quoted in Larry Stempel, "Not Even Varèse Can Be an Orphan," *The Musical Quarterly* 60, no. 1 (1974): 51; italics in original.

29. This passage from the first edition of Francis Picabia's *391*, published in New York in 1917, is among the Varèse-isms compiled in Varèse, "The Liberation of Sound," 11.

30. Varèse, "The Liberation of Sound," 12, 13, 16.

31. Mattis quotes Roche's unpublished memoirs; see Olivia Mattis, "Edgard Varèse and the Visual Arts," PhD dissertation (Stanford University, 1992), 1.

32. Paul Rosenfeld, quoted in Oja, *Making Music Modern,* 40.

33. Susan McClary, "Getting Down Off the Beanstalk," *Minnesota Composer's Forum Newsletter* (January 1987): 5–8.

34. Varèse, "The Liberation of Sound," 13.

35 Paracelsus as quoted in Varèse's score for *Arcana* (New York: Colfranc Publishing, 1964).

36. Edgard Varèse, "Statements by Edgard Varèse," *Soundings* 10 (1976): 7.

37. Paul Rosenfeld, *An Hour with American Music* (Philadelphia and London: J. B. Lippincott, 1929), 165–166.

38. Charles Baudelaire, *The Painter of Modern Life and Other Essays,* trans. Jonathan Mayne (New York and London: Phaidon Press, 1995), 12.

39. Varèse, quoted in Louise Varèse, *Looking-Glass Diary,* 123; see also Jürg Stenzl, "'Daily Life, Slavishly Imitated': Edgard Varèse and Italian Futurism," in *Varèse: Composer, Sound Sculptor, Visionary,* 142.

40. See Alexander Lee, "The Art of Noises," *History Today* 67, no. 12 (2017): https://www.historytoday.com/archive/music-time/art-noises; and Filippo Mari-

netti, "Futurist Manifesto," in Lawrence C. Rainey, Christine Poggi, and Laura Wittman, eds., *Futurism: An Anthology* (New Haven: Yale University Press, 2009).

41. Baudelaire, *The Painter of Modern Life*, 10.

42. Jürgen Habermas, *The Philosophical Discourse of Modernity: Twelve Lectures*, trans. Frederick G. Lawrence (Cambridge, MA: MIT Press, 1991), 261.

43. Michel Foucault, *The Order of Things: An Archaeology of the Human Sciences* (London and New York: Routledge, 2002 [original French 1966]), 336. "Once the order of the world was no longer God-given," that is, once the world no longer appeared as a "great chain of being" in which the human being was merely a part of a larger order already in place, "man, as we know him today, makes his appearance and becomes the measure of things." Dreyfus and Rabinow, *Michel Foucault: Beyond Structuralism*, 27–28.

44. The phrase "sheer will to cognitive self-mastery" derives from Habermas's discussion of Foucault's archaeology of the human sciences, specifically Foucault's claim that the Modern Man (or *l'homme*), the object of the human sciences and the subject who uses these sciences, is characterized by a "pretentious and never redeemed" "*will to truth*." Thus, this subject is, in Habermas's phrase, a "structurally overburdened and overstained subject," for whom "any frustration is only a spur to the renewed production of knowledge." Habermas, *The Philosophical Discourse of Modernity*, 261.

45. Paul Valéry, letter to Francis de Miomandre, quoted in the preface to Miguel Angel Asturias, *Legends of Guatemala*, trans. Kelly Washbourne (Pittsburgh: Latin American Literary Review Press, 2011), 21–22.

46 Allan Stoekl, "Introduction," in *Visions of Excess*, xx.

47. Bataille, "Nietzsche and the Fascists," in *Visions of Excess*, 182:

> The anti-Semitic falsifications of Frau Förster, Nietzsche's sister, and of Herr Richard Oehler, his cousin, are in some ways even more vulgar than Judas's deal—beyond all reckoning, they give the force of a whiplash to the maxim in which Nietzsche expressed his horror of anti-Semitism: DO NOT BEFRIEND ANYONE INVOLVED IN THIS IMPUDENT HOAX, RACISM!

48. Bataille, "Materialism," in *Visions of Excess,* 15–16; italics in original.

49 I owe this insight into the Bataille–Derrida connection via the trace and "base materialism" to Fuoco Fann (personal correspondence).

50. Bataille, "Base Materialism and Gnosticism," 48; italics in original.

51. "I admit that I have, in respect to mystical philosophies, only an unambiguous interest, analogous to that of an uninfatuated psychiatrist towards his patients." Bataille, "Base Materialism and Gnosticism," 46.

52. See Georges Bataille, *The Accursed Share*, vol. I, trans. Robert Hurley (New York: Zone Books, 1988); Jacques Derrida, "From Restricted to General Economy: A Hegelianism Without Reserve," in *Writing and Difference*, trans. Alan Bass (New York and London: Routledge, 2001), 317–350.

53. Bataille, "Base Materialism and Gnosticism," 46, 48.

54. Sylvère Lotringer, "Furiously Nietzschean," introduction to Georges Bataille, *On Nietzsche*, trans. Bruce Boone (St. Paul: Paragon House, 1992), vii–viii. To quote Jean-Michel Besnier and Amy Reid, for Bataille defending Nietzsche

> was . . . a move to preserve a Nietzschean point of view on politics, in other words an "elsewhere" beyond the categories of left and right, an attitude which could be opposed to Stalinism as well as to fascism. . . . It was a move to save independent action because it is the only weapon against the fascination of Nazism.

Jean-Michel Besnier and Amy Reid, "Georges Bataille in the 1930s: A Politics of the Impossible," *Yale French Studies* 78 (1990): 176.

55. Quoted in Mattis, "Edgard Varèse and the Visual Arts," 175, 176.

56. See Olivia Mattis, "From Bebop to Poo-wip: Jazz Influences in Varèse's *Poème électronique*," in *Varèse: Composer, Sound Sculptor, Visionary*, 309–317; Brigid Cohen, "Enigmas of the Third Space: Mingus and Varèse at Greenwich House, 1957," *Journal of the American Musicological Society* 71, no. 1 (Spring 2018): 155–211; Rosenfeld, *An Hour with American Music*. It is also conspicuous to note that Varèse, like Bataille, loved Nietzsche's writings, according to Louise Varèse:

> Early in his life there was a time when Varèse discovered and embraced Nietzsche—in fact, there was a time when he liked to think of the great poet-philosopher as his alter ego; ignoring his own protean and—in spite of his repudiation—Italian nature, he failed to see that the bond was intellectual and spiritual affinity, not consanguinity. Nietzschean he was in his moral judgments. I have spoken of his aversion to pity. He believed with Nietzsche that "pity stands opposed to the tonic emotions which heighten vitality"; so, as Varèse allowed himself to none for his own weaknesses, sufferings, depressions—only repugnance—he had succeeded in blacking them out of his memory of Berlin where only tonic emotions survived.

Louise Varèse, *Looking-Glass Diary*, 95.

57. Bataille, "Base Materialism and Gnosticism," 45. Regarding *Documents* and *Acéphale*, see David Evans, "*Documents* Against Civilization," in Martin Evans, ed., *Empire and Culture: The French Experience, 1830–1940* (Hampshire, UK, and New York: Palgrave Macmillan, 2004), 71–88; Georges Bataille, *The Sacred Conspiracy: The Internal Papers of the Secret Society of Acéphale and Lectures to the College of Sociology*, eds. Marina Galletti and Alastair Brotchie, trans. Natasha Lehrer, John Harman, and Meyer Barash (London: Atlas Press, 2017).

58. Bataille, "Base Materialism and Gnosticism," 45.

59. Bataille, "Base Materialism and Gnosticism," 48.

60. Varèse may also have come into Asturias's orbit through Heitor Villa-Lobos, one of the few composers with whom Varèse is known to have spent time

(he preferred the company of painters, poets, and dramatists). Ernst Lichtenhahn, "Varèse's *Ecuatorial* in Its Parisian Surroundings," in *Varèse: Composer, Sound Sculptor, Visionary*, 193–201; Michel Duchesneau, "Varèse in Paris, 1928–1933," in *Varèse: Composer, Sound Sculptor, Visionary*, 184–192.

61. Asturias, *Legends of Guatemala*, 53.

62. I reference the version of *Ecuatorial* conducted by Riccardo Chailly and performed by the Royal Concertgebouw as part of *Varèse: The Complete Works* (Decca Record Company Limited, London, 1998).

63. Asturias, *Legends of Guatemala*, 53.

64. The text for *Ecuatorial*, in both Spanish and English, may be found on The LiederNet Archive, accessed 20 September 2022: https://www.lieder.net/lieder/get_text.html?TextId=121111

65. After endeavors to include electronic instruments like the aerophone and *ondes* in works like *Ecuatorial*, Varèse concluded in 1936 that "our still primitive electrical instruments find it necessary to abandon staff notation and to use a kind of seismographic writing much like the early ideographic writing originally used for the voice before the development of staff notation." Varèse, "The Liberation of Sound," 13.

66. Asturias, *Legends of Guatemala*, 54.

67. Asturias, *Legends of Guatemala*, 55.

68. Bataille, "The Solar Anus," in *Visions of Excess*, 8–9.

69. Bataille, "Base Materialism and Gnosticism," 49.

70. Bataille, "Base Materialism and Gnosticism," 50. That Bataille's thought would come to exert a particular allure for generations of later French thinkers is owed to the latent ethics that we can glean from these anti-ontological pronouncements, an allure no doubt amplified by the profane package in which Bataille placed this ethics. He projects a late Marxian ideology critique—a will to "[disconcert] the human spirit and idealism before something base"—through a renegade surrealist pornographic aesthetic tied to a freewheeling ethnographic curiosity. See James Clifford's illuminating discussion of Bataille in relation to surrealist aesthetics, a theme I will take up more explicitly in the following chapter. James Clifford, "On Ethnographic Surrealism," *Comparative Studies in Society and History* 23, no. 4 (1981), 539–564.

71. Varèse, "The Liberation of Sound," 11.

72. Hegel, quoted in Jacques Derrida, *Of Grammatology*, trans. Gayatri Chakravorty Spivak (Baltimore and London: Johns Hopkins University Press, 1997), 24.

73. Derrida, *Of Grammatology*, 25.

74. Hegel, quoted in Derrida, *Of Grammatology*, 25.

75. G. W. F. Hegel, *The Philosophy of Fine Art*, vol. III, trans. Francis Plumptre Beresford Osmaston (London: G. Bell and Sons, 1920), 380–384; italics in original.

76. "It is by virtue of this twofold negation of externality, in which the root-

principle of tone consists," Hegel continued, that music resonates with the soul and spirit in the same manner as the phonetic breath:

> this resonance which, in its essential explicitness, is something more ideal than the subsistent corporeality in its independent reality, also discloses this more ideal existence, and thereby offers a mode of expression suited to the ideality of conscious life.

Hegel, *The Philosophy of Fine Art*, 384.

Chapter Three

The ideas in this chapter were originally developed in the following article: Edmund Mendelssohn, "Ontological Appropriation: Boulez and Artaud." *Twentieth-Century Music* 18, no. 2 (2021): 281–310. doi:10.1017/S1478572221000049. © Edmund Mendelssohn, 2021. Reprinted with permission.

    1. "Je dois cependant reconnaître que je choisi ce 'corpus' instrumental en fonction d'influences dues aux civilisations extra-européennes: le xylophone transpose le balafon africain, le vibraphone se réfère au gender balinais, la guitare se souvient de koto japonais." Pierre Boulez, "Dire, jouer, chanter," from Jean-Louis Barrault, *La musique et ses problèmes contemporains 1953–1963*, Collection "Cahiers Renaud-Barrault" (Paris: René Julliard, 1963), 317. Unless otherwise indicated, all translations are mine.

    2. "De fait, ni la stylistique ni l'emploi même des instruments ne se rattachent en quoi que ce soit aux traditions de ces différentes civilisations musicales." Boulez, "Dire, jouer, chanter," 317.

    3. "La musique doit être hystérie et envoûtement collectifs, violemment actuels—suivant la direction d'Antonin Artaud, et non pas une simple reconstitution ethnographique à l'image de civilisations plus ou moins éloignées de nous." Pierre Boulez, "Propositions," *Polyphonie* 2 (1948). This oft-quoted passage is from a 1947 letter from Boulez to André Souris published in Robert Wangermée, *André Souris et le complexe d'Orphée: Entre surréalisme et musique sérielle* (Liège: Mardaga 1995), 274; see also Caroline Potter, "Pierre Boulez, Surrealist," *Gli spazi della musica* 6, no. 1 (2017): 75.

    4. Boulez's approach to non-European sound was, as he wrote, "totally opposed to the unwelcome appropriation of a 'colonial' vocabulary by Europe at the beginning of this century," including "numerous and ephemeral Malagasy or Cambodian rhapsodies or other [musical] genre paintings." Boulez, "Dire, jouer, chanter," 317.

    5. See Rosângela Pereira de Tugny, "L'autre moitié de l'art," in Jean-Louis Leleu and Pascal Decroupet, eds., *Pierre Boulez: Techniques d'écriture et enjeux esthétiques* (Geneva: Éditions Contrechamps, 2006), 299–317; and Luisa Bassetto, "Ritratto del compositore come apprendista etnologo: Pierre Boulez prima dell'incontro con André Schaeffner," *Musicalia* 7 (2010): 61–82.

6. Pierre Boulez, "Sound and Word," in *Stocktakings from an Apprenticeship*, trans. Stephen Walsh (Oxford: Clarendon Press, 1991), 42.

7. Christoph Cox, *Sonic Flux: Sound, Art, and Metaphysics* (Chicago and London: University of Chicago Press, 2018); Nina Sun Eidsheim, *Sensing Sound: Singing and Listening as Vibrational Practice* (Durham and London: Duke University Press, 2015).

8. Emmanuel Lévinas, *Totality and Infinity: An Essay on Exteriority*, trans. Alphonso Lingis (The Hague, Boston, and London: Martinus Nijkoff, 1979 [original French 1961]), 43.

9. See Robert Young, *White Mythologies: Writing History and the West* (London and New York: Routledge, 1990), 14.

10. Lévinas, *Totality and Infinity*, 43–44.

11. Joan Peyser, *Boulez* (New York and London: Schirmer Books, 1976), 25.

12. Edward Campbell, *Boulez, Music, and Philosophy* (New York: Cambridge University Press, 2010), 33; Peter O'Hagan, *Pierre Boulez and the Piano: A Study in Style and Technique* (London and New York: Routledge, 2017), 74; François Meïmoun, "La Construction du langage musical de Pierre Boulez: La Première Sonate pour piano," PhD dissertation (École des Hautes Études en Sciences Sociales, 2018), esp. 165–173; Potter, "Pierre Boulez, Surrealist," 75.

13. Antonin Artaud and Ruby Cohn, "States of Mind: 1921–1945," *Tulane Drama Review* 8, no. 2 (1963): 30–73; Sylvère Lotringer, *Mad Like Artaud*, trans. Joanna Spinks (Minneapolis: Univocal Publishing, 2015), 12.

14. "Hear Antonin Artaud's Censored, Never-Aired Radio Play: *To Have Done with the Judgment of God* (1947)," *Open Culture*, September 2014: http://www.open culture.com/2014/09/antonin-artauds-censored-never-aired-radio-play.html

15. See Meïmoun, "La Construction du langage musical de Pierre Boulez," 167–170.

16. "J'aime mieux le peuple qui mange à même la terre le délire d'où il est né.... C'est ainsi que vous allez entendre la danse du TUTUGURI." Antonin Artaud, *Pour en finir avec le jugement de Dieu* (Paris: Éditions Gallimard, 2003), 28–29. According to Luisa Bassetto, Boulez intended to use the following text, the "Dance of the Tutuguri," in his unfinished *Marges*, which he conceived in or about 1961 but abandoned after 1968. Luisa Bassetto, "Marginalia, ou *l'opéra-fantôme* de Pierre Boulez," in *Pierre Boulez: Techniques d'écriture et enjeux esthétiques*, 255–298.

17. Boulez, "Sound and Word," 42.

18. David Tudor's remarks about the difficulties he had while learning to play the *Deuxième sonate* for its 1950 American premiere attest to the aesthetic and historical links between this piece and Artaudian theatricality vis-à-vis Boulez. Taking a cue from Boulez's writings, Tudor read Artaud's *Le Théâtre et son double*. "All of a sudden I saw that there was a different way of looking at musical continuity," he stated, "having to deal with what Artaud called the affective athleticism.... I had to put my mind in a state of non-continuity—not remembering—so

that each moment is alive." David Tudor, quoted in Eric Smigel, "Recital Hall of Cruelty: Antonin Artaud, David Tudor, and the 1950s Avant-Garde," *Perspectives of New Music* 45, no. 2 (2007): 173.

19. This definition of *écriture* derives in part from Antoine Bonnet, "Écriture and perception, on *Messagesquisse* by P. Boulez," *Contemporary Music Review* 2, no. 1 (1987): 209; see Jonathan Goldman, *The Musical Language of Pierre Boulez: Writings and Compositions* (Cambridge, UK, and New York: Cambridge University Press, 2011), 203 n. 15.

20. Goldman, *The Musical Language of Pierre Boulez*, 4, 63.

21. These dates of composition are attributed by Dominique Jameux, *Pierre Boulez*, trans. Susan Bradshaw (London: Faber and Faber, 1991), 38–39.

22. The *Livre* exemplifies the opposition of smooth and striated time: longer resonant "smooth" tones forming a contrast with short and percussive "striated" attacks. See Goldman, *The Musical Language of Pierre Boulez*, 12; also see Gilles Deleuze, "Boulez, Proust and Time: "Occupying Without Counting," *Angelaki* 3, no. 2 (1998): 69–74.

23. The magisterial example of analytic decoding is, of course, Lev Koblyakov, *Pierre Boulez: A World of Harmony* (Chur: Harwood Academic Publishers, 1990). See also Pascal Decroupet, "Serial Organization and Beyond: Cross-Relations of Determinants in *Le Marteau sans maître* and the Pitch-Algorithm of 'Constellation,'" and Erling E. Guldbrandsen, "Casting New Light on Boulezian Serialism: Unpredictability and Free Choice in the Composition of *Pli selon pli—portrait de Mallarmé*," in *Pierre Boulez Studies*, eds. Edward Campbell and Peter O'Hagan (Cambridge, UK: Cambridge University Press, 2016), 108–138, 193–220.

24. James Clifford, "On Ethnographic Surrealism," *Comparative Studies in Society and History* 23, no. 4 (October 1981): 541.

25. André Breton, *Manifestoes of Surrealism*, trans. Richard Seaver and Helen R. Lane (Ann Arbor: University of Michigan Press, 1969), 14.

26. André Breton, "Silence d'or," handwritten original, accessed 10 September 2020: https://www.andrebreton.fr/work/56600100198010

27. "[Poetry] is at a disadvantage compared to . . . music as regards the immediate, pervading, and uncriticizable communication of feeling." Breton, *Manifestoes of Surrealism*, 263.

28. Breton, *Manifestoes of Surrealism*, 23.

29. "The contamination of money has covered everything over," Breton declared, transforming words like "justice," "fatherland," and "duty" into empty signifiers detached from their signifieds. Breton, *Manifestoes of Surrealism*, 216.

30. Breton, *Manifestoes of Surrealism*, 264; italics in original.

31. Antonin Artaud, *The Theater and Its Double*, trans. Mary Caroline Richards (New York: Grove Press, 1958), 89.

32. Artaud, *The Theater and Its Double*, 75.

33. "A direct communication will be re-established between the spectator and

the spectacle . . . from the fact that the spectator, placed in the middle of the action, is engulfed and physically affected by it." Artaud, *The Theater and Its Double*, 96.

34. Jacques Derrida, "The Theater of Cruelty and the Closure of Representation," in *Writing and Difference*, trans. Alan Bass (London and New York: University of Chicago Press, 1978), 232–250.

35. Artaud, *The Theater and Its Double*, 61; see also Nicola Savarese, "1931: Antonin Artaud Sees Balinese Theatre at the Paris Colonial Exposition," *The Drama Review* 43, no. 3 (2001): 51–77.

36. Artaud, *The Theater and Its Double*, 111.

37. Artaud, *The Theater and Its Double*, 54.

38. Matt Sakakeeny uses the term "entextualization" to connote the process through which a composer takes "sound" or "noise" and incorporates it into musical writing. On this view, writing allows the separation of a sound from its source "in the world," including the non-European "noise" that a composer might use as sonic fodder, and the translation of these sounds into arbitrary symbols. Matt Sakakeeny, "Music," in *Keywords in Sound*, eds. David Novak and Matt Sakakeeny (Durham and London: Duke University Press, 2015), 114.

39. Roland Barthes, *Mythologies*, trans. Richard Howard and Annette Lavers (New York: Hill and Wang, 2012), 217, 218.

40. Clifford, "On Ethnographic Surrealism," 546.

41. Clifford, "On Ethnographic Surrealism," 546.

42. Artaud, *The Theater and Its Double*, 91.

43. Pierre Boulez, "Pierre Boulez's Introduction to Sonatas and Interludes for Prepared Piano by John Cage at Suzanne Tézenas's Salon," in *The Boulez–Cage Correspondence*, ed. Jean-Jacques Nattiez, trans. Robert Samuels (Cambridge, UK, and New York: Cambridge University Press, 1993), 28.

44. Pierre Boulez, "Le Concept d'écriture," in *Leçons de musique (Points de repère III): Deux décennies d'enseignement au Collège de France (1976–1995)*, eds. Jean-Jacques Nattiez and Jonathan Goldman (Paris: Christian Bourgeois Éditeur, 2005), 559.

45. Boulez, "Pierre Boulez's Introduction to Sonatas and Interludes," 27–28.

46. Pierre Boulez, *Conversations with Célestin Deliège* (London: Eulenburg Books, 1976), 118.

47. Pierre Boulez, from an unpublished interview with Sylvie de Nussac, quoted in Luisa Bassetto, "Ritratto del compositore come apprendista etnologo: Pierre Boulez prima dell'incontro con André Schaeffner," *Musicalia* 7 (2010): 62. Regarding the Balinese music he heard with Messiaen: "it was the . . . quality and resonance of the sonority, the speed of play, and the conception of time over long periodicities," with "the tam-tam [marking] the time at very long intervals while others played much more quickly," Boulez wrote, that fascinated him most. Pierre Boulez, "La tradition écartelée: un entretien de Phillippe Albèra avec Pierre Boulez," *Dissonance* 62 (1999): 11.

48. See "Chef de musique chez Renault-Barrault," in Christian Merlin, *Pierre Boulez* (Paris: Fayard, 2019).

49. Among Boulez's papers housed in the Paul Sacher Foundation, Bassetto found four handwritten transcriptions of songs as well as seven typewritten sheets that contain notes, transcriptions, and analyses of traditional Cambodian songs and texts. "It is conceivable," she writes, "that all these notes and transcriptions were taken very quickly, probably under dictation and during a session of listening to recordings (perhaps a selective transcription test given to group of candidates for the mission to Cambodia)." Bassetto, "Ritratto del compositore come apprendista etnologo," 63.

50. These documents, as Bassetto demonstrates, not only attest to the young composer's profoundly precise ears, but also "testify more generally to the state of ethnomusicological training in France after the Second World War," indicating that sound documentation had a colonialist origin. Bassetto, "Ritratto del compositore come apprendista etnologo," 63.

51. Boulez, "Pierre Boulez's Introduction to Sonatas and Interludes," 29.

52. "There is no gesture for Boulez without *écriture*," writes Goldman, "which is the medium of musical discourse and the mediation between the idea and realized sound. Without *écriture*, there is no access to the musical as such, but only to the sonorous." Goldman, *The Musical Language of Pierre Boulez*, 57.

53. Boulez, *Conversations with Célestin Deliège*, 118; emphasis added.

54. Boulez, *Conversations with Célestin Deliège*, 118.

55. Of course, Boulez's specific approach to sound evolved: the violent gestural language of the *Deuxième sonate*, the system of total serialism through which Boulez composed *Structures I* (1952), and the computers in use at IRCAM two decades later, represent different moments in Boulez's development—he was always on the move. Yet, despite the various approaches that Boulez cultivated, his essential view of sound and writing remained consistent.

56. "La caractéristique essentielle de l'espace élaboré par la culture musical occidentale, c'est son entière indépendance à l'égard de matériel sonore." Boris de Schloezer, *Introduction à J.-S. Bach* (Paris: Gallimard, 1947), 168.

57. Schloezer, *Introduction à J.-S. Bach*, 169.

58. "These innovations, these discoveries, these adventures, which belong to western musical culture" as it developed from the classical tradition through Schoenberg and dodecaphonicism, "were and are only possible by virtue of what I would like to call the 'dematerialization' of the sound space: the element of our field of action is no longer the sound of the drum or of the bagpipe; it is a number, the term of quantitative relations." Schloezer, *Introduction à J.-S. Bach*, 169.

59. "What writing betrays, in its nonphonetic moment, is life," wrote Derrida to sum up Hegel's view, claiming that "*Aufhebung* is, more or less implicitly, the dominant concept of nearly all histories of writing" following Hegel, "still to-

day"—in 1965. Jacques Derrida, *Of Grammatology*, trans. Gayatri Chakravorty Spivak (Baltimore and London: Johns Hopkins University Press, 1997), 25.

60 Pierre Boulez, "Pierre Boulez Talks About His Music," UE Interview, published on YouTube, accessed 31 October 2022: https://www.youtube.com/watch?v=ie5Ore2rjhk

61. Boulez, quoted in Campbell, "Pierre Boulez: Composer, Traveller, Correspondent," in *Pierre Boulez Studies,* 17. Joseph Salem incorrectly attributes Boulez's words to a letter to Schaeffner—this passage, also quoted by Robert Piencikowski, was for Stockhausen. Alas, there is no evidence (yet?) that Boulez discussed the instruments he found in South America with Schaeffner, although their correspondence does allude to the South American trip and demonstrates Boulez's fascination with the non-western instruments housed in the Musée de l'Homme. I agree with Salem's conviction that Boulez's endeavor to collect instruments "[confirms] both the ethnomusicological influence of his mentor [Schaeffner] and the source of new percussive combinations in both *Le Marteau* and *L'Orestie.*" Joseph Salem, "Boulez's *Künstlerroman*: Using *blocs sonores* to Overcome Anxieties and Influence in *Le Marteau sans maître*," *Journal of the American Musicological Society* 71, no. 1 (2018): 135–136; Robert Piencikowski, "Between the Text and the Margin: Varèse and Pierre Boulez, 1952–1965," in *Edgard Varèse: Composer, Sound Sculptor, Visionary* (Woodbridge: Boydell Press, 2006), 384 n. 16; Pierre Boulez and André Schaeffner, *Correspondance 1954–1970*, ed. Rosângela Pereira de Tugny (Paris: Fayard, 1998), see esp. 35 and 49–53.

62. Boulez, quoted in Campbell, "Pierre Boulez: Composer, Traveller, Correspondent," 17.

63. Boulez's words about the ineffectual rites and cults are quoted from Campbell, "Pierre Boulez: Composer, Traveller, Correspondent," 7; Jean-Louis Barrault, *Nouvelles réflexions sur le théâtre* (Paris: Flammarion, 1959).

64. Pierre Boulez, personal communication with Rosângela Pereira de Tugny, in Boulez and Schaeffner, *Correspondance 1954–1970*, 52–53 n. 1; Kelly E. Hayes, "Black Magic and the Academy: Macumba and Afro-Brazilian Orthodoxies," *History of Religions* 46, no. 4 (2007): 284.

65. Boulez and Schaeffner, *Correspondance 1954–1970*, 52–53.

66. Gerard Béhague, "Patterns of *Candomblé* Music Performance: An Afro-Brazilian Religious Setting," in *Performance Practice: Ethnomusicological Perspectives*, ed. Gerard Béhague (Westport and London: Greenwood Press, 1984), 223; Robert A. Voeks, *Sacred Leaves of Candomblé: African Magic, Medicine, and Religion in Brazil* (Austin: University of Texas Press, 1997), 41 and 69–114; see also Stephen Selka, "Mediated Authenticity: Tradition, Modernity, and Postmodernity in Brazilian Candomblé," *Nova Religio: The Journal of Alternative and Emergent Religions* 11, no. 1 (2007): 5–30.

67. O'Hagan, *Pierre Boulez and the Piano*, 330–331; Barrault, *Nouvelles réflexions*, 86.

68. Barrault, *Nouvelles réflexions*, 86.

69. I wish to thank Carol A. Hess for her comments and questions regarding an earlier conference paper version of this essay, and particularly for introducing me to Gerard Béhague's work, *Orfeu Negro*, and literature about Candomblé.

70. Pascal Decroupet, "Introduction" to Pierre Boulez, *Le Marteau sans maître: Fac-similé de l'épure et de la première mise au net de la partition* (Basel: Paul Sacher Foundation, 2005), 46.

71. Béhague, "Patterns of *Candomblé* Music Performance," 228.

72. Barrault, *Nouvelles réflexions*, 87:

Il y a bien le regarde du prêtre et son sourire, ce grand Christ suspendu, son agonie braquée sur la table, et la fumée enveloppante de l'encens, qui donnent un côté insolite à cette sorte de cocktail-party de petite mairie de campagne.

73. Barrault, *Nouvelles réflexions*, 87.

74. Barrault, *Nouvelles réflexions*, 87.

75. Barrault, *Nouvelles réflexions*, 88:

Suivons l'homme "blessé." Pour l'instant, les autres ne s'occupent pas de lui. . . . Il a l'air surpris. "O to to toï." Quelque chose comme une pointe de flèche l'a atteint au sternum. . . . Il grimace de la douleur. "Popoï da!"

76. Barrault, *Nouvelles réflexions*, 88–89:

Voici à présent quatre ou cinq secondes trépidantes, rappelant ou la fornication ou le vomissement, la secousse sexuelle ou un refus exacerbé: sa bouche se déforme, se yeux lui sortent de la tête. "Apollon! Apollon!" . . . Il semble parfois en contact avec l'Esprit qui s'accroche à sa nuque et lui parle; alors il soulève ses paupières et ses sourcils en signe d'interrogation: "Apollon, dieu des routes, où m'as-tu donc conduit?"

77. Boulez, quoted in O'Hagan, *Pierre Boulez and the Piano*, 331.

78. Béhague, "Patterns of *Candomblé* Music Performance," 232.

79. Béhague, "Patterns of *Candomblé* Music Performance," 231.

80. David Graeber, "Fetishism as Social Creativity: or, Fetishes Are Gods in the Process of Construction," *Anthropological Theory* 5, no. 4 (2005): 407–438.

81. Peter O'Hagan, "Pierre Boulez and the Project of 'L'Orestie,'" *Tempo* 61, no. 241 (2007): 45–46.

82. Barrault, *Nouvelles réflexions*, 90.

83. Barrault, *Nouvelles réflexions*, 90:

Non quelque chose d'érudit, non cette fameuse harmonie grecque de nos lycées, non la Grèce de ces statues décolorées, mais une Grèce archaïque, ju-teuse, humaine, angoissée et en contact avec le mystère de la vie: une Grèce magique.

84. Boulez, quoted in Campbell, "Pierre Boulez: Composer, Traveller, Correspondent," 7.

85. A kind of allegorizing often occurs, as Clifford contended, as a staple of ethnographic writing: moments of radical alterity become markers of a human condition beyond a specific instance, ultimately a way to universalize the human condition. "Ethnographic texts are inescapably allegorical," he wrote, claiming that "the very activity of ethnographic *writing*—seen as inscription or textualization—enacts a redemptive Western allegory." James Clifford, "On Ethnographic Allegory," in *Writing Culture: The Poetics and Politics of Ethnography* (Berkeley: University of California Press, 1986), 99.

86. Béhague, "Patterns of *Candomblé* Music Performance," 229.

87. Richard Taruskin, "Russian Folk Melodies in 'The Rite of Spring,'" *Journal of the American Musicological Society* 33, no. 3 (1980): 501–543; and *Defining Russia Musically: Historical and Hermeneutical Essays* (Princeton and Oxford: Princeton University Press, 1997), esp. 389–430, 460–465.

88 Derrida, *Writing and Difference*, 250; italics in original.

89. Ning Zhang, "Interview with Jacques Derrida: The Western Question of 'Forgiveness' and the Intercultural Relation," *Comparative and Continental Philosophy* 12, no. 1 (2020): 14.

90. Derrida, quoted in Ning Zhang, "Jacques Derrida's First Visit to China: A Summary of His Lectures and Seminars," *Dao: A Journal of Comparative Philosophy* 2, no. 1 (2002): 154.

91. Zhang, "Jacques Derrida's First Visit to China," 154; see the Prelude.

92. This clarification of the Heideggerian distinction between "Being" and "being" (*Sein* and *Seiend*) as a distinction between stasis and kinesis, or perhaps between noun and verb, is owed to Fann. Personal correspondence; and see Fann, *This Self We Deserve*, 12–13, 33–34.

93. Jacques Derrida, "Differance," in *Speech and Phenomena and Other Essays on Husserl's Theory of Signs*, trans. David B. Allison (Evanston: Northwestern University Press, 1973), 143.

94. Derrida, "Differance," 138.

95. Zhang, "Interview with Jacques Derrida," 14.

96. See Lévinas's section titled "Metaphysics Precedes Ontology" from *Totality and Infinity*, 42–48.

97. Antonin Artaud, "Le Rite des rois d'Atlantide," in *Oeuvres* (Paris: Éditions Gallimard, 2004), 756.

98. Eduardo Viveiros de Castro, "Who Is Afraid of the Ontological Wolf?: Some Comments on an Ongoing Anthropological Debate," *Cambridge Journal of Anthropology* 33, no. 1, Special Section—Remaking the Public Good: A New Anthropology of Bureaucracy (Spring 2015): 11.

99. David Graeber, "Radical Alterity Is Just Another Way of Saying 'Reality': A Reply to Eduardo Viveiros de Castro," *HAU: Journal of Ethnographic Theory* 5, no. 2 (2015): 15.

100. Viveiros de Castro, "Who Is Afraid of the Ontological Wolf?," 14.

101. Paul Rabinow, "Humanism as Nihilism: The Bracketing of Truth and Seriousness in American Cultural Anthropology," in *The Accompaniment: Assembling the Contemporary* (Chicago and London: University of Chicago Press, 2011), 14.

102. To read the right author, see Eduardo Kohn, "Anthropology of Ontologies," *Annual Review of Anthropology* 44 (2015): 311–327.

103. Eduardo Kohn, *How Forests Think: Toward an Anthropology Beyond the Human* (Berkeley: University of California Press, 2013).

104. Graeber, "Radical Alterity Is Just Another Way of Saying 'Reality,'" 34.

105. Kohn, "Anthropology of Ontologies," 312.

106. Cox, *Sonic Flux*, 2, 119.

107. Steve Goodman, *Sonic Warfare: Sound, Affect, and the Ecology of Fear* (Cambridge, MA, and London: MIT Press, 2010), 81.

108. Nina Sun Eidsheim, *Sensing Sound: Singing and Listening as Vibrational Practice* (Durham and London: Duke University Press, 2015).

109. Eidsheim, *Sensing Sound*, 3 and 54–57.

110. Brian Kane, "Sound Studies Without Auditory Cultures: A Critique of the Ontological Turn," *Sound Studies* 1, no. 1 (2015): 11.

111. I owe this insight into recent studies of sound to Nicholas Mathew.

112. See Fann, *This Self We Deserve*, 12–16, 33–34.

113. Viveiros de Castro, "Who Is Afraid of the Ontological Wolf?," 11; italics in original.

114. I am grateful to Fuoco B. Fann for his insights, through personal correspondences and lectures, into the ethnocentrism inherent in the notion of ontology as the mainstream of western philosophy. See Fann, *This Self We Deserve*, esp. 49–50.

115. Tendayi Sithole, *The Black Register* (Cambridge, UK: Polity Press, 2020), 245.

116. Sithole, *The Black Register*, 259.

117. "I would like to suggest that surrealist procedures are always present in ethnographic works, though seldom explicitly acknowledged." Clifford, "On Ethnographic Surrealism," 563.

118. Derrida, *Writing and Difference*, 250; italics in original.

Chapter Four

1. John Cage, *Silence: Lectures and Writings by John Cage* (Middletown: Wesleyan University Press, 1973), 5.

2. John Cage, from a 1948 talk at Vassar College, "A Composer's Confessions," quoted in James Pritchett, "'Silent prayer', the first silent piece," accessed 22 September 2022: https://rosewhitemusic.com/piano/2018/08/27/silent-prayer-the-first-silent-piece/

3. John Cage, *For the Birds: In Conversation with Daniel Charles* (London and New York: Marion Boyars, 2009 [original French, *Pour Les Oiseaux*, 1976]), 150, 151; italics in original.

4. Piekut wrote that in Cage's thought of the 1950s, "nature is figured at its most traditionally modernist—as raw sound." Benjamin Piekut, "Chance and Certainty: John Cage's Politics of Nature," *Cultural Critique* 84 (2013): 140; see also Holly Watkins, "On Not Letting Sounds Be Themselves," *CR: The New Centennial Review* 18, no. 2 (2018): 75–98.

5. Michel Foucault, "Language to Infinity," in *Aesthetics, Method, and Epistemology: Essential Works of Foucault 1954–1984*, vol. II, ed. James D. Faubion, trans. Robert Hurley and others (New York: New Press, 1998), 91.

6. Foucault, "Language to Infinity," 91; also quoted and explicated in Fuoco B. Fann, *This Self We Deserve: A Quest After Modernity* (Berkeley: Philosophy and Art Collaboratory, 2020), 16–24.

7. I borrow the phrase "modern phonetic language" from Fann, who draws from Foucault's archaeology of the human sciences and from Derrida's grammatology to suggest that phonetic languages in western countries, joined by geographic proximity and by epistemological affinities, became ever more autonomous after the turn of the nineteenth century. This autonomy arose not just through the creation of new sciences of language (like philology, for Foucault an indication that "language [had] folded in upon itself," becoming a discipline among others), but through a particular manner of approaching and using language, something like a *mentalité*. As Fann clarifies, citing Foucault's *The Order of Things*,

> the nineteenth-century practice of analyzing grammatical structures indeed separated phonetic language from its bonds with judgement, attribution, and affirmation in the West. "The ontological transition provided by the verb *to be* between thinking and speaking is removed." As phonetic language became "an autonomous organic structure," it "acquire[d] a being proper to itself. And it is this being that contains the laws that govern it." The modern phonetic language thus exists in its own name, and has its own life.

Fann, *This Self We Deserve*, 4. This modern phonetic language is, above all, a vehicle through which the Modern Man indulges in a kind of unbridled egotism: hence Foucault's archaeology may be seen to lay ground for a critique of the modern self, an anthropocentric and structurally overloaded "double" of self that, as Fann suggests, makes us (modern westerners) malfunction in everyday life. I am also indebted to Fann's suggestions, in personal correspondence, regarding the link between metaphysical assumptions held by scholars of performance (and by Cage) and the metaphysics of phonetic language (from a Derridean standpoint) explored later in this chapter. See also, *This Self We Deserve*, 4–5, 6–7, 25–30, 73–87, 132–142, and 166–170.

8. Dreyfus and Rabinow summarize:

> Suddenly, according to Foucault's story, somewhere at the end of the eighteenth century there occurred one of the most dramatic epistemic shifts which Foucault's archaeology is designed to chart. A "profound upheaval," "an archaeological mutation" occurred which signaled the collapse of the Classical Age and made possible the emergence of man. Representation suddenly became opaque. As long as discourse provided a transparent medium of representation whose linguistic elements corresponded to primitive elements in the world, representation was not problematic. God had arranged a chain of being and arranged language in preestablished correspondence with it. . . . In the major change with which we are here concerned, man, as we know him today, makes his appearance and becomes the measure of all things. . . . Man, who was once himself a being among others, now is a subject among objects. But Man is not only a subject among objects, he soon realizes that what he is seeking to understand is not only the objects of the world but himself. Man becomes the subject and object of his own understanding.

Hubert L. Dreyfus and Paul Rabinow, *Michel Foucault: Beyond Structuralism and Hermeneutics* (Chicago: University of Chicago Press, 1983), 27–28. See Fann, *This Self We Deserve*, esp. Lecture One, "Words Are Cheap and Expensive," 3–34.

9. Michel Foucault, *The Order of Things: An Archaeology of the Human Sciences* (London and New York: Routledge, 2002 [original French 1966]), 322.

10. Foucault, "Language to Infinity," 91.

11. I owe this insight into the connection between Derrida and Foucault's ideas about phonetic language, its ontological status and the presence of speech, to Fann's work and personal correspondence. See *This Self We Deserve*, 140: "In 'Language to Infinity' (1963), Foucault already anticipates the questions and doubts that Derrida voices in 'Writing Before the Letter' (1965)." See also:

> Derrida affirms that ontology is a Greek thing and thus foreign to the Chinese, while Foucault argues that only phonetic language sustains an "ontological status". . . . While Derrida and Foucault argued over [other] issues, they had one thing in common: the question of phonetic language, specifically, the privilege granted to phonetic language. (37)

12. Jacques Derrida, *Of Grammatology*, trans. Gayatri Chakravorty Spivak (Baltimore and London: Johns Hopkins University Press, 1997), 3.

13. Yet with the epochal changes that marked the birth of European modernity, Derrida implies, "phonetic writing . . . limits itself even as it is in the process of imposing its laws upon the cultural areas that had escaped it." *Of Grammatology*, 10.

14. John Lagerwey, "Écriture et corps divine en Chine," in *Le Corps des dieux* (Paris: Gallimard, 1986), this translation from Fann, *This Self We Deserve*, 7–8. Recall Lagerwey's clarification:

in *Voice and Phenomena* and *Of Grammatology*, Derrida denounces the Western metaphysical prejudice against writing—a prejudice that he traces from Plato through Rousseau to Lévi-Strauss—and he also critiques the constituent opposition between the "dead letter" and the "living voice." In admirable pages on Plato, he shows the equivalences in the Platonic system between the notions of father, sun, voice, and life, in opposition to mother, moon, writing, and death. . . . The Latin West will think in terms at once ethical and metaphysical regarding the lexical couples of body/soul, matter/spirit, woman/man, politics/religion (or State/Church), always giving a negative value to the first term of each couple.

John Lagerwey, "Dieu-Père/Dao-Mère: dualismes occidentaux et chinois," *Extrême-Orient Extrême-Occident*, Hors-série (2012). Translation is mine.

15. Lagerwey, "Écriture et corps divine en Chine."

16. Lagerwey, personal correspondence, and "Dieu-Père/Dao-Mère."

17. Fann, *This Self We Deserve*, 11–12.

18. Hegel, quoted in Derrida, *Of Grammatology*, 23.

19. Fann, *This Self We Deserve*, 10.

20. Nicholas Mathew, "Omniaudience," conference paper delivered at UC Berkeley, Fall 2021.

21. Maurice Blanchot, *The Work of Fire*, trans. Charlotte Mandell (Stanford: Stanford University Press, 1995), 301.

22. For a description of the glass house in which Cage lived, and behind which he "hunted" for mushrooms, see Branden Joseph, "John Cage and the Architecture of Silence," *October* 81 (Summer 1997): 80–104.

23. The only specific form of music (of which I am aware) for which the philosopher openly expressed his love was the Andalusian classical music performed by singer and violinist Lili Labassi (aka Elie Moyal, 1897–1969). The 1999 documentary by Safaa Fathy, *D'Ailleurs Derrida*, shows the philosopher listening to Labassi during a car ride across Paris to the École Normale Supérieure. He avows that if he could have learned to sing like Labassi, he would never have become a philosopher. Aside from Labassi's song—and a brief run-in with Ornette Coleman in 1997 during which Derrida read a text onstage while Coleman and his band improvised (and was quickly booed off the stage)—the philosopher seems not to have paid much attention to music. See Jeremy F. Lane, "Theorising Performance, Performing Theory: Jacques Derrida and Ornette Colemen at the Parc de la Villette," *French Cultural Studies* 24, no. 3 (2013): 319–330.

24. Derrida, *Of Grammatology*, 14.

25. John Cage, "The Future of Music: Credo," and "Experimental Music," in *Silence: Lectures and Writings by John Cage* (Hanover: Wesleyan University Press, 1961), 5, 10.

26. Peggy Phelan, *Unmarked: The Politics of Performance* (London and New York: Routledge, 1993), 146; Erika Fischer-Lichte, *The Transformative Power of*

Performance: A New Aesthetics, trans. Saskya Iris Jain (London and New York: Routledge, 2008), see esp. 38–74.

27. In short, while some believe in "pure" presence, holding an ontological view about the being of performance, others contend that presence is always "written." While there is some crossover between these two poles, the overall stakes of the debate may be understood according to this binarism: either presence *is* . . . or presence "is" only in retrospect. See also Philip Auslander, *Liveness: Performance in a Mediatized Culture* (London and New York: Routledge, 1999); Rebecca Schneider, *Performing Remains: Art and War in Times of Theatrical Reenactment* (London and New York: Routledge, 2011); and Amelia Jones, "'Presence' in Absentia: Experiencing Performance as Documentation," *Art Journal* (Winter 1997): 11–18.

28. See David Patterson's study, drawing from the Black Mountain College archive and from interviews with audience members, in "Two Cages, One College: Cage at Black Mountain College, 1948 and 1952," *Black Mountain Studies Journal*, online, accessed September 2016: http://www.blackmountainstudiesjournal.org/volume4/4-11-david-patterson/; see also Brigid Cohen, "Musical Cosmopolitans at Black Mountain College," in Helen Molesworth and Ruth Erickson, eds., *Leap Before You Look: Black Mountain College 1933–1957* (New Haven and London: Yale University Press, 2015), 202–206.

29. Phelan, *Unmarked*, 148.

30. As Patterson noted, Cage and company seem to have taken certain prescriptions from Artaud's first *Manifesto of the Theater of Cruelty* literally, including his imperative that "a direct communication will be re-established between the spectator and the spectacle, between the actor and the spectator, from the fact that the spectator, placed in the middle of the action, is engulfed and physically affected by it." Antonin Artaud, *The Theater and Its Double*, trans. Mary Caroline Richards (New York: Grove Press, 1958), 96. Cage wrote to Boulez on 22 May 1951:

> I have been reading a great deal of Artaud. (This because of you and through Tudor who read Artaud because of you.) I hope I have made a little clear to you what I am doing. I have the feeling of just beginning to compose for the first time. I will soon send you a copy of the first part of the piano piece [*Music of Changes*]. The essential underlying idea is that each thing is itself, that its relations with other things spring up naturally rather than being imposed by any abstraction on an "artist's" part. (see Artaud on an objective synthesis).

See *The Boulez–Cage Correspondence*, ed. Jean-Jacques Nattiez, trans. Robert Samuels (Cambridge, UK, and New York: Cambridge University Press, 1993), 96; see Patterson, "Two Cages, One College."

31. "Metaphor works to secure a vertical hierarchy of value and is reproductive" whereas "[m]etonymy is additive and associative." Throughout *Unmarked*, Phelan

used examples of artworks that foreground, in the manner of Artaud's Theater of Cruelty, the limits of representation, including "hardship art" or "ordeal art" in which an artist's own physical pain becomes a feature of a work. See, for instance, Phelan's description of Angelika Festa's 1987 *Untitled Dance (with fish and others)*. Phelan, *Unmarked*, 148, 153–158.

32. Michael Kirby and Richard Schechner, "An Interview with John Cage," *Tulane Drama Review* 10, no. 2 (Winter 1965): 52–53.

33. For M.C. Richard's sketch, see "Untitled Event—Fragments on its Historiography and Myth-Making," Black Mountain Research online, accessed 18 February 2022: https://black-mountain-research.com/2015/07/06/untitled-event/

34. Various auditors recalled Cage, for instance, standing or sitting on a step ladder or at a raised lectern; among those who recalled that Rauschenberg's painting were on display, some remember seeing his *White Paintings* and others insist the paintings were black. See Patterson, "Two Cages, One College."

35. Kirby and Schechner, "Interview with John Cage," 52.

36. Patterson, "Two Cage's, One College," n. 104.

37. John Cage, "On Robert Rauschenberg, Artist, and His Work," in *Silence*, 102.

38. See John Cage, "Defense of Satie," in *John Cage: An Anthology*, ed. Richard Kostelanetz (New York: Da Capo Press, 1970), 81.

39. Phelan, *Unmarked*, 147:

The fact that these descriptions vary considerably—even at times wildly—only lends credence to the fact that the interaction between the art object and the spectator is, essentially, performative—and therefore resistant to the claims of validity and accuracy endemic to the discourse of reproduction.

40. Whereas modernists had, by and large, obsessed over paint and ink, after Duchamp redirected the artistic "creative act" away from the medium and toward the mind of the artist or of the receiver, the specific medium, in Krauss's phrase (drawing a parallel to her own experience of losing memory after suffering a stroke), "washed away." Rosalind E. Krauss, *Under Blue Cup* (Cambridge, MA: MIT Press, 2011), see esp. 55–69.

41. Schneider, *Performing Remains*.

42. Phelan seems to leap right into the gap, the incommensurability between what an event *was*, what actually happened live, and how the event may be remembered "now": this gap in fact defines what a work of performance *is*. With music in view, it becomes easy to sense that the scholarly debate about presence in performance, though it attempts to step outside a Derridean framework, is "always already" caught up in its terms, since Derridean thought, like Cageian musical practice, concerns the philosophical question of the now.

43. The well-known Cage aphorism appeared in published form in *A Year from Monday* and reads: "PERMISSION GRANTED. BUT NOT TO DO WHATEVER

YOU WANT." John Cage, *A Year from Monday: New Lectures and Writings by John Cage* (Middletown: Wesleyan University Press, 1967), 28.

44. Cage wrote in "Diary: How to Improve the World (You Will Only Make Matters Worse) 1965," in *A Year from Monday*, 12: "Music as discourse (jazz) doesn't work. If you're going to have a discussion, have it and use words." He echoed an idea from "45' for a Speaker" (1954): "Communication if it is required is a way of calling attention to one's own psychology." Cage, in *Silence*, 172.

45. Benjamin Piekut, *Experimentalism Otherwise: The New York Avant-Garde and Its Limits* (Berkeley: University of California Press, 2011), 57.

46. Allan Kaprow, "Happenings in the New York Scene (1961)," in *Essays on the Blurring of Art and Life*, ed. Jeff Kelley (Berkeley: University of California Press, 1993), 16.

47. John Cage, in Richard Kostelanetz, *Conversing with Cage* (New York and London: Routledge, 2003), 119.

48. Cage wrote to Tudor in 1951: "Loving you from this side with you so close and so far is what loses me." While it is unlikely that Cage's "overflowing [. . .] of desire" for Tudor, a straight man, ever culminated in a sexual relationship, nevertheless their correspondence indicates that Tudor—who addressed Cage playfully as "lonely heart"—reciprocated Cage's affection with some of the most exacting and technically detailed inquiries about musical performance imaginable. To take a cue from Eve Sedgwick, Cage and Tudor's relationship can be termed "homosocial." The desire undergirding Cage and Tudor's musical innovations extended to Cage's other collaborators—especially to Cunningham, whose sexual and artistic relationship with Cage has been well documented. Homosociality functioned as a kind of affective glue for those in Cage's mid-century circle, and perhaps Cage's aesthetic position can be said to have taken shape through an intersubjective process of male homosocial desire. See Eve Kosofsky Sedgwick, *Between Men: English Literature and Male Homosocial Desire* (New York: Columbia University Press, 1985); Martin Iddon, ed., *John Cage and David Tudor: Correspondence on Interpretation and Performance* (New York: Cambridge University Press, 2013). I am grateful to Mary Ann Smart for suggesting the connection between Cage and Tudor's milieu and the pattern of male homosocial desire that Sedgwick described.

49. Cage, *Silence*, 12.

50. Biographer Kenneth Silverman has suggested that Cage's presentism—his call to "just be"—reflected the influence of American transcendentalism à la Emerson and Thoreau. See Kenneth Silverman, *Begin Again: A Biography of John Cage* (New York: Knopf, 2010), 108–109.

51. The phrase "intellectual Gordian knot" comes from Kuspit's description of Duchamp's readymades. See Donald Kuspit, *The End of Art* (Cambridge, UK: Cambridge University Press, 2004).

52. Derrida, *Of Grammatology*, 295.

53. The video of this event, titled "Musik im technischen Zeitalter," is available

on YouTube as "John Cage + David Tudor—Musik Im Technischen Zeitalter 1963, accessed 30 April 2021: https://www.youtube.com/watch?v=9IAWKjvt6A4&t=674s

54. James Pritchett, *The Music of John Cage* (Cambridge, UK: Cambridge University Press, 1993), 126; italics in original.

55. During a memorial event for Tudor in 1996, Christian Wolff recalled a performance in Germany of Cage's "Cartridge Music" that took place sometime in the mid 1950s. Adorno attended the performance and afterward gave a short lecture about the relevance of this music. Tudor allegedly responded: "You haven't understood a thing." From David Patterson, "Celebrating a Life," *davidtudor.org*, accessed 15 May 2021: https://davidtudor.org/Life/memorial.html

56. The seminal survey of these various approaches is Pritchett, *The Music of John Cage.*

57. Jacques Derrida, "Differance," in *Speech and Phenomena and Other Essays on Husserl's Theory of Signs*, trans. David B. Allison (Evanston: Northwestern University Press, 1973), 142.

58. John Cage, "Composition as Process," in *Silence*, 48.

59. See Richard Taruskin, *Music in the Late Twentieth Century: The Oxford History of Western Music,* vol. 5 (New York: Oxford University Press, 2010).

60. His turn to chance has been explained via Cage's biography. Reading Cage's 1944 *Perilous Night* for prepared piano as an expression of the composer's emotional turmoil after realizing his homosexuality, David Revill suggests 1944 as a breaking point. Cage was distraught, according to Revill, after a music critic compared the clanging, crashing, and percussive timbres of his *Perilous Night* for prepared piano to a "woodpecker in a church belfry." As Taruskin suggested, the critic's words equipped Cage with a bitter resentment. Cage's quiet recalcitrance, his abnegation of self-expression, can be seen as his response. David Revill, *The Roaring Silence; John Cage: A Life* (New York: Arcade Publishing, 1992), 86–88; Richard Taruskin, "Indeterminacy," in *Music in the Late Twentieth Century.*

61. Cage, *A Year from Monday*, 50.

62. See Branden W. Joseph, "HPSCHD—Ghost or Monster?," in Hannah B. Higgins and Douglas Kahn, eds., *Mainframe Experimentalism: Early Computing and the Foundations of the Digital Arts* (Berkeley: University of California Press, 2012), 147–169.

63. Pritchett, *The Music of John Cage*, 159.

64. John Cage, "McLuhan's Influence," in *John Cage: An Anthology*, 170.

65. One of Cage's students, John Brockman, recounted receiving a copy of Wiener from his mentor in 1965. See Christina Dunbar-Hester, "Listening to Cybernetics: Music, Machines, and Nervous Systems, 1950–1980," *Science, Technology, & Human Values* 35, no. 1 (2010): 120.

66. Cybernetics arose as Wiener dialogued with colleagues in various sciences during the 1940s and 50s, with Leibniz as his "patron saint," since his philoso-

phy "centers around two closely related concepts—that of a universal symbolism and that of a calculus of reasoning." Norbert Wiener, *Cybernetics: Or Control and Communication in the Animal and the Machine* (Cambridge, MA: MIT Press, 1948), 11, 12.

67. Cage, in Larry Austin, "An Interview with John Cage and Lejaren Hiller," *Computer Music Journal* 16, no. 4 (Winter 1992): 16.

68. See Roger Moseley, *Keys to Play: Music as a Ludic Medium from Apollo to Nintendo* (Berkeley: University of California Press, 2016).

69. Austin, "An Interview with John Cage and Lejaren Hiller," 17.

70. Wiener, *Cybernetics*, 14.

71. Derrida, *Of Grammatology*, 9; italics in original.

72. "It could be argued that the transition from 'language' to 'writing' was already implicit within structuralism itself," Johnson continued.

> Structuralism in fact combined models of interpretation drawn from linguistics with concepts of a higher level of abstraction taken from cybernetics: communication, control, feedback, program, code, information, message.... In this sense, it could be said that cybernetics performed a kind of revealing function essential to the emergence of grammatology.

Christopher Johnson, "The Cybernetic Imaginary," in *Reading Derrida's Of Grammatology*, eds. Sean Gaston and Ian Maclachlan (London and New York: Continuum, 2011), 12–13.

73. Wiener, *Cybernetics*, 23.

74. Wiener, *Cybernetics*, 19.

75. Derrida, *Of Grammatology*, 9.

76. Derrida, *Of Grammatology*, 324 n. 3.

77. As Mumma wrote in 2006, the instrumental loudspeakers "added and subtracted harmonics and occasionally created complex inter-modulations with the electronic sound sources." He continued:

> attached to each "instrumental loudspeaker" was a small microphone that allowed the acoustically modified sound to be further amplified and resonantly distributed by conventional loudspeakers throughout the performance space.

Gordon Mumma, *Cybersonic Arts: Adventures in American New Music,* ed. Michelle Fillion (Urbana, Chicago, and Springfield: University of Illinois Press, 2015), 154; see also Matt Rogalsky, "Idea and Community: The Growth of David Tudor's *Rainforest,* 1965–2006," PhD dissertation (City University London, 2006), 102.

78. The performance was the culmination of a month of rigorous rehearsals and workshops towards the end of the Merce Cunningham Dance Company's month-long residency prior to the Second Buffalo Festival of the Arts Today. Rogalsky, "Idea and Community," 94.

79. David Vaughan, *Merce Cunningham: Fifty Years*, ed. Melissa Harris (New York: Aperture, 1999), 162.

80. Vaughan, *Merce Cunningham: Fifty Years*, 162.

81. Cunningham commented years later: "the piece suggests a little community of six people, but you only see two or three of them at a time." Merce Cunningham, *The Dancer and the Dance: Merce Cunningham in Conversation with Jacqueline Lesschaeve* (New York and London: Marion Boyars, 1985), 113. As *New York Times* reviewer Alastair Macaulay wrote after a 2011 re-realization of the original choreography:

> Feet and hands move like paws; bodies crawl along the floor; heads nuzzle or butt or, as if sensing alarm signals, turn sharply or slowly. In one image that often causes laughs in the audience, a man softly shoves a supine woman with his head and she rolls like a log. In an even more striking image, a woman swings upside down from a man's arm like a monkey on a branch.

Alastair Macaulay, "Jungle Gymnasts on a Farewell Tour," *New York Times*, 11 July 2011: http://www.nytimes.com/2011/07/12/arts/dance/merce-cunningham -dance-company-review.html?_r=0

82. Roger Copeland, *Merce Cunningham: The Modernizing of Modern Dance* (New York and London: Routledge, 2004), 13:

> In the world of Cunningham's dances, the driving impulse is to hurry up, then stop: Race to the street corner, but then stop at the traffic light; run for the elevator; but then wait—impatiently—while it descends to the ground floor. There is no need to commission backdrops painted with likeness of traffic lights or stop signs. (14)

83. See John Driscoll and Matt Rogalsky, "David Tudor's *Rainforest*: An Evolving Exploration of Resonance," *Leonardo Music Journal* 14 (2004): 26; and Nicholas Collins, "Introduction: Composers Inside Electronics: Music After David Tudor," *Leonardo Music Journal* 14 (2004): 1–3.

84. David Tudor, in "John Cage & David Tudor Interview (Part II), 1972," published on YouTube: https://www.youtube.com/watch?v=YR2lpLvQjEQ

85. Mumma, *Cybersonic Arts*, 39–40.

86. Cage, "Diary: How to Improve the World (You Will Only Make Matters Worse) 1965," in *A Year from Monday*, 17–18.

87. Cage, "Composition as Process," 43.

88. In Rudolf Arnheim's words, modern art reflects on one hand "an almost desperate need to wrest order from a chaotic environment," and on the other, "the frank exhibition of bankruptcy and sterility wrought by that same environment." Donald Kuspit extends Arnheim's notion of entropy by linking it to the death drive and suggesting that "instead of understanding modern art in terms of movements . . . one understand it in terms of the dialectic of entropy and creativ-

ity, or, to use Arnheim's terms, the morbid catabolic and healthy anabolic forces that make it self-contradictory." Kuspit, *The End of Art*, 51.

89. Kuspit, *The End of Art*, 67–68:

> Tinguely's *Homage to New York* . . . is about as far as . . . technology-dependent art goes toward "aesthetic" excitement. . . . Tinguely's self-annihilating machine certainly takes what Duchamp called the nihilism of Dada—which first declared the meaninglessness and valuelessness of art in the modern world—to a new extreme.

90. John Cage, "Julliard Lecture," in *A Year from Monday*, 95–98. This lecture is available in audio recording via Julliard's digital archive: http://jmedia.juilliard .edu/digital/collection/p16995coll3/id/10933

91. Cage, "Julliard Lecture," 100.

92. Caroline A. Jones, "Finishing School: John Cage and the Abstract Expressionist Ego," *Critical Inquiry* 19, no. 4 (1993): 628–665.

93. There is also reason to question Suzuki's own authenticity vis-à-vis the Chan/Zen tradition: in Bernard Fauré's words, though Suzuki eventually denounced the antinomianism that he had earlier advocated, his "vision remained to the very end imbued with a nostalgia for naturalness and a deep bias against ritualism." Suzuki's Zen was a nostalgic Zen, a noncontingent and "radically antinomian teaching free from any formalism or ritualism." Fauré demonstrates, however, that Suzuki's ideal Zen was a twentieth-century replication of something that had occurred over and over through the history of Chan Buddhism, a nostalgia for "'pure' practice": yet even "Suzuki himself . . . had to admit that life in Japanese Zen monasteries is a far cry from the idealized version for Western consumption." Suzuki therefore promulgated a "pious reconstruction of the 'golden age' of Zen," a "simplistic image of its mythic past." Bernard Fauré, *The Rhetoric of Immediacy: A Cultural Critique of Chan/Zen Buddhism* (Princeton: Princeton University Press, 1991), 19, 284. However one might envision this rigidly ritualized and disciplined lifestyle, it is surely a far cry from Suzuki's own lifestyle as a Zen celebrity in New York, and an even further cry from anything that ever "happened" at Black Mountain College.

94. See Edward Crooks, "John Cage's Entanglement with the Ideas of Coomaraswamy," PhD dissertation (University of York, 2011) and David Patterson, "Cage and Asia: History and Sources," in *The Cambridge Companion to John Cage*, ed. David Nicholls (Cambridge, UK: Cambridge University Press, 2002). For examples of biographers who have taken Cage's word for it, see Rob Haskins, *John Cage* (London: Reaktion Books, 2012), Revill, *The Roaring Silence*, and, finally, Kay Larson's quite nauseating *Where the Heart Beats: John Cage, Zen Buddhism, and the Inner Life of Artists* (New York: Penguin Press, 2012).

95. While Caroline Jones (in "Finishing School") lauded Cage as a "Zen master" to the mid-century avant-garde, casting his use of silence in his music, his

frequent refusal to answer his critics, and his persona as a soft-spoken resistance to an otherwise phallocentric New York avant-garde, Jonathan D. Katz affirmed that Zen served a therapeutic function for Cage, allowing him critical distance as a gay man from an otherwise homophobic and sometimes outright hostile mid-twentieth-century cultural scene. Jonathan D. Katz, "John Cage's Queer Silence; or, How to Avoid Making Matters Worse," *GLQ* 5, no. 2 (1995): 231–252. Finally, Pulitzer Prize–winning biographer Kenneth Silverman affirms, in a similar self-empowering mode, that the Zen concept of "no-mind" allowed Cage a unique experience of freedom and "self-reliance." Kenneth Silverman, *Begin Again: A Biography of John Cage* (Evanston: Northwestern University Press, 2012), 108.

96. Patterson, "Cage and Asia," 58–59.

97. Aldous Huxley, *The Perennial Philosophy* (New York and London: Harper Perennial, 2009 [original 1945]).

98. Sharf refers here to the conception of Zen Buddhism promulgated in the west by Japanese proselytizers including Shaku Sōen, Sōen's student D. T. Suzuki, and Suzuki's lifelong friend Nishida Kitarō, in the late nineteenth and early twentieth centuries. Robert H. Sharf, "The Zen of Japanese Nationalism," in *Curators of the Buddha: The Study of Buddhism Under Colonialism*, ed. Donald S. Lopez Jr. (Chicago and London: University of Chicago Press, 1995), 124–132. This conception surfaced in works and writings by avant-garde artists and musicians, the "counterculturalists" of the 1940s and 50s fighting the "technocratic machine," and abides in the popular culture to the present day. See R. John Williams, "Technê-Zen and the Spiritual Quality of Global Capitalism," *Critical Inquiry* 37 (Autumn 2011): 20–21, 59–70.

99. Fann, *This Self We Deserve*, 164.

100. Cage, *Silence*, xi.

101. This lecture is available in audio recording via Julliard's digital archive: http://jmedia.juilliard.edu/digital/collection/p16995coll3/id/10933

102. Foucault, "Language to Infinity," 89.

103. Foucault quotes a passage from Claude Duret's 1613 *Trésor de l'histoire des langues*:

> the stork, so greatly lauded for its charity towards its father and its mother, is called in Hebrew *Chasida*, which is to say, meek, charitable, endowed with pity . . . The horse is named *Sus*, thought to be from the verb *Hasas*, unless that verb is rather derived from the noun, and it signifies to rise up, for among all four-footed animals the horse is most proud and brave. . . .

Duret's words are one example, for Foucault, of the fundamental role played by resemblance in Renaissance-era thought. He also draws from alchemists like Crollius, botanists like Aldrovandi, and from Paracelsus to suggest that the human world was ontologically interwoven with the natural world and the cosmos. According to this *episteme*, plants are arranged on earth to mirror the stars arranged in the sky; there are the same number of fish in the sea as animals on earth and as stars in the sky; a person's eyes are the mirror of the sun and moon.

> The world is covered with signs that must be deciphered, and those signs, which reveal resemblances and affinities, are themselves no more than forms of similitude. To know must therefore be to interpret: to find a way from the visible mark to that which is being said by it and which, without that mark, would lie like unspoken speech, dormant within things.

Foucault, *The Order of Things*, 36, 40.

104. Crollius, quoted in Foucault, *The Order of Things*, 22–23.

105. Whereas during the Renaissance words bore a profound resemblance to the things they signified—the world was *like* a language, with a hidden Text underneath, waiting to be revealed through *commentary*, and even words themselves were thought to have intrinsic meaning (just like the things of the world)—in the Classical Age "the primary text is effaced, and with it, the entire, inexhaustible foundation of the words whose mute being was inscribed in things; all that remains is representation, unfolding in the verbal signs that manifest it, and hence becoming *discourse*." Foucault, *The Order of Things*, 88; italics in original. Representation replaces resemblance as the backbone of all possible knowledge. In Dreyfus and Rabinow's words,

> The Classical Age set itself the project of constructing a universal method of analysis which would yield perfect certainty by perfectly ordering representations and signs to mirror the ordering of the world, the order of being— for being, in the Classical Age, had a universal order.

In this order, "man was not *the* maker, *the* artificer—God—but as the locus of clarification, he was *an* artificer." In modernity, however, Man emerges and becomes the measure of things. Dreyfus and Rabinow, *Michel Foucault: Beyond Structuralism and Hermeneutics*, 19–20; italics in original.

106. See Jürgen Habermas, *The Philosophical Discourse of Modernity: Twelve Lectures*, trans. Frederick G. Lawrence (Cambridge, MA: MIT Press, 1991), 260–265.

107. Foucault, *The Order of Things*, 52, 53:

> *Don Quixote* is a negative of the Renaissance world; writing has ceased to be the prose of the world; resemblances and signs have dissolved their former alliance; similitudes have become deceptive and verge upon the visionary or madness; . . . words wander off on their own, without content, without resemblance to fill their emptiness. . . . Magic, which permitted the decipherment of the world by revealing the secret resemblances beneath its signs, is no longer of any use except as an explanation, in terms of madness, of why analogies are always proved false.

108. Foucault, *The Order of Things*, 229. "Sade attains the ends of Classical discourse and thought." Violence, desire, and sexuality henceforth "extend, below the level of representation, an immense expanse of shade which we are now attempting to recover . . . in our discourse, in our freedom, in our thought." In other words, Sade symbolizes for Foucault a broader endeavor among modern people to try and intensify freedom by plunging into the murky shade below the level of representation—for Sade, the area of battering desire, sexuality, violence, death, etc. "But our thought is so brief, our freedom so enslaved, our discourse so repetitive, that we must face the fact that that expanse of shade below is really a bottomless sea" (229).

109. Foucault, *The Order of Things*, 311; italics in original. Translation modified from "The whole being of language is now one of sound" to "the whole being of language is now sonorous." See the French original: *Lets mots et les choses: Une archéologie des sciences humaines* (Paris: Gallimard, 1966), 298.

110. Foucault, *The Order of Things*, 322.

111. Foucault, *The Order of Things*, 48.

112. Foucault, "Language to Infinity," 91.

113. Eckhart, cited in John Cage's "Forerunners of Modern Music," in *Silence*, 62.

114. Eckart, cited in Cage, "Forerunners of Modern Music," 64.

115. See John Cage's "Lecture on Something," in *Silence*, 145.

116. These two citations to Eckhart may be found in "Forerunners of Modern Music" and "45' for a Speaker," in *Silence*, 64 and 193.

117. Fann, *This Self We Deserve*, 140–141; italics in original.

118. Foucault, *The Order of Things*, 264–265.

Postlude

1. A clip of this obscure television special is available on YouTube as "John Cage, John Lennon & Yoko Ono," accessed 30 April 2021: https://www.youtube.com/watch?v=O6fYyw-XcfE

2. Ono's first husband, composer Toshi Ichiyanagi, studied with Cage in New York during the 1950s, bringing Ono to Cage's classes at the New School, and Ono is alleged to have met Cage separately while attending the Suzuki lectures at Columbia University. See Mark Swed, "A Dean of Japanese Music Talks Boundaries, John Cage and Life with Yoko Ono," *Los Angeles Times*, 15 May 2015: https://www.latimes.com/entertainment/arts/la-ca-cm-toshi-ichiyanagi-profile-20150517-column.html

3. This is how Taruskin classed performance art: "recording and electro-acoustical technologies . . . spurred the professional revival in the late twentieth century of age-old oral practices normally associated with folklore, giving rise to the genre that is known, for want of a better term, as performance art." Richard Taruskin, *Music in the Late Twentieth Century: The Oxford History of Western Music,* vol. 5 (New York: Oxford University Press, 2010), 481.

4. John Cage, *M: Writings '67–'72* (London: Calder and Boyars, 1973), ix.

5. John Cage, *Mureau,* recorded 3 October 1972 and released as a cassette by Edition S Press. Published on YouTube, accessed 15 May 2021: https://youtu.be/R2t3JdtYGzM

6. David Tudor and John Cage, "Mesostics re Merce Cunningham (Untitled)," in *The Art of David Tudor,* vol. 3 (Brooklyn: Anthology of Recorded Music, 2013). Audio recording, accessed 15 May 2021: https://youtu.be/1NXA1N6YO3g

7. And Cage's appropriation of the *I Ching* demands a chapter-length analysis.

8. Jacques Derrida, *Of Grammatology,* trans. Gayatri Chakravorty Spivak (Baltimore and London: Johns Hopkins University Press, 1997), 9.

9. Jacques Derrida, "Differance," in *Speech and Phenomena and Other Essays on Husserl's Theory of Signs,* trans. David B. Allison (Evanston: Northwestern University Press, 1973), 156; see also Fuoco B. Fann, *This Self We Deserve: A Quest After Modernity* (Berkeley: Philosophy and Art Collaboratory, 2020), 13, 142, 152.

INDEX

・・・ **Sensing Media**
Aesthetics, Philosophy,
and Cultures of Media
EDITED BY WENDY HUI KYONG CHUN
AND SHANE DENSON

What does it mean to think, feel, and sense with and through media? In this cross-disciplinary series we present books and authors exploring this and related questions: How do media technologies, broadly defined, transform artistic practices and aesthetic sensibilities? How are practices, encounters, and affects entangled with the deep infrastructures and visible surfaces of the media environment? How do we "make sense"—cognitively, perceptually, and culturally—of media?

We are especially interested in contributions that open our understanding of media aesthetics beyond the narrow confines of Western art and aesthetic values. We seek works that reestablish the environmental connections between art and technology as well as between the aesthetic, the sensible, and the philosophical. We invite alternative epistemologies and phenomenologies of media rooted in the practices and subjectivities of Black, Indigenous, queer, trans, and other communities that have been unjustly marginalized in these discussions. Ultimately, we aim to sense the many possible worlds that media disclose.

—

Ioana B. Jucan, *Malicious Deceivers: Thinking Machines and Performative Objects*

Vilém Flusser, *Communicology: Mutations in Human Relations?*, edited by Rodrigo Maltez Novaes, foreword by N. Katherine Hayles

Mark Amerika, *My Life as an Artificial Creative Intelligence*